POPULAR PLAYS

by Women

IN THE RESTORATION
AND EIGHTEENTH CENTURY

For Reiner, the better editor

POPULAR PLAYS

by Women

IN THE RESTORATION
AND EIGHTEENTH CENTURY

EDITED BY

Tanya Caldwell

broadview press

© 2011 Tanya Caldwell

Library and Archives Canada Cataloguing in Publication

Popular plays by women in the Restoration and eighteenth century / edited by Tanya Caldwell.

Includes bibliographical references.
ISBN 978-1-55111-916-8

1. English drama—Women authors. 2. English drama—Restoration, 1660-1700. 3. English drama—18th century. I. Caldwell, Tanya, [date]

PR708.W6P66 2011   822'.40809287   C2011-902626-0

Broadview Press is an independent, international publishing house, incorporated in 1985.

We welcome comments and suggestions regarding any aspect of our publications — please feel free to contact us at the addresses below or at broadview@broadviewpress.com / www.broadviewpress.com.

North America

Post Office Box 1243
Peterborough, Ontario
Canada K9J 7H5
2215 Kenmore Ave.
Buffalo, New York
USA 14207
tel: (705) 743-8990
fax: (705) 743-8353
customerservice
@broadviewpress.com

*UK, Europe, Central Asia,
Middle East, Africa, India and
Southeast Asia*

Eurospan Group
3 Henrietta St., London
WC2E 8LU, UK
tel: 44 (0) 1767 604972
fax: 44 (0) 1767 601640
eurospan
@turpin-distribution.com

Australia and New Zealand

NewSouth Books
c/o TL Distribution
15-23 Helles Ave.
Moorebank, NSW
Australia 2170
tel: (02) 8778 9999
fax (02) 8778 9944
orders@tldistribution.com.au

Edited by Denis Johnston.
Book design by Michel Vrana.

Broadview Press acknowledges the financial support of the Government of Canada through the Canadian Book Fund for our publishing activities.

The interior of this book is printed on paper containing 100% post-consumer fibre.

Printed in Canada

CONTENTS

ACKNOWLEDGMENTS

This project was begun before Georgia State University had access to Early English Books Online (EEBO) and Eighteenth Century Collection Online (ECCO); finally gaining that access has made all the difference. I was also able to work with the Larpent manuscript of *The Runaway* at The Huntington Library in San Marino, California, where I was fortunate to encounter David Worrall and benefit from his enormous knowledge of the Larpent collection and eighteenth-century drama. This anthology is much better for the generous help of Katherine West Scheil and of Brian Corman, who got me hooked on drama in the first place. I would also like to acknowledge the advice of Murray Brown, Nancy Copeland, and Melinda Finberg, whose fine anthology, *Eighteenth-Century Women Dramatists* (Oxford, 2001), provided me, as a novice editor, with a guide. Jane Spencer's *The Rover and Other Plays* (Oxford, 1995) and earlier Broadview editions of Restoration and eighteenth-century plays have also provided fine examples. My first-rate research assistants deserve more credit than I can express here: Sabrina Abid can track down anything, and Sarah Higinbotham's sharp eye and insightful comments greatly augmented this project. I am especially grateful to Noel Chevalier for allowing me to include his edition of *The Rehearsal; or, Bays in Petticoats*, first published in his *The Clandestine Marriage, Together with Two Short Plays* (Broadview, 1995). He has been a pleasure to work with and helpful throughout; he also suggested the Leapor poem that appears in the final section of critical comments by women playwrights. I wish also to thank the Huntington Library for allowing us to use its copy of the title page of *The Runaway*. Just as Cowley's children—as she writes in the prologue to *The Runaway*—provided her with a muse, so mine, Hannah and Madeleine, bring perspective to a life otherwise consumed by old texts.

INTRODUCTION

Virginia Woolf's famous quip about Aphra Behn earning women the right to speak their minds does not come close to explaining how women managed to have any plays at all performed on the London stage in the eighteenth century.[1] All the playwrights included in this anthology were anomalies, as was any woman whose dramatic creations were staged in the period. As Ellen Donkin points out, from the re-opening of the London theaters in 1660 to the end of the eighteenth century, women averaged only seven per cent of the playwrights whose works appeared on stage in any given season (1). The challenges they faced were formidable, for drama is an intrinsically public medium. Hannah Cowley highlights how little control the playwright ultimately had over what happened on stage when she calls her play *The Town Before You* (1795) "rather the Comedy which the Public have chosen it to be, than the Comedy which I intended" (Preface). The frustration she expresses is a common refrain throughout this period. Any aspiring playwright had to face numerous hurdles in the path to the stage—hurdles involving, as Donkin shows in detail, theater managers, censors, actors, and the whims of fickle audiences whose tastes were unpredictable. Susanna Centlivre sums up the consequent insecurity of any playwright's existence when she calls writing "a kind of Lottery in this fickle Age" and the dramatist's lot "as precarious as the Cast of a Die," for "we see our best Authors sometimes fail" (Preface to *Love's Contrivance*). Women faced additional challenges in having to infiltrate what remained a male-dominated infrastructure and negotiate social prohibitions that, at best, restricted their activities in the public sphere and, at worst, would not have them there at all. Even when they overcame the odds, like the women whose plays are presented here, history was not kind to them, critics and anthology makers over the centuries using defamation and silence, those powerful critical tools, to distort the tale of the Restoration and eighteenth-century stage.[2]

Yet, the women and their plays included in this anthology were vastly successful—not just for female playwrights, but for their time. Behn, Centlivre, and Cowley all wrote plays, and first plays at that, which enjoyed runs often far surpassing those of the male peers who vastly outnumbered them. Just

1   Woolf said, "All women together ought to let flowers fall on the tomb of Aphra Behn, which is, most scandalously but rather appropriately, in Westminster Abbey, for it was she who earned them the right to speak their minds" (98).
2   The sheer popularity of Centlivre's plays often dictated their inclusion in early anthologies, however.

nine years after the opening of her first play, as Deborah Payne points out,[3] Behn had become a mainstay in the Duke's Company. Centlivre was perhaps the most successful of all eighteenth-century playwrights, writing more plays than most and enjoying hits with several of them. Cowley, meanwhile, came late, as an unknown to the theater world, yet was able to boast the triumph of a play that, she says, "has all the crudeness of a first attempt": it "succeeded ... on the Stage, far beyond my most sanguine expectations" and "was one of the most profitable Plays, both to the Author and Manager, that appears on the records of the Treasury-Books at either House" despite a run curtailed "by the Benefits" (Preface to *Albina*). Against even greater odds, in the post-Garrick theater world that was hostile to women, she went on to produce more outstanding stage successes. Catherine—Kitty—Clive, too, was confident enough in her celebrity status to appeal to the public in response to what she felt was a deliberate injustice to her by the managers of both patent houses. However, David Garrick, the most influential of all dramatic personae in this period, best underscored the achievement of these women, for he chose to end his acting career in the role of Don Felix in Centlivre's *The Wonder*, while the last new play performed in his long run as manager at Drury Lane was Cowley's first, *The Runaway*.

The purpose of this anthology is to supplement the *Broadview Anthology of Restoration and Early Eighteenth-Century Drama* by making readily available more plays by women that enjoyed success similar to phenomena such as Behn's *The Rover* and Centlivre's *A Bold Stroke for a Wife*. Thanks to a huge surge recently in scholarly interest in early modern women writers and the simultaneous response to student interest on the part of presses such as Broadview, which has produced a number of fine editions of individual plays by seventeenth- and eighteenth-century women, the face of eighteenth-century literature and drama is quite different in the second decade of the twenty-first century than it was even in the early 1990s. Still, change occurs slowly, as Brian Corman pointed out in a discussion of the drama canon in 1992, for the critical tradition deeply affects what texts are available for performance or teaching. The exclusion of women writers in general from the canon began with critics such as Alexander Pope, who, in his *Life of Curll*, famously dismissed Centlivre as "the Cook's Wife in Buckingham Court." In the cause of maintaining literary standards, he ridiculed her and many of her female—and male—contemporaries in a more sustained fashion in *The Dunciad* (1728). By the time his poem appeared, the neoclassical standards he defended were already anachronistic, but he and his contemporaries set

---

3   In Schofield and Macheski, eds., *Curtain Calls* 113.

critical precedents for the treatment of women writers that lasted until the late twentieth century.

The critical assaults were not always as direct as Pope's. As a Restoration writer, Behn suffered worst of all. While her plays, like her other texts, have qualities equal to those of the best writers in English, she wrote them for audiences that demanded bawdy content. By the early eighteenth century, her works had lost favor because that content had brought her a reputation as a fallen woman. While Stephen Jones grudgingly includes "Aphara [*sic*] Behn" in *A New Biographical Dictionary*, his stance is typical of his time. After giving basic factual information, his entry for the revised edition of 1799 reads, "Her works are extremely witty but not remarkably chaste."[4] Centlivre's outstanding successes on stage kept her plays in the repertoires and so in early anthologies. Lord Byron, indeed, grumbled that, "Congreve gave up writing because Mrs. Centlivre's balderdash drove his comedies off," while around 1800 Robert Bisset included Centlivre among eight individual examples of writers, including Shakespeare but excluding Dryden, "whose excellencies time cannot diminish" (Bowyer 97; Bisset 3: 35). Yet, as Byron's snide observation indicates, the critical attention Centlivre won frequently diminished or subverted her achievements. An entry in Sir Richard Steele's *Tatler*, for example, acknowledges her *Busy Body*, but attributes its worth to "that subtilty of spirit which is peculiar to females of wit, and is very seldom well performed by those of the other sex, in whom craft in love is an act of invention, and not, as with women, the effect of nature and instinct" (No. 19, May 24, 1709). Another entry contains a note in which the author feels compelled to remark that the "authoress" had "no inconsiderable share of beauty" before suggesting that Steele includes her at all because she was "of his own party" in adhering to "whig principles even in the most dangerous times" (No. 15, May 13, 1709). Silence—simply ignoring the existence of the women and their vastly popular plays—was another powerful critical tactic. Donkin argues that, as early as 1698, Jeremy Collier, in his influential pamphlet *A Short View of the Immorality and Profaneness of the English Stage* (1698), just "erased" the presence of women as playwrights: "Women play an important role in his argument as actresses, but as playwrights they simply never appear" (24-25).

---

4   The title page of the second edition states that the *Biography* is "Corrected: With Considerable Additions and Improvements" (1796). The entry for Behn reads, "A celebrated English poetess in the reign of Charles I and II. She wrote 17 plays, some histories and novels, died April 16, 1689, and was buried in the cloisters of Westminster Abbey." The third edition (1799), which claims to be "Corrected: With Very Considerable Additions," adds the sentence quoted here.

The revolutionary activity that assailed England on many fronts at the end of the eighteenth century stymied any progress that women had made in the struggle to speak their minds and influence critical and canonical traditions. Catherine Burroughs points out that the most popular female playwrights in the British and American repertoires (Centlivre, Cowley, and Elizabeth Inchbald) favored "variations of social comedy, which seem to have allowed female authors to participate in topical debates without alienating those audiences who would be resistant to the idea of an 'unfeminine'—that is, politically serious—woman writer" (4). Cowley and Inchbald, despite their successes, took care to distance themselves from any feminist or subversive (which was the same thing) activity. Despite the judicious political insights made implicitly or in passing throughout her plays, Cowley claims in the "Advertisement" to her *A Day in Turkey* (1792) to "know nothing about politics" for such interests are suited neither to a female mind ("I never in my mind could attend to their discussion") nor female pursuits: "will Miss Wollstonecraft forgive me—whose book contains such a body of mind as I hardly ever met with—if I say that politics are *unfeminine*?" In the last decade of her life, moreover, she edited out of her plays for the sake of (obsessive) modesty much of the vibrant language and situations that contributed to their literary and dramatic impact. This posthumous 1813 edition was the last time her works appeared in print until Frederick Link's facsimile edition (1979). Inchbald was similarly "self-conscious," as Katherine Rogers puts it, "about daring to be a critic [as well as an actress, playwright, and novelist] and perhaps, as a beautiful woman used to charming men, she was particularly reluctant to displease them" (*Curtain Calls* 281). Sharing the moral high ground of Cowley and their male contemporaries, she condemns Centlivre's *A Bold Stroke for a Wife*, which, as Rogers notes, "actually is quite clean" and which Inchbald concedes "was no worse than other plays of its time"—as frequent performance testified (281-82).

Anthologies and student editions of popular and worthy seventeenth- and eighteenth-century plays have come a long way even since the early 1990s. Particularly helpful have been sound scholarly paperback editions of Behn's plays (together and separately) and Centlivre's plays, and anthologies such as *Eighteenth-Century Women Dramatists* (Oxford, 2001). While plays such as *The Rover, A Bold Stroke for a Wife*, and *The Belle's Stratagem* are now familiar to students of the period, there are many more that were acclaimed in their time but lie neglected because of the forces just described. The plays currently available also suggest a much narrower generic range for women playwrights than was actually the case. This anthology offers more comedies because of their great appeal to audiences, and demonstrates some of the variety that these dramatists offered their audiences. Here are three main pieces and one afterpiece, a mode usually not associated with women. Behn's *The Emperor of the Moon* demonstrates her dexterity in spectacle as well as her talent in satire and addresses the new world of scientific exploration, a male bastion. Centlivre's *The Gamester*, like *The Emperor of the Moon*, is a fine example of how popular continental plays were adapted into palatable English fare. Clive's *The Rehearsal* is a reminder not only that women wrote more than main-piece comedies but also that there were enjoyable "extras" that helped make up an evening's performance. With its warning about the miseries of marriage mismatches, Cowley's *The Runaway* is perhaps most obviously a "woman's" play, yet its appeal crosses gender lines.

The selections here also reflect waves of female playwriting that Judith Stanton and Ellen Donkin each outlines. Stanton points out that most of the plays by women in the 1670s were Aphra Behn's (*Curtain Calls* 327). Behn's activity in the Restoration continued into the 1690s and early eighteenth century thanks to the productivity of "the Female Wits," who included Centlivre, Mary Pix, Delariviere Manley, and Catharine Trotter. Women produced few new plays in the middle part of the century, Clive's *The Rehearsal* (1751) among the even fewer popular ones (*Curtain Calls* 327). Still, Stanton observes, the "overall falling off of new plays staged from 1720 to 1759 contrasts sharply with the number of women's plays actually being staged during those years" so that "a theater-goer would have had the impression that more and more women were writing plays all the time" (*Curtain Calls* 328). Greater general productivity in the 1760s went hand in hand with "a slow but steady rise in new productions by women playwrights, which accelerated noticeably in 1779, and continued through to the end of the century" (Donkin 19). After 1800, Donkin records, there was a "rapid tapering off" of plays by women on stage and "no one emerges to replace Elizabeth Inchbald or Hannah Cowley ... until Catherine Gore in the 1830s" (19, 31).

The female playwrights themselves offer the best insights into the challenges facing women and the ways in which they met them. In the process, they have provided a significant body of criticism that furthers knowledge about the ways in which society and the practical aspects of the theater shaped drama. This anthology offers a sampling of that criticism. Often apologetically delivered and residing in prologues, epilogues, and prefatory essays, the insights of these early women writers into the function and development of English drama have been ignored while literary history reveres the critical poems and essays of such Restoration and eighteenth-century commentators as John Dryden, Thomas Rymer, Charles Gildon, Nicholas Rowe, Alexander Pope, and Samuel Johnson. Yet in the same period that Dryden, in his *Essay of Dramatick Poesie* (1668), urges his readers to consider the idiosyncrasies of English drama and audiences and so to rethink the usefulness of Aristotle's rules, Behn—and her successors, who take their cue from her and not Dryden—point out the impossibility of pleasing an audience by adhering to the Ancients' "musty rules of unity." In her "Epistle to the Reader" prefaced to *The Dutch Lover* (1673), for example, Behn disparages those who "discourse as formally about the rules" of drama, "as if 'twere the grand affair of human life." At a time when Shakespeare's plays were acceptable to audiences largely in adapted form, she then succinctly weighs Ben Jonson against Shakespeare, as Dryden does at length in his *Essay*, preferring, as he does, the latter for his lack of pretension and genuine entertainment. In their blunt commentary on social prejudices and theater politics and procedures, these critical essays also collectively reveal how particular groups—in this case, women—are cut out of history and the canon.

Like any pioneers, Behn and Centlivre faced the greatest challenges. Behn was not the first woman to have a play performed on the Restoration stage, but she was the first major English female playwright and the first woman in England to earn a living by her pen. Centlivre, who enjoyed the company of her fellow "Female Wits," was the first major eighteenth-century female playwright. Their presence in the theater world can be traced to Charles 11's modified patent for the theaters, published in 1662, which officially permitted actresses as part of the stage business and so just as officially opened to women a domain that in England had always been exclusively male. Yet, just as the king could not endow respectability or full public acceptance along with the titles and estates he conferred upon his mistresses, so too any woman—actress or writer—involved with the stage remained vilified by the public and a virtual outsider. In effect, Behn and Centlivre had to become honorary men as they confronted the obstacles before them. Winning the confidence of the theater manager was just the start. Petulant and vengeful critics, audiences, and actors remained much greater challenges for female playwrights than their male peers. By the time Cowley wrote for the stage in the last quarter of the eighteenth century, women had won some acceptance, but daunting challenges remained. Yet, throughout the period, women found ways in which to extend the existing parameters of the theater world even as they struggled within its boundaries.

The biggest problem of all was simply that of being known to be a woman—or as Behn summed it up, "a devil on't, the woman damns the poet." In an excerpt included here from her "Epistle to the Reader" from *The Dutch Lover* (1673), she tells of the "fop" who entered the pit to announce to "those that sat about it, that they were to expect a woeful play, God damn him, for it was a woman's" (p. 281 below). This has a parallel in Centlivre's account, also included here, of the "spark" who loved her *Gamester* and visited the bookseller for a copy only to discover that it was a woman's play, whereupon he "threw down the book, and put up his money, saying he had spent too much after it already" (p. 293 below). A particular dilemma for Behn, in the Restoration, was that audiences demanded bawdiness in their drama—but could not accept it from women. In the Preface to *The Lucky Chance* she condemns as ridiculous the charge commonly made against her plays "that 'tis not fit for the ladies": as if, she says of her male accusers "the ladies were obliged to hear indecencies only from their pens and plays" (p. 285 below). The complaint runs like a refrain through her commentaries. As plays became more moral and women more accepted, however, the moral hypocrisy seemed to intensify rather than abate. At the end of the eighteenth century, Cowley lamented that a "Novelist may use the boldest tints" and "seize Nature for her guide," but as a woman writing for the stage she felt "encompassed with chains when I write": "They will allow me, indeed, to draw strong character, but it must be without speaking its language. I may give vulgar or low bred persons, but they must converse in a stile of elegance" ("An Address" before *A School for Greybeards*).

Still, a century after Behn, Cowley suggests that the public, to which she attributes a characteristically English "gallantry," will indulge her *Runaway* precisely because the author is a woman, whereas if it were written by a man it "would have incurred the severest lash of criticism" (p. 197 below). Donkin too wonders if being a woman writer—and so a curiosity—may have helped a playwright gain attention in the eighteenth century, when, as George Colman remarked after becoming manager at Drury Lane, "cartloads of trash [were] annually offer'd to the Director of a London Theatre" (Donkin 6; Jenkins 512). Donkin further illustrates how Garrick's fatherly treatment of female authors gave many a start in the theater. Yet, as she also argues, such patronage—or patronizing—backfired when they were left without protection after his retirement in 1776 (26-31; passim). Cowley sketches, in the Preface to her *Albina*, a horror story of how Sheridan, in his first season as Garrick's successor at Drury Lane, had no interest in her *Runaway* even as "the last piece which was produced by his able successor," so that "my Comedy, to use the technical term, was *shelf'd*." Worse, as she labored to have her tragedy *Albina* staged, Sheridan and Harris, the manager at Covent Garden, froze her out, costing her "a reasonable prospect of several hundred pounds," a messy public controversy with Hannah More, whom she suspected of plagiarizing from her play when it lay neglected in manuscript, and "years of fruitless anxiety and trouble."

While theater managers might prevent a play from getting off the ground and vociferous critics might damn it, actors, who frequently expressed their biases against female playwrights, had the power to make or break it on the boards. Centlivre pinpoints their omnipotence when she claims that poets "like Mushrooms rise and fall of late" but "no scene takes place without the moving player" (Prologue to *Love's Contrivance*). Three quarters of a century later, Cowley stresses that no matter how good or bad the lines a playwright provides for the actors, the ultimate success of the play lies entirely in their hands. A "great Actor, holding a sword in his left hand and making awkward pushes with it," she says "charms the audience infinitely more" than by any "wit and observation which the ingenious Author might have given him" (Preface to *The Town Before You*).

For all her dynamic scripts, Behn was an early victim of the omnipotent actors, who clearly enjoyed their power over women playwrights. She complains to her reader in the "Epistle" of *The Dutch Lover* that the play "was hugely injured in the acting," especially by the actor who ad-libbed his lines: "My Dutch Lover spoke little of what I intended for him, but supplied it with a deal of idle stuff." Sometimes, actors would reject a part in a woman's play; Robert Wilks, for example, "refused for some time" to act in *The Busy Body*, as the *Tatler* records (No. 15, May 13, 1709). Despite this setback and audience prejudice, the play "forced a run of thirteen nights" and became Centlivre's greatest success. On the other hand, actors could support playwrights through outstanding performances of their characters, as Garrick certainly did. In one season he played Marplot in *The Busy Body*, and, as Bowyer explains, after Garrick took the role of Don Felix in *The Wonder*—which he played for twenty years—the play came to be regarded as Centlivre's masterpiece (Bowyer 183). As already noted, this was the role he chose as a finale to his stellar acting career, and Bowyer quotes from Fizgerald's *Life of David Garrick* to argue that the performance marked a signal moment for English comedy: "The occasion afforded 'one last glimpse of true comedy, the like of which it may be suspected no one has seen since,' and the crowded, magnificent, and responsive audience may be regarded as unique in the history of the English stage" (183).

As one of Garrick's "favorite performers," Clive was in an ideal position to foreground difficulties that women faced as playwrights and performers and to retaliate against them (Bowyer 182). In *The Rehearsal* she sensationalizes the figure of the female playwright as a social misfit, and her portrayal of Mrs. Hazard is, in many ways, as cruel a satire as Pope's Phoebe Clinket in *Three Hours after Marriage* (a figure often associated with Centlivre). Yet through Mrs. Hazard she brings to life on stage the frustrations of the woman writer and reveals a playwright's anxieties about the actors—and she does so in a humorous self-mocking way. Played by Clive, the character simultaneously highlights the actress's own power and her vulnerability as a woman when she protests that Mrs. Clive is "so conceited, and insolent" that she won't readily accept a part in her (Mrs. Hazard's) play because she claims—and here Clive as Hazard mimics Clive the actress/playwright—"I have been a great sufferer already, by the manager's not doing justice to my genius; but I hope I shall next year convince the Town, what fine judgment they have: for I intend to play a capital tragedy part for my own benefit" (p. 178 below). Clive wrote *The Rehearsal* with Garrick's support for her own benefit night—but here she benefits all struggling women playwrights.

As Clive's stratagem suggests, women employed active and passive tactics in their battles. One of the latter was anonymous presentation and publication of their plays, though this was not always successful. After Sheridan ignored her *Albina*, Cowley had "a Lady of Rank" present her play to Harris at Covent Garden "with the name and sex of the Author concealed," though the rest of her story reveals that Harris knew indeed whose play it was (Preface to *Albina*). Cowley's attempt at anonymity had many precedents. For whatever reasons, the play that would be Behn's most successful, *The Rover* (1677), first appeared anonymously, and, as Anne Russell points out, a line in the prologue calls the author "he" and "him" (14). Yet, prior to *The Rover*, Behn had published six plays with title pages announcing the author as Mrs. Behn or the more ambiguous A. Behn. Moreover, the prologue of *The Forced Marriage* (1670), her first play, toys with the idea of female manipulation of audiences (see p. 283 below). Centlivre employed similar strategies, identifying authorship and gender in her first plays, then retreating behind anonymity. Her biographer John Bowyer suggests that what we would now call feminist activity early in Queen Anne's reign ("some even believing that Queen Anne could be persuaded to build a college for women") enabled Centlivre to publish her first play "with her name on the title page." The prologue, furthermore, "boasted that [the play] was a lady's: *And here's To-night, what doubly makes it sweet, / A private Table, and a Lady's Treat.*" For her second play, too, she was "allowed immediate credit" (Bowyer 41-42). Yet the next ones were published anonymously. Her third and fourth plays, *The Beau's Duel; or, A Soldier for the Ladies* and *The Stolen Heiress; or, the Salamanca Doctor Outplotted* respectively, both performed in 1702 and published in 1703, suggest male authorship by employing the pronoun "he" to refer to the author in prefatory material. Both also have dedications that engage in the male system of patronage with its heroic language of generosity, achievement, and noble lineage. Her fifth play, *The Gamester*, was also published anonymously and, as already noted, passed for a man's until word spread that it was not. *The Basset-Table* (1705), which followed and was also extremely popular, coyly refused to announce its female authorship yet did not renounce it either, the title page referring to the author as that "of *The Gamester*" and the dedication claiming that the author felt for the play "the fondness of a Mother." ·

Often female playwrights simply spoke out against the prejudices they confronted, especially when objections to the supposed quality of their work involved their education. Behn is first to confront this problem directly, arguing that there is no problem for "plays have no great room for that which is men's advantage over women: that is, learning." She uses as her prime example Shakespeare, "who was not guilty of much more of this than often falls to women's share" and yet whose plays "have better pleased the world than Jonson's works, though by the way 'tis said that Benjamin was no such rabbi neither." She dismisses the Ancients' rules as "enough intelligible and practicable by a woman," if actually "they meant anything." Like Dryden in his *Essay of Dramatick Poesie*, however, she suggests that a playwright is better occupied studying what entertains an English audience—and, she adds, "avoiding of scurrility" (see p. 282). Centlivre reinforces the point, arguing that while the "Criticks cavil most about Decorums, and crie up Aristotle's Rules as the most essential part of the Play," they will "never persuade the Town to be of their Opinion, which relishes nothing so well as Humour lightly tost up with Wit, and drest with Modesty and Air." Taking care not to decry the unities, she claims her preferences lie with the town's, for the freer way of writing "gives the Poet a larger Scope of Fancy, and with less Trouble, Care, and Pain, serves his and the Players End." Why, therefore, she asks, "shou'd a Man torture, and wrack his Brain for what will be no Advantage to him" for "the Town will ne'er be entertain'd with Plays according to the Method of the Ancients, till they exclude this Innovation of Wit and Humour, which yet I see no likelihood of doing" (Preface to *Love's Contrivance*, 1703).

Cowley too, in the prologue to *The Runaway*, introduces herself, a newcomer to the London theater world, as a "woman" who is "untutored in the school, / Nor Aristotle knows, nor scarce a rule." There is doubtless irony here, for the education her father gave her, informal though it may have been, would have rivaled that of many male contemporaries, and her prologue itself provides evidence of schooling in ancient authors. Yet she places confidence in the simple "rural, playful" fare she has to offer the audience—presentations of human nature that derive from a mother's special insights. In her final play, *The Town Before You*, she is still aware that "Laugh! Laugh! Laugh! is the demand" from audiences. Far from excusing her education, she stakes a high moral ground as frustrated social educator: "I invoke the rising generation, to correct a taste which, to be gratified, demands neither genius or intellect" (Preface).

More subtly, women infiltrated and expanded the possibilities of patronage, that essentially male institution, which was so central to theater operations. For Clive, an insider's stance as a popular actress and important member of Garrick's company enabled her, at mid-century, to arrange her own benefit night for her play, *The Rehearsal* (1753). When she felt gypped with regard to her earnings, moreover, she went over the theater managers' heads, appealing to those most powerful patrons of all, the theater-going public, in *The Case of Mrs. Clive, Submitted to the Public* (1744). Her predecessors were necessarily more surreptitious. In her early dedications especially, Centlivre assimilated herself into the male poet-patron system by flattering her patrons in the customary masculine language of the institution, as mentioned above. Yet, while she begins the dedication of *The Basset Table* in a familiar way by lauding the worthiness of the patron and noting the unworthiness of the poet, she then subtly feminizes the language by claiming "the fondness of a Mother for her Production." Behn, as Russell points out, managed to produce "her first seven plays (including *The Rover*) without dedications to patrons, an unusually long period for a writer to remain without patronage, and an indication of" her outsider's status (14). Having thus proved the system not omnipotent after all, she insinuates her way into and parodies it in *The Feigned Courtesans* (1679). Behn dedicates the play to the king's mistress and former actress and orange girl, Nell Gwyn, lauding her innate generosity and applying the equally customary language of noble lineage to Gwyn's illegitimate children by the king. In this way, Behn, the sensational but disrespectable playwright, and Gwyn, the king's sensational but disrespectable mistress, outsiders both, appropriate and undermine a time-honored male institution. Such tactics as Behn and Centlivre employed doubtless opened the way for such as Cowley who came from nowhere to claim for her first play the support of England's most famous theater personality. Cowley went so far as to assert, in her prologue, that its merits emanate from her role as a mother, for her children were her muse and the sketches of human nature in the play a re-creation of her children's passions.

Women also used their plays to question and expand social boundaries, even when they seemed to reinforce male prejudices.[5] In *The Basset Table*, for example, Centlivre creates a female virtuoso (what we might call a mad scientist) who is a key source of the play's humor. Yet while we laugh at her virtuoso behavior (a stock butt of comedy), we can sympathize with her situation in being subject to the whims of a tyrannical father—and with her determination that nothing can "enslave" the mind, as she declares in

---

5   Nancy Cotton argues that when "women wrote like men, they expressed male prejudices," pointing to Lady Knowell in Behn's *Sir Patient Fancy* and Valeria in Centlivre's *The Basset Table* as key examples (210).

Act Two. Like Behn in *The Emperor of the Moon*, moreover, Centlivre shows her dexterity in the language and concepts of another exclusively male domain, that of scientific exploration. Similarly, while Behn's *Rover*, for example, is as irreverent as any play by her male contemporaries, it subtly draws audience attention and sympathy towards women and their problems. The play opens with a conversation between witty women. It provides a female equivalent of the well-loved rake hero. It highlights throughout the mercenary and miserable nature of forced marriages. It even presents a highly sympathetic character who is as much an outsider as the playwright herself—a high-priced, self-sufficient courtesan. As Clive's and Cowley's plays included here indicate, by mid-century women could unabashedly focus on "women's issues" and win audience favor for doing so. The editor of the 1813 edition of Cowley's plays observes that, "her dramas differ from others in that women are generally made the leading characters" (x). *The Runaway* is typical of Cowley in this and in its focus on marriage as well as the type of female characters presented: they generally embody "the purest innocence of conduct with the greatest vivacity of manners" (x).

Successful as they were, these women wrote not merely for their own pleasure in the craft: they worked to support themselves and their dependent families. As the first professional woman writer in England, Behn famously commented, in her "Note" to *Sir Patient Fancy*, that she was "forced to write for bread and not ashamed to own it," even if she felt that writing, as she did, for vulgar tastes was "a way which even I despise as much below me." Financial exigency certainly proved an effective muse, for Behn's output was second only to John Dryden's in the Restoration. Before and after Centlivre's first stage productions (she was then known as Susannah Carroll), she worked as a strolling player to support herself. In 1707, she married Joseph Centlivre, who, as a chief royal cook, bore the delightful title Yeoman of the Mouth. Bowyer suggests that this marriage (despite the pre-nuptial contract Joseph insisted upon) allowed her a degree of financial freedom for the first time so that she "relaxed before trying another play." The result was a "greater originality than usual," which won her "popular favor" for *The Busy Body* (1709) "her most successful comedy" (94). Perhaps because of the relative financial freedom marriage offered, she went on to produce other outstanding hits.

Marriage and her growing family had the opposite effect for Cowley. With the unexpected success of *The Runaway*, she realized she had "opened a new prospect of advantage to my family, which I have since pursued with alacrity" (Preface to *Albina*). Clearly this new prospect was sorely needed. Sheridan's shelving of *The Runaway* and the debacle over *Albina* hurt more than her pride, as she says with reluctance in her Preface to the tragedy: "This may appear a vulgar topic; but to me it is a very serious subject of complaint, that, by the conduct of the Winter Managers, I have been deprived of a reasonable prospect of several hundred pounds." The situation was indeed serious; in late 1780 Hannah's father, Philip Parkhouse, appealed on behalf of his daughter's family to Lord Harrowby, former MP of Tiverton, where the Parkhouse family lived. Harrowby's response was to assign Thomas Cowley a commission in the East India Company, which effectively left his wife still managing her family's affairs, especially after Thomas died in India in 1797 (de la Mahotiere 46-47). Her situation was not unusual. Donkin adds Charlotte Lennox, Elizabeth Inchbald, Frances Brooke, Sophia Lee, and Frances Burney to the list of women for whom "there is clear evidence that the prime motivating factor for undertaking playwriting in the first place was a struggle for economic survival for themselves and their dependent families" (18). A letter from Lennox to Garrick in 1775 sounds remarkably similar to Cowley's story: "I am not indifferent to theatrical rewards; could I obtain them, they would assist me to bring up my little boy and my girl ..." (Donkin 14). The degree of urgency that Clive felt at her unfair treatment financially at the hands of both major theater managers drove her twice to publish the details in appeals to the public.

In the century that this anthology covers, then, from Behn's plays through Cowley's, women made their mark in the realm of playwriting, perhaps the hardest of all literary media to crack. Cowley's retreat from the stage because of the restrictions dictating what she could (and could not) put in the mouths of her characters and her bowdlerization, as the 1813 editor puts it, of her own plays in the name of morality suggest no progress at all had been made since Behn bore the slings and arrows of slander. The intervening years, however, had seen dynamic women make a real impact on every aspect of the London theater world. Despite the ostensible lack of progress, moreover, Behn had paved a path down which her successors were careful to follow, consciously placing themselves in a tradition and creating a female lineage as determinedly as Dryden did an English one. Tracing her literary ancestry to Behn, Centlivre, as Bowyer points out, called herself "Astraea" in a series of literary correspondence (10). She also publicly acknowledged her debt to her predecessor, as Mary Pix did (Finberg xvii). Janet Todd adds Ariadne, Catharine Trotter, and Delariviere Manley to the list of playwrights immediately following Behn who "saw her as their most important predecessor" (14). Clive, meanwhile, chose to close her acting career with a play by Centlivre, and Cowley imitated plays by Behn and Centlivre. Their impact is revealed in a complaint in *The St. James Chronicle* in 1779 that the "Success of the Amazonian leaders brought forth a Mrs. Griffith, a Mrs. Cowley, and a Miss More" (Donkin 67).

The legacy female playwrights left is remarkable, even as it continues to emerge. Problems abound, including the paucity of information about their lives and critical tendencies that have "thoroughly gendered" what limited accounts exist of their lives and works, to use Copeland's observation about Centlivre (*Bold Stroke* 8). As the plays presented here demonstrate, however, some of the best entertainments to grace the English stage in the long eighteenth century were the work of women's pens.

APHRA BEHN, *THE EMPEROR OF THE MOON* (1687)

This was Behn's second most popular play, after *The Rover* (1677). From its debut in December 1687 until the mid-eighteenth century, *The Emperor of the Moon* enjoyed over 130 performances, and continued to be performed periodically until 1748. After that, records show only a 1777 production at the Patagonian Theatre,[6] in which the play was, Summers says, "very unnecessarily altered" (3: 339).

The early performances maximized the capacities for spectacle of the Dorset Garden Theatre, which had housed the Duke's Company before it merged with King's Company, forming the United Company in 1682. Before the merger, Behn wrote for the Duke's Company, perhaps, Jane Spencer suggests, because it was under the control of a woman—William Davenant's widow—at the time Behn's playwriting career began (viii-ix). However, audiences loved the elaborate effects in which the Duke's Company, with its "unparalleled resources," excelled; and as *The Emperor of the Moon* so well demonstrates, Behn's great talent lay in her full use of the stage area (Hughes 12). From her innovative prologue with its talking head, she relies heavily on the physical capabilities of the theater: with its constant action, characters concealed from other characters but visible to the audience, discovery scenes (including Parnassus and a temple), fights, blanket tossing, human tapestry, and grand finale of the zodiac descent and dance, this play targets the senses of the audience for its impact.[7] The sheer number of stage directions indicate the degree to which action—the movement of bodies and props on stage—shapes the play.

Also typical of Behn's drama in general is the obvious influence in this farce-based play of continental drama, for which Charles II developed an enthusiasm during his Interregnum-period exile. Behn had begun *The Emperor of the Moon* during Charles's reign, but shelved it following his

---

6   The Patagonian Theatre opened in 1776 in London, run by a Dublin group. It was mostly associated with puppet shows and pantomimes.
7   Jane Spencer provides a fine discussion of Behn's stagecraft in her introduction to the plays.

sudden death in 1685, the ensuing political unrest of James II's succession, and the unexpected losses that the United Company suffered with the flop of Dryden's elaborate political spectacle, *Albion and Albanius* (Hughes 158-59). In her dedication to the Marquis of Worcester, she declares that the play was "calculated for His late Majesty of Sacred Memory, that Great Patron of Noble Poetry, and the Stage." She then stresses her adaptation of continental sources to English taste: "A very barren and thin hint of the Plot I had from the Italian, and which, even as it was, was acted in France eighty odd times without Intermission. 'Tis now much altered and adapted to our English Theater and Genius...." Her main source was *Arlequin Empereur dans la Lune* (1684), a French farce. As Summers points out, the "Italian" scenes came from the "impromptu comedy" *Commedia dell'Arte all'Improviso* (3:386-87).[8]

Derived from European farce traditions and heavily dependent on its entertainment value, the play has long escaped serious critical analysis. In 1948, Leo Hughes and A.H. Scouten argued that even the "romantic plot has almost disappeared under the farcical scenes heaped upon it with no higher motive than to provide laughs" and that what remains "is treated with no sign of seriousness" (43). Over fifty years later, Derek Hughes too cautioned that the "play must not be overinterpreted" (171). Yet, just as much as Behn's full-length and less explicitly farcical plays, this one both reflects and critiques complex philosophical, social, and political issues of its time. As an attempt to create an idiosyncratically English drama from continental sources, the play also consciously participates in the development of English drama, the tradition of which Behn directly confronts in her dedicatory epistle and the opening of her prologue.

Admittedly, the main plot seems clichéd, especially for a female playwright, as it presents the hilarious intrigues of two witty young couples who are desperate to free themselves from a tyrannical father figure, and who ultimately win his sympathy as well as the audience's. Yet like Behn's other plays and those of her contemporaries, *The Emperor of the Moon* engages in Hobbesian theories of natural vs. social law beginning with Elaria's bold song that opens the play with a curse upon the "faithless maid, / Who first her sex's liberty betrayed; / Born free as man to love and rage." This theme is augmented by the challenge to patriarchal power and the wit of the female

---

8   Leo Hughes and A.H. Scouten discuss Behn's source in detail, challenging some of Summers's suggestions about her use of the French play (40-41). Hughes gives the Italian title of the French-Italian production that Behn used: "This was derived from *Arlecchino, imperatore nella luna*, a farsa by Nolant de Fatouville which had been performed in 1684 by the Italian comedians in Paris (and which, via Goldoni, was to be the ultimate source of Haydn's opera *Il Mondo della luna*)."

leads (also typical of Behn's drama), while the servant Mopsophil is just as determined to have her own choice of a husband. The play thus offers an interesting complement to Behn's daring poems and novels, with their freedom-loving female characters.

The act itself of undertaking a play about a virtuoso (with the pseudo-scientific language this involves) was a further assertion on Behn's part of the equal powers of a woman's mind—more so than in the later case of Centlivre's female virtuoso, Valeria, whom critics and audiences can construe as ridiculous. Around the time she completed *The Emperor of the Moon*, Behn also translated from French *A Discovery of New Worlds* (1688), and attached to it "a preface, by way of essay on translated prose; wherein the arguments of Father Tacquet, and others against the system of Copernicus (as to the motion of the earth) are likewise considered and answered." In her preface, she claims that part of the appeal of "this little book" lay in "the author's introducing a woman as one of the speakers in these five discourses," for "I thought an English woman might adventure to translate any thing, a French woman may be supposed to have spoken." While she modestly admits that "I found the task not so easy as I believed at first" and professes only to go as far as "a woman's reasoning allows" and "not venture upon the astronomical part," she assesses current theories of the Ptolemaic and Copernican systems and their theological implications—while providing a theory of translation. Apologetic though it may be, the woman's voice rings out here as an equal participant in the intellectual spheres of the late seventeenth century, just as her witty and enduring presentation of Doctor Baliardo conveys the female playwright's full comprehension of contemporary scientific debates.

As critics have begun to notice, moreover, *The Emperor of the Moon* goes beyond gentle mockery of the Royal Society and its empirical investigations. Behn herself ties her ingenious commentary on perception to a political warning by regretting in her dedicatory epistle that the stage is now "quite undone by the misapprehension of the ignorant and misrepresenting of the envious," while "the only diversion of the town now, is high dispute, and public controversies in taverns, coffee houses, & c. And those things which ought to be the greatest mysteries in religion, and so rarely the business of discourse are turned into ridicule, and look but like so many fanatical stratagems to ruin the pulpit as well as the stage." Arguing that the play is an attack on "excessive credulity," Al Coppola underlines Behn's concern with spectacle in all spheres of public life and demonstrates how the play "stimulates the viewer's uncritical gaze only to retrain it" (483). Barbara Benedict, likewise, puts the play in the contexts of Restoration science fiction fads and the culture of exploration, remarking that "Behn contrasts the different ways of seeing: idealism, love, empirical curiosity, and exploration" (60). As they suggest, *The Emperor of the Moon* is at the heart of Restoration culture and offers audiences far more than light French-flavored entertainment.

SUSANNA CENTLIVRE, *THE GAMESTER* (1705)

Centlivre's twentieth-century biographer John Bowyer is correct to bestow upon her "the rank of the most popular woman dramatist in English," for, as he notes, she "was the most prolific playwright in England from 1700 to 1722," and her plays remained in the repertoires of English and American theaters through the nineteenth century. "Most of the great actors and actresses of the eighteenth and nineteenth centuries," he also notes, "won reputation in her comedies" (v). Of her nineteen plays, *The Gamester* ranks amongst the five most popular, and was unusual in winning its author a benefit performance on the twelfth night of its first run. It was the first play for which she had a star cast (Bowyer 59, 62).

Like Behn in *The Emperor of the Moon*, Centlivre stresses in her dedication that she has taken a French source for her play but adapted it to the tastes and habits of an English audience: "Part of it, I own myself obliged to the French for, particularly the character of the Gamester; but he is entirely ruined in the French. Whereas I, in complaisance to the many fine gentlemen that play in England, have reclaimed him...." As critics have pointed out, Mottley identifies Centlivre's source for the play as Jean Francois Regnard's *Le Joueur* (1696) (Bowyer 60). Bowyer observes that Centlivre was doubtless encouraged in looking to the French play by her success the previous year with *Love's Contrivance; or, Le Médecin Malgré Lui*. Structurally, *The Gamester* is made more English through the addition of Lovewell, so as to provide the two pairs of lovers that audiences expected (Bowyer 61). However, the specifically English nature of *The Gamester* lies, as Centlivre's dedication underscores, in its moral: "the ill consequences of gaming." It resides also in the way it develops English comedy as a genre in the presentation of that moral.

By the time Centlivre composed her play, gambling was a social problem, and was long established as a prevalent topic in literature. In 1674 Charles Cotton had published *The Compleat Gamester; or, Instructions how to play at billiards, trucks, bowls and chess. Together with all manner of usual and most gentile games either on cards or dice. To which is added, the arts and mysteries of riding, racing, archery, and cockfighting.* His purpose, he claimed, was not to moralize (after all, even the "Stoick" must at some point "unbend his mind"); rather, gaming had become such a social phenomenon that he would fully instruct his readers in the games in which they might "pass away their spare minutes in harmless recreation" so that they "may observe the cheats and abuses, and so be armed against the injuries may accrue thereby" ("Epistle to the Reader"). Centlivre's character Cogdie seems designed as a similar warning to an eighteenth-century audience concerning cheats, though, as her play indicates, by this point gambling, far from being a "harmless recreation," had become a social contagion. Just two years after *The Gamester*, Colley Cibber remarked in the dedication to *The Lady's Last Stake* (1707) that "Gambling is a Vice, that has undone more innocent Principles, than any one Folly that's in Fashion" (quoted by Evans 26). The extent of the damage it wreaked upon the upper classes, in particular, Amanda Foreman shows comprehensively in her biography of the late eighteenth-century aristocrat Georgiana, Duchess of Devonshire (1998).

Gambling was already a recurrent theme in comedy too by 1705. James Evans traces its evolution through Restoration social comedy into the eighteenth century, highlighting the association between libertinism and gambling. As he says, however, there is a marked difference between the libertinism of Charles II's reign and that of subsequent monarchies: "in an era with more sober courts providing examples of conduct and promoting the reformation of manners, Centlivre created a very different kind of libertine gambler than her predecessor" (25). Valere might be addicted to gambling but he is not the sexual free-ranger that his predecessors are. Indeed, his father and his beloved stipulate throughout that he must choose between his destructive gambling and his love, while "the bourgeois ideology of *The Gamester* requires that Valere demonstrate his inner worth before he can marry the heiress" (27). In its sentimental tone and the clarity of its moral, the play contributes in its own way to what has been labeled the "reform movement" in eighteenth-century comedy.[9]

Centlivre's dedication demonstrates her consciousness of the power of the stage over social mores and the newly heightened social awareness of drama's moral function. Echoing the language of Jeremy Collier's attack on the stage and the essay warfare that ensued, she claims that her main design, "according to the first intent of plays," is to "recommend morality." She is careful to "affirm there is nothing immodest, nor immoral in it." However, despite its two conversion scenes, in which Valere and Lady Wealthy regret their errors, and its explicit morality, especially in Valere's last speech, the play engages the audience in the dilemmas of the time rather than offering straightforward instruction. Valere's addiction as he expresses it, for

---

9   Jacqueline Pearson argues that Centlivre was resistant to reform comedy that was actively promoted by "some women dramatists, like Catharine Trotter and Mary Pix" (203-04).

example, ties the temptation of gambling to the imperatives of a society in which money reigns supreme:

> Who is happier than a gamester? Who more respected—I mean those that make any figure in the world? Who more caressed by lords and dukes? Or whose conversation more agreeable? Whose coach finer in the ring? Or finger in the side box produce more luster? Who has more attendance from the drawers, or better wine from the master? Or nicer served by the cook? In short, there is an air of magnificence in't. A gamester's hand is the philosopher's stone that turns all it touches into gold. (p. 135 below)

Hector is quick to retort "and gold into nothing," yet an audience member already lured by gaming would doubtless feel inclined to cheer Valere's words. Similarly, the long gaming scene in Act Four with its mounting tensions may serve as well for a "fix" for those in the audience already addicted to the suspense of the game as it does for a warning about the ease with which great stakes are lost.

While this play showcases the gentleman gambler and suggests how easily estates can be lost at the toss of a die, Centlivre's next, *The Basset Table*—an attempt to capitalize on the success of *The Gamester*—focuses on the habits of a merchant's wife, Mrs. Sago. The main plot again depends upon the reform of an aristocrat, a woman this time; however, the play's harshest attack is on the citizen's wife, who wheedles goods from her husband that she sells in order to play at the basset table—where she is only accepted because she always loses. Just as Hector in *The Gamester* offers moral commentary on his master's addiction throughout, moreover, and begins the play with a complaint about gaming, so servants are the most sensible and morally upright characters in *The Basset Table*. The opening scene is especially remarkable in its focus on a group of servant characters, who announce the problems that the play explores. *The Gamester* and *The Basset Table*, indeed, are typical of Centlivre's drama in particular and women's plays in general in the amount of stage time devoted to the servant class. As the playwright addresses gambling as a plague in the eighteenth century, in short, she is careful to show its impact throughout society, not just amongst those with power.

The impact of *The Gamester* is hard to pin down. It appeared on stage fairly regularly until 1745; then in 1789, it was produced as a three-act comedy under the title *The Pharo Table* at Covent Garden. Its influence on other plays, as Bowyer suggests, is probable: "[e]ven Charles in Sheridan's *The School for Scandal* shows many resemblances to Valere." As he also says, however, "direct borrowings" are "difficult to prove" (66). What is certain is that Centlivre achieved in this play, as in her others, lively and sympathetic characters, allowing audiences to feel their predicaments and engage in moral consideration of pressing social issues.

CATHERINE CLIVE, *THE REHEARSAL*;
OR, BAYS IN PETTICOATS (1753). BY NOEL CHEVALIER[10]

At the time she composed *The Rehearsal; or Bays in Petticoats*, Catherine "Kitty" Clive was one of the most celebrated performers in her day. Clive's biography, as interpreted by historians such as Charles Lee Lewes in his 1805 *Memoirs*, is a fantastic rags-to-riches story. Lewes includes a tale of her discovery that is the eighteenth-century equivalent of the Hollywood legend of Lana Turner's being discovered in Schwab's Pharmacy:

> When Mrs. Clive lived with Miss Knowles, who then lodged at Mrs. Snell's, a fan-painter in Church-Row, Houndsditch, Mr. Watson, many years box-keeper of Drury-Lane and Richmond, kept the Bell Tavern, directly opposite to Mrs. Snell's. At this house was held the Beef-Steak Club, instituted by Mr. Beard, Mr. Dunstall, Mr. Woodward, Stoppalear, Bencraft, Giffard, &c. &c. Kitty Rafter, being one day washing the steps of the door, and singing, the windows of the club-room being open, they were instantly crowded by the company, who were all enchanted by her natural grace and simplicity. This circumstance alone led her to the stage, under the auspices of Mr. Beard and Mr. Dunstall. (2: 195-96)

This story has by no means been verified, but it exemplifies Clive's persona: unassuming, full of "natural grace and simplicity." The anecdote mentions her singing talent; it does not mention her considerable talent for comedy, which made her a central figure at Drury Lane at a time when stage comedy provided the most lucrative entertainment.

Clive also managed to maintain a public reputation as a respectable woman of the stage, ironically in part because of her failed marriage. She had married George Clive, a lawyer, in 1733, but the marriage was over by 1734. Clive and her husband separated in 1735, but never divorced. Despite the separation, Clive respected her marriage vows, and therefore was able to move freely among her male colleagues without scandal. In fact, her chastity became part of her endearing persona.

---

10   This portion of the Introduction is written by Dr. Noel Chevalier, who has adapted it from his Introduction to *The Clandestine Marriage, Together with Two Short Plays* (Broadview, 1995).

Bays in Petticoats, the first of only two plays that Clive composed, was written partly as a piece of self-parody. Clive had actually played the part of the pompous hack poet in a revival of Buckingham's *Rehearsal* (1671)—originally a satirical dig at John Dryden that remained one of the most popular comedies of the eighteenth century—but by 1750, critics such as "Harry Rambler" were only too eager to point out that Clive was no longer attractive enough to play breeches parts. As a response, Clive created Mrs. Hazard, the female counterpart to Buckingham's Bayes.[11] Clive carries the parallel only so far: Mrs. Hazard begins as a comic figure, but ends up being presented in a more sympathetic light than Buckingham's original poet.

In the 1671 play, Bayes really is a bad playwright: overly conventional, bombastic, and too proud of his own ideas to approach them critically, no matter how ridiculous they appear. While Buckingham satirizes all the conventions of heroic drama, a good deal of his attack is also directed at Bayes's refusal to receive any constructive advice on how to improve his play. At the opening of *Bays in Petticoats* we are tempted to see Mrs. Hazard in the same way. Gatty, her maid, notes her ill temper, while Tom, her footman, mentions that she has become a laughing-stock in the Town because of her play: "I fancy this farce of hers is horrid stuff: for I observe, all her visitors she reads it to (which is indeed every body that comes to the house) whisper as they come down stairs, and laugh ready to kill themselves." Indeed, when Mrs. Hazard first appears, she is as nasty and as ill-tempered as Gatty has described her. For the moment, Mrs. Hazard is only a more irascible version of Bayes.

With the appearance of Witling, however, the perspective changes. Witling's name identifies him as a satirical figure, part of the foppish social circle that Mrs. Hazard moves in. Witling inadvertently reveals part of the reason why Mrs. Hazard has become such a laughing-stock—no one expects to take seriously any play written by a woman: "I'll swear," Witling reports himself saying, "I believe Mrs Hazard can write a very pretty play, for she has a great deal of wit and humour.—Wit and humour! says [Frank Surly], why, there are not ten women in the creation that have sense enough to write a consistent *N.B.*—" (see p. 176 below). Frank Surly is not alone in his belief: the group of witlings who interrupt Mrs. Hazard's rehearsal in Act II refuse to take any of it seriously without actually having seen much of it.

Mrs. Hazard's attackers represent a variety of types. The three women who show up at the theater—Miss Sidle, Miss Giggle, and Miss Dawdle—are women who care for nothing but gossip and fashion; their names alone suggest their silliness. Mrs. Hazard is rightly outraged that Miss Giggle

---

11   While Buckingham's character is Bayes, it is spelled Bays in the title of Clive's play.

would use the theater as a kind of makeshift drawing room to entertain her friends; Witling himself reveals that he has brought this party to the theater precisely to be revenged on Mrs. Hazard for making him "sick to death with her stuff." The most condescending remarks, however, come from Sir Albany Odelove, an old rake who also presumes, because he has had the advantage of a level of formal education denied to all women at that time, to offer advice on how to write plays:

> I say, Madam, will you give me leave, as you're going to entertain the Town (that is, I mean endeavour, or attempt to entertain them), for let me tell you, fair lady, 'tis not an easy thing to bring about. If men, who are properly graduated in learning, who have swallowed the tincture of a polite education, who, as I may say, are hand and glove with the classics, if such geniuses as I'm describing, fail of success in dramatical occurrences, or performances ('tis the same sense in the Latin), what must a poor lady expect, who is as ignorant as the dirt?

Mrs. Hazard, rightly furious, suspends her rehearsal shortly afterward, and stomps off the stage. Witling, unfazed by the outburst, calls for a dance, and on that note the play ends.

The brutality of the witlings' behavior in Act II marks them, and not Mrs. Hazard, as the object of satire here. In Buckingham's play we clearly sympathize with the wits who ridicule Bayes, mainly because Bayes himself is so unaware that he is being ridiculed. The wits and even the actors make fun of his play as it is being rehearsed, and the piece is so laughably awful that it is clear that the whole genre of heroic drama as exemplified by Dryden is being satirized as much as Bayes's inept handling of its conventions. Clive, on the other hand, redirects the focus of Buckingham's piece to show the frustration felt by a woman of some literary talent who wants to be taken seriously as a writer. Mrs. Hazard's burletta (a portion of which is sung in Act II) is no worse than other examples of its genre, such as Charles Burney's highly successful *The Cunning-Man*. Peter Holman argues that the burletta had been performed independently prior to its inclusion in *The Rehearsal*,[12] and the fact that no less a figure than William Boyce composed the music lends it considerable authority. Clive presents the text without comment—significantly, the witlings arrive to laugh at the piece only after we have heard most of it. Furthermore, there is nothing to indicate that the

---

12   In booklet for CD *Peleus and Thetis and Other Theatre Music* by William Boyce, Peter Holman, conductor (Hyperion CDA 66935., 1997), 3. At the time of this writing, the CD is available as a paid download at www.hyperion-records.co.uk and the booklet without charge.

burletta is played farcically: Mrs. Hazard (Clive herself) sings the part of Marcella, as a "stand-in" for the actress Mrs. Clive. This last detail shows that Clive is only too happy to indulge in some jokes at her own expense—a feature which no doubt delighted the audience—but that same mockery doesn't extend to her writing.

Clive satirizes herself as a performer; she satirizes fashionable London society; she satirizes attitudes towards women writers that she no doubt encountered herself; but she does not satirize Mrs. Hazard. She is far too wronged in Act II for the reader to see her as an object of ridicule. Indeed, her very name suggests the great risks involved in any woman's attempting to be taken seriously as a dramatist. *Bays in Petticoats* is a farce, but it is a dark farce, a comedy which questions the notion of public taste, and which reveals the sexism inherent in the theater that would later receive fuller treatment in playwright and opera-house manager Frances Brooke's novel *The Excursion* (1778). In Clive's play, unfortunately, the witlings triumph: Mrs. Hazard declares that she is "not sure [she] will ever have another" rehearsal, and tears her manuscript to pieces as she leaves the stage. Witling laconically comments that "her tearing it, will only save the audience the trouble of doing it for her." In that, he misses the point: no one has attacked the play itself, and Mrs. Hazard's great frustration lies in her being questioned that, as a woman, she is capable of writing one at all.

Bays in Petticoats premiered 15 March 1750, at a benefit night for Clive. The mainpiece that night was *Hamlet*, in which Clive performed Ophelia. Prompter Richard Cross, who plays himself in the farce, notes that her play was well received; it was performed five more times during the 1749-50 season. After that, it remained unperformed until 10 March 1753, when Clive included a revised version of the second act. This revised version was the one published, and has formed the basis of the present text. A manuscript version of the play is in the Larpent Collection (Larpent 89), although no text version, it must be noted, can ever represent fully what was seen and heard in the theater. On April 3 the piece was again performed "by desire," but by October 31 the public seems to have grown tired of it: Cross notes that on this night the piece was "hiss'd a little." Its final performance during Garrick's tenure was 22 March 1762, again at a benefit night for Clive. This time, it was presented with further alterations to the burletta portion. The text of these alterations seems not to have survived.

HANNAH COWLEY, *THE RUNAWAY* (1776)

Like Behn, Centlivre, and Clive, most female playwrights had their start in the theater through inside contacts or as performers. Cowley's story is unusual in the unpremeditated nature of her career. Beginning with the preface to the 1813 edition of her works, commentators claim (perhaps apocryphally), that as a content country wife and mother, she attended the theater one evening with her husband and was inspired to try her own hand: "So delighted with this? she said to him—why I could write as well myself! His laugh, without notice, was answered in the course of the following morning by sketching the first Act of *The Runaway*, and, though she had never before written a literary line, the Play was finished with the utmost celerity" (1813 *Works* viii). Cowley herself declares that the "idea of writing for the stage struck me by mere accident" (Preface to *Albina*).

In her dedication to the play, she states publicly that she submitted it as an outsider to David Garrick, who was so impressed that he selected it as the last new play he would stage in his illustrious career as theater manager. The theater manuscript, now part of the Larpent collection, reveals that Garrick edited the play himself, and that the changes he made served, for the most part, simply to tighten an overly lengthy text. As mentioned above (p. 10), it was immediately successful, enjoying a run of seventeen nights—more than any other that season—and would have continued longer but for the start of the season's benefit plays.

Despite her later struggles with subsequent theater managements (see p. 15 above), Cowley went on to produce a number of popular and generically diverse plays. Her most successful was *The Belle's Stratagem* (1780), which opened with a 28-night run and became a Covent Garden staple, enjoying 118 performances before 1800.[13] Her father proudly claimed, "That Mrs. Cowley is the first literary female in Europe cannot be disputed," and, as de la Mahotiere points out, "he had good grounds for this claim." Her plays appealed to audiences as far away as America and the continent. The publication history of *The Runaway* alone (see p. 277 below) suggests an eager reading public. The play was also published in Dublin in 1776, probably, as de la Mahotiere suggests, as a piracy, and it was "translated into German as 'Der schoene Fleuchtung' and published in Altenburg the same year and in Vienna in 1777" (49).

Almost as unusual as her beginnings in the public theater was her education at the hands of a father who remained, throughout his life, her biggest fan. Philip Parkhouse attended the prestigious Blundell's grammar school in Tiverton, Devon—which now accepts girls. His classical education prepared him for a church career until "family circumstances" made this impossible, according to Tiverton's historians. He opened Tiverton's first bookshop in the town center instead, and dedicated himself to sharing his learning

---

13   Melinda Finberg outlines the success of Cowley's plays in her introduction (xl).

and his books with his talented daughter (de la Mahotiere 17). Parkhouse's civic role as town councilor as well as his bookshop would have brought Cowley into contact with people of from all walks of life, giving her fodder for her plays.

Indeed, Cowley's great talent (as in *The Runaway*) lies, as Finberg puts it, in "writing fluid, sparkling dialogue and creating sprightly memorable comic characters" (xxxv). The Justice in *The Runaway*, with his delightful local dialect, was doubtless modeled on just such country officials as crossed her path, while the servants' mannerisms and Lady Dinah's pomposity demonstrate her talent for capturing the language and style of all classes. In her "Address" before *A School for Greybeards* (1786), Cowley proudly quotes what she sees as "very high praise" from a critic of the play: "When Mrs. Cowley gets possession of the spirit and turn of a character, she speaks the language of *that* character better than *any* of her dramatic cotemporaries [*sic*]" (v). Her achievement—the creation of her vibrant characters—is all the more admirable given the restrictions on her in this period of stringent morality: for, immediately after citing the critic's praise of *Greybeards*, she explains how she felt hamstrung by critics and audiences, who forbade her to express the language of "vulgar or low bred persons" because a woman writer must "not deviate from the line of politeness" (v).

Public impatience with women who meddle in politics further inhibited Cowley's talents, even as she professed to concur with the prevailing sentiment. In the same essay in which she chides Mary Wollstonecraft for being "unfeminine" in engaging in politics, she points to the folly of ignoring events that rocked the late eighteenth century: "How then could I, pretending to be a comic poet, bring an emigrant Frenchman before the public at this day, and not make him hint at the events which had just passed, or were passing in his native country?" Cowley's patriotism and awareness of social issues, indeed, run through her plays, from *The Runaway* onward, in subtle but insistent allusions that she employs to buttress her moral and social messages.

Avoiding the outright attacks that her predecessors endured, as Anne K. Mellor suggests, Cowley assails "patriarchal domestic ideology from within" (52). Mellor argues that the public and private spheres become one in her plays, positing, for example, that Lady Dinah "identifies herself with France's ancien régime" when she announces "I must be rid of her, yet I know not how. Oh, France! For thy Bastille, for thy Lettres de Cachet" (p. xxx below). Mellor also sees Mr. Hargrave's concern that Mr. Drummond will, after his death, cut down his fences and open his lands as "resistance [to] a democratic political revolution in England" (54). More generally, however, Mr. Drummond embodies moral decency, while Lady Dinah provides a counter-example of some of the most reprehensible elements of the aristocracy and moneyed classes. The young couples, meanwhile, are so likeable that audiences have no choice but to sympathize with their plights and approve the success of George and Emily's polite but determined resistance to patriarchal commands. Consequently, as Mellor concludes, Cowley's comedies are quietly revolutionary in their presentation of marriage as a union that ought to be "based on mutual respect, intense love, sexual desire, trust, and the recognition by both parties that women will have, as Jean Gagen puts it, 'the deciding vote' in the selection of their husbands" (56-57; Gagen 115).

According to her contemporaries, Cowley herself exhibited a deep sense of morality in this age of gambling, affairs, and political dissipation—a characteristic she shared with Queen Charlotte, royal consort to George III, to whom she dedicated *The Belle's Stratagem*. This personal morality seems ultimately to have driven her from the stage that she lamented as no longer sustaining "a word … that looks like instruction, or a sentence which ought to be remembered." In the same farewell essay to the theater world (1795), she expresses great regret that a "mother" currently cannot "now lead her daughters to the great National School, the Theatre, in the confidence of their receiving either polish or improvement" (Preface to *The Town Before You*). She subsequently retreated from London too, returning to Tiverton, where she set about editing her works for what would become the 1813 edition.

NOTE ON THE TEXTS AND EDITING PRINCIPLES

For each of the texts included here I have used the first edition as copy text, except for Behn's *The Emperor of the Moon* (see p. xxx below). In the case of the plays, I have listed textual variations between copies of editions that were published in the century they debuted (the two seventeenth-century editions for Behn's play and the eighteenth-century editions for the others). Throughout, I have silently modernized spelling and punctuation, converted capitalized common nouns into lower case, and expanded elisions, except where they affect pronunciation; for example, "lur'd" becomes "lured" and "wou'd" becomes "would" but "ne'er" remains the same. I have interpolated a few stage directions where the action of the play seems clearly to call for it; these interpolated directions are indicated by square brackets. Those in parentheses are the author's.

EMPEROR
OF THE
MOON:
A
FARCE.

As it is Acted by Their
Majesties Servants,
AT THE
QUEENS THEATRE.

Written by Mrs. *A. Behn.*

LONDON:
Printed by *R. Holt*, for *Joseph Knight*, and *Francis Saunders*, at the *Blew-Anchor* in the lower Walk of the *New Exchange*, 1687.

DRAMATIS PERSONAE

Doctor Baliardo	Mr. Underhill
Scaramouch, his man	Mr. Leigh
Pedro[1], his boy	
Don Cinthio,	Young Mr. Powell
Don Charmante,	Mr. Mumford[2]
both nephews to the viceroy, and lovers of Elaria and Bellemante.	
Harlequin,[3] Cinthio's Man,	Mr. Jevon
Officer and clerk	
[Page]	

Elaria, daughter to the doctor,	Mrs. Cooke
Bellemante, niece to the doctor,	Mrs. Mumford[4]
[Florinda]	
Mopsophil, governante to the young ladies,	Mrs. Corey

The persons in the moon are Don Cinthio (Emperor), Don Charmante (Prince of Thunderland), their attendants (persons that represent the court cards).
Kepler and Galileus, two philosophers.
Twelve Persons, representing the figures of the twelve signs of the zodiac.
Negroes, and persons that dance.
Musick, kettledrums, and trumpets.

The Scene: Naples.

PROLOGUE

Spoken by Mr. Jevon

Long, and at vast expense, th'industrious stage
Has strove to please a dull ungrateful age:

---

1   Both the 1688 copy text and 1687 first edition (see p. 102 below) alternate arbitrarily between calling this character Pedro and Peter. I have reproduced this textual feature.
2   I.e., William Mountford.
3   Scaramouch and Harlequin are the names of stock characters from the *commedia dell'arte* tradition.
4   I.e., Susanna Mountford.

With heroes and with gods we first began,
And thundered to you in heroic strain:
Some dying love-sick queen each night you enjoyed,
And with magnificence at last were cloyed:
Our drums and trumpets frighted all the women;
Our fighting scared the beaux and billet-doux men.
So spark,[5] in an intrigue of quality,
Grows weary of his splendid drudgery;
Hates the fatigue, and cries, "A pox upon her,
What a damned bustle's here with love and honor?"
In humbler comedy we next appear,
No fop or cuckold, but slap-dash we had him here;
We showed you all, but you, malicious grown,
Friends' vices to expose, and hide your own,
Cry, "Damn it—this is such, or such a one."
Yet, nettled, "Plague,[6] what does the scribbler mean,
With his damned characters, and plot obscene?"
No woman without vizard[7] in the nation
Can see it twice, and keep her reputation—that's certain,"
Forgetting—
That he himself, in every gross lampoon,
Her lewder secrets spreads about the town;
Whilst their feigned niceness is but cautious fear,
Their own intrigues should be unraveled here.
Our next recourse was dwindling down to farce,
Then—"Zounds,[8] what stuff's here? 'Tis all o'er my—"
Well, gentlemen, since none of these has sped,
'Gad, we have bought a share i'th' speaking head.[9]
So there you'll save a sice,[10]
You love good husbandry in all but vice;
Whoring and drinking only bears a price.

The head rises upon a twisted post, on a bench, from under the stage.
After, Jevon speaks to its mouth.

---

5   Young man elegantly dressed or foppish in character.
6   "A plague on it"—a curse.
7   I.e., no respectable woman; prostitutes wore vizard masks when attending the theater.
8   "God's wounds"—an exclamation.
9   I.e., a disembodied head. There are many legends of speaking heads dating back to antiquity; evidently there was a contemporary popular novelty with which the play here competes.
10   Sixpence (slang).

Oh!—Oh!—Oh!
STENTOR.[11] Oh!—Oh!—Oh!

After this it sings "Sawny,"[12] laughs, cries "God bless the king," in order.

STENTOR. (*Answers.*) Speak louder, Jevon, if you'd have me repeat—

Plague of this rogue, he will betray the cheat.
    He speaks louder; it answers indirectly.[13]

—Hum—There 'tis again,
Pox of your echo with a northern strain.
Well—this will be but a nine days wonder too;
There's nothing lasting but the puppets' show.
What lady's heart's so hard, but it would move,
To hear Philander and Irene's[14] love?
Those sisters too, the scandalous wits do say,
Two nameless, keeping beaux have made so gay;
But those amours are perfect sympathy,
Their gallants being as mere machines as they.
Oh! How the city wife, with her [nown] ninny,[15]
Is charmed with, "Come into my coach, Miss Jinny, Miss Jinny."
But overturning, Frible[16] cries, "Adznigs,[17]
The juggling rogue has murdered all his kids."
The men of war cry, "Pox on't, this is dull,
We are for rough Sports—Dog Hector, and the Bull."[18]
Thus each in his degree, diversion finds,
Your sports are suited to your mighty minds;
Whilst so much judgment in your choice you show,
The puppets have more sense than some of you.

---

11   A loud and far-reaching voice (here, the speaking head).
12   "Sawny, the Scot," a popular Scots song, likely included because of the theater tradition of connections between the occult and Shakespeare's *Macbeth*.
13   As Jane Spencer points out, the "He" here is most plausibly Jevon and "it" the head, with Jevon speaking the lines that follow.
14   Conventional names of lovers.
15   Own fool.
16   The name means "frivolous" or "trifling."
17   An exclamation.
18   Dog fighting and bull baiting were popular entertainments. The name here is mock-heroic—Hector was a Trojan prince celebrated in Homer's *Iliad* for his bravery.

ACT I

Scene I

A Chamber.

Enter Elaria and Mopsophil.

I.

A curse upon that faithless maid,
Who first her sex's liberty betrayed;
Born free as man to love and range,
Till nobler nature did to custom change,
Custom, that dull excuse for fools,
Who think all virtue to consist in rules.

II.

From Love our fetters never sprung;
That smiling god, all wanton, gay, and young,
Shows by his wings he cannot be
Confined to a restless slavery;
But here and there at random roves,
Not fixed to glittering courts, or shady groves.

III.

Then she that constancy professed,
Was but a well dissembler at the best;
And that imaginary sway
She feigned to give, in seeming to obey,
Was but the height of prudent art,
To deal with greater liberty her heart.

After the song Elaria gives her lute to Mopsophil.

ELARIA. This does not divert me;
Nor nothing will, till Scaramouch return,
And bring me news of Cinthio.
MOPSOPHIL. Truly I was so sleepy last night, I know nothing of the
    adventure, for which you are kept so close a prisoner today, and more
    strictly guarded than usual.

ELARIA. Cinthio came with music last night under my window, which, my father hearing, sallied out with his myrmidons[19] upon him; and clashing of swords I heard, but what hurt was done, or whether Cinthio were discovered to him, I know not; but the billet[20] I sent him now by Scaramouch will occasion me soon intelligence.

MOPSOPHIL. And see, madam, where your trusty Roger[21] comes. (*Enter Scaramouch, peeping on all sides before he enters.*) You may advance, and fear none but your friends.

SCARAMOUCH. Away, and keep the door.

ELARIA. Oh, dear Scaramouch! Hast thou been at the viceroy's?

SCARAMOUCH. (*In heat.*) Yes, yes—

ELARIA. And hast thou delivered my letter to his nephew, Don Cinthio?

SCARAMOUCH. Yes, yes, what should I deliver else?

ELARIA. Well—and how does he?

SCARAMOUCH. (*Fanning himself with his cap.*) Lord, how should he do? Why, what a laborious thing it is to be a pimp!

ELARIA. Why, well he should do.

SCARAMOUCH. So he is, as well as a night-adventuring lover can be—he has got but one wound, madam.

ELARIA. How! Wounded say you? Oh heavens! 'Tis not mortal?

SCARAMOUCH. Why, I have no great skill—but they say it may be dangerous.

ELARIA. I die with fear; where is he wounded?

SCARAMOUCH. Why, madam, he is run—quite through the—heart. But the man may live, if I please.

ELARIA. Thou please! Torment me not with riddles.

SCARAMOUCH. Why, madam, there is a certain cordial balsam,[22] called a fair lady, which outwardly applied to his bosom, will prove a better cure than all your weapon-salve or sympathetic powder,[23] meaning your ladyship.

ELARIA. Is Cinthio then not wounded?

SCARAMOUCH. No otherwise than by your fair eyes, madam; he got away unseen and unknown.

---

19   Loyal followers—here servants.
20   A note or short letter.
21   Roger was used as a generic name—here for servants.
22   Oily medicinal preparation for soothing wounds.
23   Ointment and powder respectively, thought to heal a wound by sympathetic agency when applied to the weapon that made the wound.

ELARIA. Dost know how precious time is, and dost thou fool it away thus? What said he to my letter?

SCARAMOUCH. What should he say?

ELARIA. Why, a hundred dear soft things of love, kiss it as often, and bless me for my goodness.

SCARAMOUCH. Why, so he did.

ELARIA. Ask thee a thousand questions of my health after my last night's fright.

SCARAMOUCH. So he did.

ELARIA. Expressing all the kind concern love could inspire, for the punishment my father has inflicted on me, for entertaining him at my window last night.

SCARAMOUCH. All this he did.

ELARIA. And for my being confined a prisoner to my apartment, without the hope or almost possibility of seeing him any more.

SCARAMOUCH. There I think you are a little mistaken; for, besides the plot that I have laid to bring you together all this night, there are such stratagems a-brewing, not only to bring you together, but with your father's consent too. Such a plot, madam!

ELARIA. Aye, that would be worthy of thy brain. Prithee what?

SCARAMOUCH. Such a device—

ELARIA. I'm impatient.

SCARAMOUCH. Such a conundrum! Well, if there be wise men and con-jurers in the world, they are intriguing lovers.

ELARIA. Out with it.

SCARAMOUCH. You must know, madam, your father (my master, the doctor) is a little whimsical, romantic, or Don-Quicksottish,[24] or so.

ELARIA. Or rather mad.

SCARAMOUCH. That were uncivil to be supposed by me; but lunatic[25] we may call him, without breaking the decorum of good manners, for he is always traveling to the moon.

ELARIA. And so religiously believes there is a world there, that he discourses as gravely of the people, their government, institutions, laws, manners, religion, and constitution, as if he had been bred a Machiavel[26] there.

SCARAMOUCH. How came he thus infected first?

---

24   A pun: Don Quixote-ish and sottish.
25   Insanity was thought to be connected with the changes of the moon—*luna* in Latin.
26   An intriguer or schemer.

ELARIA. With reading foolish books, Lucian's *Dialogue of Icaromenippus*,[27] who flew up to the moon, and thence to heaven; an heroic business, called *The Man in the Moon*, if you'll believe a Spaniard, who was carried thither, upon an engine drawn by wild geese;[28] with another philosophical piece, *A Discourse of the World in the Moon*;[29] with a thousand other ridiculous volumes, too hard to name.

SCARAMOUCH. Aye, this reading of books is a pernicious thing. I was like to have run mad once, reading Sir John Mandeville.[30] But to the business—I went, as you know, to Don Cinthio's lodgings, where I found him with his dear friend Charmante, laying their heads together for a farce.

ELARIA. A farce!

SCARAMOUCH. Aye, a farce, which shall be called *The World in the Moon*, wherein your father shall be so imposed on, as shall bring matters most magnificently about.

ELARIA. I cannot conceive thee, but the design must be good, since Cinthio and Charmante own it.

SCARAMOUCH. In order to this, Charmante is dressing himself like one of the cabalists[31] of the Rosicrucian order,[32] and is coming to prepare my credulous master for the greater imposition. I have his trinkets here to play upon him, which shall be ready.

ELARIA. But the farce, where is it to be acted?

SCARAMOUCH. Here, here, in this very house; I am to order the decoration, adorn a stage, and place scenes proper.

ELARIA. How can this be done without my father's knowledge?

SCARAMOUCH. You know the old apartment next the great orchard, and the worm-eaten gallery that opens to the river, which place for several

---

27 Lucian's tale of Menippus, who traveled to the moon, became available in Ferrand Spence's translation of Lucian's *Works* (1684); Spence followed Nicolas Perrot D'Ablancourt's version, first published in 1634 and reissued in Paris in 1654.

28 Francis Godwin's *The Man in the Moone, or a Discourse of a Voyage thither by Domingo Gonsales* was published in 1638.

29 John Wilkins's *The discovery of a world in the moone, or, A discourse tending to prove, that 'tis probable there may be another habitable world in that planet* appeared in 1638 and was republished in 1684. English versions of Cyrano de Bergerac's tale of a moon voyage also appeared in 1659 and 1687.

30 Mandeville's *The voyages and trauailes of Sir John Maundeuile knight*, dating from the late fifteenth century, was reprinted frequently throughout the seventeenth century.

31 A secret intriguer.

32 A secret society of Protestant mysticism, reputedly founded by Christian Rosenkreuz in 1484, but first mentioned in 1614; members were said to claim various forms of secret and magic knowledge (*Oxford Companion to English Literature*).

years nobody has frequented; there all things shall be acted proper for our purpose.

Enter Mopsophil running.

MOPSOPHIL. Run, run, Scaramouch; my master's conjuring for you like mad below. He calls up all his little devils with horrid names: his microscope, his horoscope, his telescope, and all his scopes.
SCARAMOUCH. Here, here—I had almost forgot the letters; here's one for you, and one for Mrs. Bellemante. (*Runs out.*)

Enter Bellemante with a book.

BELLEMANTE. Here, take my prayer book, oh *ma très chère*.[33] (*Embraces her.*)
ELARIA. Thy eyes are always laughing, Bellemante.
BELLEMANTE. And so would yours, had they been so well employed as mine, this morning. I have been at the chapel, and seen so many beaus, such a number of *plumés*,[34] I could not tell which I should look on most; sometimes my heart was charmed with the gay blonding, then with the melancholy *noire*,[35] anon the amiable brunette; sometimes the bashful, then again the bold; the little now, anon the lovely tall. In fine, my dear, I was embarrassed on all sides, I did nothing but deal my heart *tout autour*.[36]
ELARIA. Oh, there was then no danger, cousin.
BELLEMANTE. No, but abundance of pleasure.
ELARIA. Why, this is better than sighing for Charmante.
BELLEMANTE. That's when he's present only, and makes his court to me. I can sigh to a lover, but will never sigh after him—but oh, the beaus, the beaus, cousin, that I saw at church.
ELARIA. Oh, you had great devotion to heaven, then!
BELLEMANTE. And so I had, for I did nothing but admire its handiwork, but I could not have prayed heartily, if I had been dying. But a deuce[37] on't, who should come in and spoil all but my lover Charmante, so dressed, so gallant, that he drew together all the scattered fragments

---

33   My very dear one (French).
34   Young men with plumed feathers in their hats.
35   Person with black hair.
36   All around (French).
37   A mild curse; "deuce" is a euphemism for "devil."

of my heart, confined my wandering thoughts, and fixed 'em all on him. Oh, how he looked, how he was dressed!

Sings.

Chevalier à cheveux blonds,
Plus de mouche, plus de poudre,
Plus de ribbons et cannons.[38]

—Oh, what a dear ravishing thing is the beginning of an amour![39]

ELARIA. Thou'rt still in tune; when wilt thou be tame, Bellemante?
BELLEMANTE. When I am weary of loving, Elaria.
ELARIA. To keep up your humor, here's a letter from your Charmante.
BELLEMANTE. (*Reads.*) "Malicious creature, when wilt thou cease to torment me, and either appear less charming, or more kind? I languish when from you, and am wounded when I see you, and yet I am eternally courting my pain. Cinthio and I are contriving how we shall see you tonight. Let us not toil in vain; we ask but your consent: the pleasure will be all ours. 'Tis therefore fit we suffer all the fatigue. Grant this, and love me, if you will save the life of—Your Charmante."—Live then, Charmante! Live as long as love can last!
ELARIA. Well, cousin, Scaramouch tells me of rare designs a-hatching, to relieve us from this captivity; here are we mewed up to be espoused to two moon-calves[40] for aught I know, for the devil of any human thing is suffered to come near us without our governante,[41] and keeper, Mr. Scaramouch.
BELLEMANTE. Who, if he had no more honesty and conscience than my uncle, would let us pine for want of lovers? But heaven be praised, the generosity of our cavaliers has opened their obdurate hearts with a golden key, that lets 'em in at all opportunities. Come, come, let's in, and answer their billets doux.[42]
Exeunt.

---

38   "Fair-haired cavalier, / No more patches, no more powder, / No more ribbons and lace" (French song).
39   Courtship.
40   Lunatics or simpletons.
41   Governess, chaperone.
42   Love-letters.

Scene 2

A garden.

Enter Doctor, with all manner of mathematical instruments hanging at his girdle; Scaramouch bearing a telescope twenty (or more) foot long.

DOCTOR. Set down the telescope. Let me see, what hour is it?
SCARAMOUCH. About six o'clock, sir.
DOCTOR. Then 'tis about the hour, that the great monarch of the upper
    world enters into his closet. Mount, mount the telescope.
SCARAMOUCH. What to do, sir?
DOCTOR. I understand, at certain moments critical, one may be snatched
    of such a mighty consequence, to let the sight into the secret closet.
SCARAMOUCH. How, sir, peep into the king's closet? Under favor, sir,
    that will be something uncivil.
DOCTOR. Uncivil! It were flat treason if it should be known; but thus
    unseen, and as wise politicians should, I take survey of all. This is the
    statesman's peeping-hole, through which he steals the secrets of his
    king, and seems to wink at distance.
SCARAMOUCH. The very keyhole, sir, through which, with half an eye, he
    sees him even at his devotion, sir.

A knocking at the garden gate.

DOCTOR. Take care none enter.

Scaramouch goes to the door.

SCARAMOUCH. Oh, sir, sir, here's some strange great man come to wait
    on you.
DOCTOR. Great man! From whence?
SCARAMOUCH. Nay, from the moon world, for aught I know, for he
    looks not like the people of the lower orb.
DOCTOR. Ha! And that may be; wait on him in. (*Exit Scaramouch.*)

Enter Scaramouch bare,[43] bowing before Charmante, dressed in a strange fantastical habit, with Harlequin; [Charmante] salutes the doctor. [Exit Scaramouche.]

---

43   I.e., without a hat.

CHARMANTE. Doctor Baliardo, most learned sir, all hail! Hail from the great cabala—of Eutopia.

DOCTOR. Most reverend bard, thrice welcome. (*Salutes him low.*)

CHARMANTE. The fame of your great learning, sir, and virtue, is known with joy to the renowned society.

DOCTOR. Fame, sir, has done me too much honor, to bear my name to the renowned cabala.

CHARMANTE. You must not attribute it all to fame, sir; they are too learned and wise to take up things from fame, sir. Our intelligence is by ways more secret and sublime: the stars, and little daemons of the air inform us all things, past, present, and to come.

DOCTOR. I must confess the Count of Gabalist[44] renders it plain, from writ divine and human, there are such friendly and intelligent daemons.

CHARMANTE. I hope you do not doubt that doctrine, sir, which holds that the four elements are peopled with persons of a form and species more divine than vulgar mortals. Those of the fiery regions we call the salamanders:[45] they beget kings and heroes, with spirits like their deietical sires. The lovely inhabitants of the water, we call nymphs. Those of the earth are gnomes or fairies. Those of the air are sylphs. These, sir, when in conjunction with mortals, beget immortal races, such as the first-born man, which had continued so, had the first man ne'er doted on a woman.

DOCTOR. I am of that opinion, sir; man was not made for woman.

CHARMANTE. Most certain, sir, man was to have been immortalized by the love and conversation of these charming sylphs and nymphs, and woman by the gnomes and salamanders, and to have stocked the world with demigods, such as at this day inhabit the empire of the moon.

DOCTOR. Most admirable philosophy and reason! But do these sylphs and nymphs appear in shapes?

CHARMANTE. Of the most beautiful of all the sons and daughters of the universe. Imagination itself—imagination is not half so charming. And then so soft, so kind! But none but the cabala and their families are blest with their divine addresses. Were you but once admitted into that society—

---

44   Abbé De Montfaucon de Villars's *Comte de Gabalis* (Paris, 1670) was published in English in 1680 as *The Count of Gabalis, or, The Extravagant Mysteries of the Cabalists Exposed in Five Pleasant Discourses on the Secret Services.*

45   Spirits or lizard-like creature supposed to live in fire.

DOCTOR. Aye, sir, what virtues or what merits can accomplish me for that great honor?

CHARMANTE. An absolute abstinence from carnal thought, devout and pure of spirit; free from sin.

DOCTOR. I dare not boast my virtues, sir. Is there no way to try my purity?

CHARMANTE. Are you very secret?

DOCTOR. 'Tis my first principle, sir.

CHARMANTE. And one, the most material in our Rosicrucian order. Please you to make a trial?

DOCTOR. As how, sir, I beseech you?

CHARMANTE. If you be thoroughly purged from vice, the optics of your sight will be so illuminated, that glancing through this telescope, you may behold one of these lovely creatures that people the vast region of the air.

DOCTOR. Sir, you oblige profoundly.

CHARMANTE. Kneel then, and try your strength of virtue, sir. Keep your eye fixed and open. (*[Doctor] looks in the telescope. While he is looking, Charmante goes to the door to Scaramouch, who waited on purpose without, and takes a glass with a picture of a nymph on it, and a light behind it, that as he brings it, it shows to the audience. Goes to the end of the telescope.*) —Can you discern, sir?

DOCTOR. Methinks, I see a kind of glorious cloud drawn up—and now—'tis gone again.

CHARMANTE. Saw you no figure?

DOCTOR. None.

CHARMANTE. Then make a short prayer to Alikin, the spirit of the east; shake off all earthly thoughts, and look again.

He prays. Charmante puts the glass into the mouth of the telescope.

DOCTOR. Astonished! Ravished with delight! I see a beauty young and angel-like, leaning upon a cloud.

CHARMANTE. Seems she on a bed? Then she's reposing, and you must not gaze—

DOCTOR. Now a cloud veils her from me.

CHARMANTE. She saw you peeping then, and drew the curtain of the air between.

DOCTOR. I am all rapture, sir, at this rare vision—is't possible, sir, that I may ever hope the conversation of so divine a beauty?

CHARMANTE. Most possible, sir. They will court you. Their whole delight is to immortalize—Alexander[46] was begot by a salamander, that visited his mother in the form of a serpent, because he would not make King Philip jealous; and that famous philosopher Merlin[47] was begotten on a vestal nun, a certain king's daughter, by a most beautiful young salamander; as indeed all the heroes, and men of mighty minds are.

DOCTOR. Most excellent!

CHARMANTE. The nymph Egeria,[48] enamored on Numa Pompilius,[49] came to him invisible to all eyes else, and gave him all his wisdom and philosophy. Zoroaster,[50] Trismegistus,[51] Apuleius,[52] Aquinas,[53] Albertus Magnus,[54] Socrates[55] and Virgil[56] had their zilphid,[57] which the foolish called their daemon or devil. But you are wise, sir.

DOCTOR. But do you imagine, sir, they will fall in love with an old mortal?

CHARMANTE. They love not like the vulgar; 'tis the immortal part they dote upon.

DOCTOR. But, sir, I have a niece and daughter, which I love equally; were it not possible they might be immortalized?

CHARMANTE. No doubt on't, sir, if they be pure and chaste.

DOCTOR. I think they are, and I'll take care to keep 'em so; for I confess, sir, I would fain have a hero[58] to my grandson.

CHARMANTE. You never saw the emperor of the moon, sir, the mighty Iredonozar?

DOCTOR. Never, sir; his court I have, but 'twas confusedly too.

---

46 Alexander the Great.
47 Wizard of Arthurian legend.
48 In Roman mythology, water spirit and wife or mistress of Numa Pompilius.
49 Second king of Rome.
50 Persian prophet and founder of the religion Zoroastrianism.
51 Hermes Trismegistus was the mythical founder of Hermeticism, an art involving alchemy.
52 Second-century Roman writer best known as author of *The Golden Ass*; he was put on trial for practicing magic.
53 Thomas Aquinas, thirteenth-century Roman Catholic theologian; Count Gabalis mentions him and many of the above.
54 Thirteenth-century scientist, philosopher, theologian.
55 Fifth-century BCE Greek philosopher tried for his unorthodox teachings.
56 First-century BCE Roman poet best known for his epic *The Aeneid*.
57 Sylph, an invisible being of the air.
58 Traditionally, a hero had one mortal and one immortal parent.

CHARMANTE. Refine your thoughts, sir, by a moment's prayer, and try
again.

He prays. Charmante claps the glass with the emperor on it; he looks in and sees it.

DOCTOR. It is too much, too much for mortal eyes! I see a monarch
seated on a throne—but seem most sad and pensive.
CHARMANTE. Forbear then, sir; for now his love-fit's on, and then he
would be private.
DOCTOR. His love-fit, sir!
CHARMANTE. Aye, sir, the emperor's in love with some fair mortal.
DOCTOR. And can he not command her?
CHARMANTE. Yes, but her quality being too mean, he struggles, though a
king, 'twixt love and honor.
DOCTOR. It were too much to know the mortal, sir?
CHARMANTE. 'Tis yet unknown, sir, to the cabalists, who now are using
all their arts to find her, and serve his majesty, but now my great affair
deprives me of you. Tomorrow, sir, I'll wait on you again; and now
I've tried your virtue, tell you wonders.
DOCTOR. I humbly kiss your hands, most learned sir.

*Charmante goes out. Doctor waits on him to the door, and returns: to him
Scaramouch. All this while Harlequin was hid in the hedges, peeping now and
then, and when his master went out he was left behind.*

SCARAMOUCH. [*Aside.*] So, so, Don Charmante has played his part most
exquisitely; I'll in and see how it works in his pericranium.[59]—Did
you call, sir?
DOCTOR. Scaramouch, I have, for thy singular wit and honesty, always
had a tenderness for thee above that of a master to a servant.
SCARAMOUCH. I must confess it, sir.
DOCTOR. Thou hast virtue and merit that deserves much.
SCARAMOUCH. Oh lord, sir!
DOCTOR. And I may make thee great; all I require, is, that thou wilt
double thy diligent care of my daughter and my niece, for there are
mighty things designed for them, if we can keep 'em from the sight of
man.
SCARAMOUCH. The sight of man, sir!
DOCTOR. Aye, and the very thoughts of man.

---

59   Brain (humorous).

SCARAMOUCH. What antidote is there to be given to a young wench, against the disease of love and longing?

DOCTOR. Do you your part, and because I know thee discreet and very secret, I will hereafter discover wonders to thee. On pain of life, look to the girls; that's your charge.

SCARAMOUCH. Doubt me not, sir, and I hope your reverence will reward my faithful services with Mopsophil, your daughter's governante, who is rich, and has long had my affection, sir.

HARLEQUIN (*Peeping, cries.*) Oh traitor!

DOCTOR. Set not thy heart on transitories mortal; there are better things in store. Besides, I have promised her to a farmer for his son. Come in with me, and bring the telescope.

Exeunt Doctor and Scaramouch. Harlequin comes out on the stage.

HARLEQUIN. My mistress Mopsophil to marry a farmer's son!
What, am I then forsaken, abandoned by the false fair one?
If I have honor, I must die with rage;
Reproaching gently, and complaining madly.
—It is resolved: I'll hang myself.—No—when did I ever hear of a hero that hanged himself? No, 'tis the death of rogues. What if I drown myself? No—useless dogs and puppies are drowned; a pistol or a caper on my own sword would look more nobly, but that I have a natural aversion to pain. Besides, it is as vulgar as rats-bane,[60] or the slicing of the weasand.[61] No, I'll die a death uncommon, and leave behind me an eternal fame. I have somewhere read in an author, either ancient or modern, of a man that laughed to death. I am very ticklish, and am resolved—to die that death. Oh, Mopsophil, my cruel Mopsophil! (*Pulls off his hat, sword and shoes.*) —And now, farewell the world, fond love, and mortal cares.

He falls to tickle himself, his head, his ears, his armpits, hands, sides, and soles of his feet, making ridiculous cries and noises of laughing several ways, with antic leaps and skips; at last falls down as dead.

Enter Scaramouch.

---

60   Poison.
61   Trachea or windpipe.

SCARAMOUCH. Harlequin was left in the garden; I'll tell him the news of Mopsophil. (*Going forward, tumbles over him.*) Ha, what's here? Harlequin dead! (*[Scaramouche] heaving him up, [Harlequin] flies into a rage.*)

HARLEQUIN. Who is't that thus would rob me of my honor?
SCARAMOUCH. Honor? Why, I thought thou'dst been dead.
HARLEQUIN. Why, so I was, and the most agreeably dead.
SCARAMOUCH. I came to bemoan with thee, the common loss of our mistress.
HARLEQUIN. I know it, sir, I know it, and that thou'rt as false as she. Was't not a covenant between us, that neither should take advantage of the other, but both should have fair play, and yet you basely went to undermine me, and ask her of the doctor. But since she's gone, I scorn to quarrel for her—but let's, like loving brothers, hand in hand, leap from some precipice into the sea.
SCARAMOUCH. What, and spoil all my clothes? I thank you for that; no, I have a newer way. You know I lodge four pair of stairs high; let's ascend thither, and after saying our prayers—
HARLEQUIN. Prayers! I never heard of a dying hero that ever prayed.
SCARAMOUCH. Well, I'll not stand with you[62] for a trifle. Being come up, I'll open the casement, take you by the heels, and fling you out into the street; after which, you have no more to do, but to come up and throw me down in my turn.
HARLEQUIN. The achievement's great and new, but now I think on't I'm resolved to hear my sentence from the mouth of the perfidious trollop,[63] for yet I cannot credit it.
  I'll to the gipsy, though I venture banging,
  To be undeceived, 'tis hardly worth the hanging.

Exeunt.

SCENE 3

The chamber of Bellemante.

Enter Scaramouch groping.

---

62 I.e., fight with you.
63 Slovenly or morally loose woman.

SCARAMOUCH. So, I have got rid of my rival, and shall here get an opportunity to speak with Mopsophil; for hither she must come anon, to lay the young ladies' night-things in order. I'll hide myself in some corner till she come. (*Goes on to the further side of the stage.*)

Enter Harlequin groping.

HARLEQUIN. So, I made my rival believe I was gone, and hid myself till I got this opportunity to steal to Mopsophil's apartment, which must be hereabouts; for from these windows she used to entertain my love. (*Advances.*)
SCARAMOUCH. Ha, I hear a soft tread—if it were Mopsophil's, she would not come by dark.

Harlequin advancing runs against a table, and almost strikes himself backwards.

HARLEQUIN. What was that? A table. There I may obscure my self. (*Groping for the table.*)
—What a devil, is it vanished?
SCARAMOUCH. Devil! Vanished! What can this mean? 'Tis a man's voice. If it should be my master, the doctor, now, I were a dead man. He can't see me, and I'll put myself into such a posture, that if he feel me, he shall as soon take me for a church spout as a man.

He puts himself into a posture ridiculous, his arms akimbo,[64] *his knees wide open, his backside almost touching the ground, his mouth stretched wide, and his eyes staring. Harlequin, groping, thrusts his hand into his mouth. He bites him; the other dares not cry out.*

HARLEQUIN. Ha, what's this? All mouth, with twenty rows of teeth. Now dare not I cry out, lest the doctor should come, find me here, and kill me. I'll try if it be mortal.

Making damnable faces and signs of pain, he draws a dagger. Scaramouch feels the point of it, and shrinks back, letting go his hand.

SCARAMOUCH. Who the devil can this be? I felt a poniard, and am glad I saved my skin from pinking.[65] (*Steals out.*)

---

64   Hands on hips with elbows turned outwards.
65   Being pierced.

Harlequin, groping about, finds the table, on which there is a carpet,[66] *and creeps under it, listening.*

Enter Bellemante, with a candle in one hand, and a book in the other.

BELLEMANTE. I am in a *belle*[67] humor for poetry tonight; I'll make some
   boremes[68] on love. (*She writes and studies.*)
                    Out of a great curiosity,
                    A shepherd did demand of me.
—No, no— *A shepherd this implored of me.*
(*Scratches out, and writes anew.*) Aye, aye, so it shall go.
               Tell me, said he,
               Can you resign?—
—Resign, aye—what shall rhyme to resign?
               Tell me, said he.

*She lays down the tablets, and walks about. Harlequin peeps from under the table,
takes the book, writes in it, and lays it up before she can turn.*

BELLEMANTE. (*Reads.*) Aye, aye, so it shall be—
               Tell me, said he, my Bellemante,
               Will you be kind to your Charmante?
(*Reads those two lines, and is amazed.*) —Ha! Heavens! What's this? I am
amazed! And yet I'll venture once more. (*Writes and studies; writes.*)
               I blushed, and veiled my wishing eyes.
(*Lays down the book, and walks as before.*)
               Wishing eyes—

Harlequin writes as before. She turns and takes the tablet.
               —*And answered only with my sighs.*
   —Ha, what is this? Witchcraft, or some divinity of love? Some Cupid
sure invisible.
Once more I'll try the charm.

Bellamante writes.

               —*Could I a better way my love impart?* (*Studies and walks.*)

---

66   Thick fabric cover, commonly of wool.
67   Tender.
68   Corrupted form of bouts-rimés (end rhymes).

Impart— (*[Harlequin] writes as before.*)
                    And, without speaking, tell him all my heart?
—'Tis here again, but where's the hand that writ it? (*Looks about.*)
—The little deity that will be seen
But only in his miracles. It cannot be a devil,
For here's no sin nor mischief in all this.

Enter Charmante. She hides the tablet; he steps to her and snatches it from her and reads.

CHARMANTE. (*Reads.*) *Out of a great curiosity,*
                    A shepherd this implored of me.
                    Tell me, said he, my Bellemante,
                    Will you be kind to your Charmante?
                    I blushed, and veiled my wishing eyes,
                    And answered only with my sighs.
                    Could I a better way my love impart?
                    And, without speaking, tell him all my heart.
—Whose is this different character? (*Looks angry.*)
BELLEMANTE. 'Tis yours for aught I know.
CHARMANTE. Away, my name was put here for a blind. What rhyming
    fop have you been clubbing wit withal?
BELLEMANTE. Ah! *Mon dieu!* Charmante jealous!
CHARMANTE. Have I not cause? Who writ these boremes?
BELLEMANTE. Some kind assisting deity, for aught I know.
CHARMANTE. Some kind assisting coxcomb, that I know. The ink's yet
    wet; the spark is near I find.
BELLEMANTE. Ah, *malheureuse!*[69] How was I mistaken in this man?
CHARMANTE. Mistaken! What, did you take me for an easy fool to be
    imposed upon? One that would be cuckolded by every feathered fool,
    that you should call a beau, *un gallant homme?*[70] 'Sdeath! Who would
    dote upon a fond she-fop? A vain conceited amorous coquette? (*Goes
    out, she pulls him back.*)

Enter Scaramouch running.

SCARAMOUCH. Oh madam! Hide your lover, or we are all undone.

---

69   Wretched one (French); she refers to herself.
70   A fine man (French).

CHARMANTE. I will not hide, till I know the thing that made the verses.
(*The doctor calling as on the stairs.*)

DOCTOR. Bellemante! Niece! Bellemante!

SCARAMOUCH. She's coming, sir.—Where, where shall I hide him? Oh,
the closet's open! (*Thrusts him into the closet by force.*)

Enter Doctor.

DOCTOR. Oh niece! Ill luck, ill luck! I must leave you tonight: my brother,
the advocate, is sick, and has sent for me. 'Tis three long leagues and,
dark as 'tis, I must go. They say he is dying. Here, take my keys (*pulls
out his keys, one falls down*), and go into my study, and look over all my
papers, and bring me all those marked with a cross and figure of three;
they concern my brother and I.

She looks on Scaramouch, and makes pitiful signs, and goes out.

—Come, Scaramouch, and get me ready for my journey; and, on your
life, let not a door be opened till my return. (*Exeunt.*)

Enter Mopsophil. Harlequin peeps from under the table.

HARLEQUIN. Ha! Mopsophil, and alone!

MOPSOPHIL. Well, 'tis a delicious thing to be rich; what a world of lovers
it invites. I have one for every hand, and the favorite for my lips.

HARLEQUIN. Aye, him would I be glad to know. (*And peeping.*)

MOPSOPHIL. But of all my lovers, I am for the farmer's son, because he
keeps a calash[71]—and I'll swear a coach is the most agreeable thing
about a man.

HARLEQUIN. Ho, ho!

MOPSOPHIL. Ah me, what's that?

HARLEQUIN. (*Answers in a shrill voice.*) The ghost of a poor lover, dwindled into a hey-ho.

*He rises from under the table, and falls at her feet. Scaramouch enters.
[Mopsophil] runs off squeaking.*

SCARAMOUCH. Ha, my rival and my mistress! Is this done like a man of
honor, Monsieur Harlequin, to take advantages to injure me? (*Draws.*)

---

71   A light carriage with a removable folding hood.

HARLEQUIN. All advantages are lawful in love and war.

SCARAMOUCH. 'Twas contrary to our league and covenant; therefore, I defy thee as a traitor.

HARLEQUIN. I scorn to fight with thee, because I once called thee brother.

SCARAMOUCH. Then thou art a poltroon;[72] that's to say, a coward.

HARLEQUIN. Coward! Nay, then I am provoked; come on—

SCARAMOUCH. Pardon me, sir; I gave the coward, and you ought to strike.

They go to fight ridiculously, and ever as Scaramouch passes, Harlequin leaps aside, and skips so nimbly about, he cannot touch him for his life, which after a while endeavoring in vain, he lays down his sword.

—If you be for dancing, sir, I have my weapons for all occasions.

Scaramouch pulls out a flute doux,[73] and falls to playing. Harlequin throws down his, and falls a dancing; after the dance, they shake hands.

HARLEQUIN. Hey, my *bon ami.*[74] Is not this better than dueling?

SCARAMOUCH. But not altogether so heroic, sir. Well, for the future, let us have fair play—no tricks to undermine each other, but which of us is chosen to be the happy man, the other shall be content.

ELARIA. (*Within.*) Cousin Bellemante, Cousin.

SCARAMOUCH. 'Slife, let's be gone, lest we be seen in the ladies' apartment. (*Scaramouch slips Harlequin behind the door.*)

Enter Elaria.

ELARIA. How now, how came you here?

SCARAMOUCH. (*Signs to Harlequin to go out.*) I came to tell you, madam, my master's just taking mule to go his journey tonight, and that Don Cinthio is in the street, for a lucky moment to enter in.

ELARIA. But what if anyone by my father's order, or he himself should by some chance surprise us?

SCARAMOUCH. If we be, I have taken order against a discovery. I'll go see if the old gentleman be gone, and return with your lover. (*Goes out.*)

---

72 A general term of abuse.
73 High-pitched flute.
74 Good friend (French).

ELARIA. I tremble, but know not whether 'tis with fear or joy.

Enter Cinthio.

CINTHIO. My dear Elaria— (*Runs to embrace her; she starts from him.*) Ha!
   Shun my arms, Elaria!
ELARIA. Heavens! Why did you come so soon?
CINTHIO. Is it too soon, whene'er 'tis safe, Elaria?
ELARIA. I die with fear. Met you not Scaramouch? He went to bid you
   wait a while; what shall I do?
CINTHIO. Why this concern? None of the house has seen me. I saw your
   father taking mule.
ELARIA. Sure you mistake; methinks I hear his voice.
DOCTOR. (*Below.*) My key! The key of my laboratory! Why, knave
   Scaramouch, where are you?
ELARIA. Do you hear that, sir? Oh, I'm undone! Where shall I hide you?
   He approaches. (*She searches where to hide him.*) Ha! My cousin's closet's
   open—step in a little. (*He goes in; she puts out the candle. Enter the Doctor.
   She gets round the chamber to the door, and as he advances in, she steals out.*)
DOCTOR. Here I must have dropped it; a light, a light—there—

Enter Cinthio, from the closet, pulls Charmante out, they not knowing each other.

CINTHIO. Oh, this perfidious woman! No marvel she was so surprised
   and angry at my approach tonight.
CHARMANTE. Who can this be? But I'll be prepared— (*Lays his hand on his
   sword.*)
DOCTOR. Why, Scaramouch, knave, a light! (*Turns to the door to call.*)

*Enter Scaramouch with a light, and, seeing the two lovers there, runs against
his master, puts out the candle, and flings him down and falls over him. At the
entrance of the candle, Charmante slipped from Cinthio into the closet. Cinthio
gropes to find him, when Mopsophil and Elaria, hearing a great noise, enter
with a light. Cinthio, finding he was discovered, falls to acting a madman;
Scaramouch helps up the doctor, and bows.*

Ha—a man—and in my house. Oh dire misfortune! Who are you, sir?
CINTHIO. Men call me Gog Magog,[75] the spirit of power:

---

75   Statues of Gog and Magog, legendary giants who protected the city of London,
stood at Guildhall until they were destroyed in the Great Fire of London, 1661.

My right hand riches holds, my left hand honor.
Is there a city wife would be a lady?
Bring her to me;
Her easy cuckold shall be dubbed a knight.
ELARIA. Oh heavens! A madman, sir.
CINTHIO. Is there a tawdry[76] fop would have a title?
A rich mechanic that would be an alderman?
Bring 'em to me,
And I'll convert that coxcomb, and that blockhead, into Your Honor
and Right-Worshipful.
DOCTOR. Mad, stark mad! Why, sirrah,[77] rogue—Scaramouch! How got
this madman in?

While the doctor turns to Scaramouch, Cinthio speaks softly to Elaria.

CINTHIO. (*Aside to her.*) Oh, thou perfidious maid! Who hast thou hid in
yonder conscious closet?
SCARAMOUCH. Why, sir, he was brought in a chair for your advice; but
how he rambled from the parlor to this chamber, I know not.
CINTHIO. Upon a winged horse, ycleped[78] Pegasus,
     Swift as the fiery racers of the sun
     —I fly—I fly—
     See how I mount, and cut the liquid sky. (*Runs out.*)
DOCTOR. Alas, poor gentleman, he's past all cure. But, sirrah, for the
future take you care that no young mad patients be brought into my
house.
SCARAMOUCH. I shall, sir, and see, here's your key you looked for.
DOCTOR. That's well; I must be gone. Bar up the doors, and upon life or
death let no man enter. (*Exeunt doctor, and all with him, with the light.*)

Charmante peeps out, and by degrees comes all out, listening every step.

CHARMANTE. Who the devil could that be that pulled me from the
closet? But at last I'm free, and the doctor's gone; I'll to Cinthio, and
bring him to pass this night with our mistresses. (*Exit.*)

As he is gone off, enter Cinthio groping.

---

76   Showy or cheaply gaudy.
77   An address expressing contempt or reprimand.
78   Called.

CINTHIO. Now for this lucky rival, if his stars will make this last part of his adventure such. I hid myself in the next chamber, till I heard the doctor go, only to return to be revenged. (*He gropes his way into the closet, with his sword drawn.*)

Enter Elaria with a light.

ELARIA. Scaramouch tells me Charmante is concealed in the closet, whom Cinthio surely has mistaken for some lover of mine, and is jealous; but I'll send Charmante after him, to make my peace and undeceive him. (*Goes to the door.*) Sir, sir, where are you? They are all gone; you may adventure out. (*Cinthio comes out.*) Ha, Cinthio here?
CINTHIO. Yes, madam, to your shame.
Now your perfidiousness is plain, false woman.
'Tis well your lover had the dexterity of escaping; I'd spoiled his making love else. (*Goes from her; she holds him.*)
ELARIA. Prithee hear me.
CINTHIO. But, since my ignorance of his person saves his life, live and possess him, till I can discover him. (*Goes out.*)
ELARIA. Go, peevish fool—
Whose jealousy believes me given to change,
Let thy own torments be my just revenge. (*Exit.*)

The end of the first act.

ACT II

Scene 1

An antic dance.

After the music has played, enter Elaria; to her Bellemante.

ELARIA. Heavens, Bellemante! Where have you been?
BELLEMANTE. Fatigued with the most disagreeable affair, for a person of my humor, in the world. Oh, how I hate business, which I do no more mind, than a spark does the sermon, who is ogling his mistress at church all the while. I have been ruffling over twenty reams of paper for my uncle's writings.

Enter Scaramouch.

SCARAMOUCH. So, so, the old gentleman is departed this wicked world, and the house is our own for this night. Where are the sparks? Where are the sparks?

ELARIA. Nay, heaven knows.

BELLEMANTE. How! I hope not so; I left Charmante confined to my closet, when my uncle had like to have surprised us together. Is he not here?

ELARIA. No, he's escaped, but he has made sweet doings.

BELLEMANTE. Heavens, cousin! What?

ELARIA. My father was coming into the chamber, and had like to have taken Cinthio with me, when, to conceal him, I put him into your closet, not knowing of Charmante's being there, and which, in the dark, he took for a gallant of mine. Had not my father's presence hindered, I believe there had been murder committed; however, they both escaped unknown.

SCARAMOUCH. Pshaw, is that all? Lovers' quarrels are soon adjusted; I'll to 'em, unfold the riddle, and bring 'em back. Take no care, but go in and dress you for the ball. Mopsophil has habits[79] which your lovers sent to put on: the fiddles, treat, and all are prepared. (*Exit.*)

Enter Mopsophil.

MOPSOPHIL. Madam, your cousin Florinda, with a lady, is come to visit you.

BELLEMANTE. I'm glad on't; 'tis a good wench, and we'll trust her with our mirth and secret. (*They go out.*)

Scene 2. Changes to the street.

Enter page with a flambeaux,[80] followed by Cinthio; passes over the stage. Scaramouch follows Cinthio in a campaign coat.[81]

SCARAMOUCH. 'Tis Cinthio—Don Cinthio. (*Calls; he turns.*) —Well, what's the quarrel? How fell ye out?

CINTHIO. You may inform yourself I believe, for these close intrigues cannot be carried on without your knowledge.

SCARAMOUCH. What intrigues, sir? Be quick, for I'm in haste.

CINTHIO. Who was the lover I surprised i'th' closet?

---

79   Clothing—here costumes.
80   Torch.
81   Military coat.

SCARAMOUCH. *Deceptio visus,*[82] sir: the error of the eyes.

CINTHIO. Thou dog—I felt him too; but since the rascal escaped me, I'll be revenged on thee—

(*Goes to beat him; he running away, runs against Harlequin, who is entering with Charmante, and like to have thrown 'em both down.*)

CHARMANTE. Ha! What's the matter here?

SCARAMOUCH. Seignior Don Charmante. (*Then he struts courageously in with them.*)

CHARMANTE. What, Cinthio in a rage! Who's the unlucky object?

CINTHIO. All man and womankind: Elaria's false.

CHARMANTE. Elaria false! Take heed, sure her nice[83] virtue is proof against the vices of her sex.

　　　—Say rather Bellemante;

　　　She who by nature's light and wavering.

　　　The town contains not such a false impertinent.

　　　This evening I surprised her in her chamber,

　　　Writing of verses, and between her lines

　　　Some spark had newly penned his proper stuff.

　　　Curse of the jilt; I'll be her fool no more.

HARLEQUIN. I doubt you are mistaken in that, sir, for 'twas I was the spark that writ the proper stuff. To do you service.

CHARMANTE. Thou!

SCARAMOUCH. Aye, we that spend our lives and fortunes here to serve you—to be used like pimps and scoundrels. Come, sir, satisfy him who 'twas was hid i'th' closet, when he came in and found you.

CINTHIO. Ha—is't possible? Was it Charmante?

CHARMANTE. Was it you, Cinthio? Pox on't, what fools are we, we could not know one another by instinct?

SCARAMOUCH. Well, well, dispute no more this clear case, but let's hasten to your mistresses.

CINTHIO. I'm ashamed to appear before Elaria.

CHARMANTE. And I to Bellemante.

SCARAMOUCH. Come, come, take heart of grace; pull your hats down over your eyes; put your arms across; sigh and look scurvily.[84] Your simple looks are ever a token of repentance. Come—come along. (*Exeunt omnes.*)

82　Optical illusion (Latin).
83　Punctilious; there is a pun here since "nice" can also mean wanton or lascivious.
84　Sorrily.

Scene 3. Changes to the inside of the house.

The front of the scene is only a curtain or hangings, to be drawn up at pleasure.

Enter Elaria, Bellemante, Mopsophil, [Florinda,] and ladies, dressed in masking habits.

ELARIA. I am extremely pleased with these habits, cousin.
BELLEMANTE. They are à la gothic and uncommune.[85]
FLORINDA. Your lovers have a very good fancy, cousin; I long to see 'em.
ELARIA. And so do I. I wonder Scaramouch stays so, and what success he has.
BELLEMANTE. You have no cause to doubt, you can so easily acquit yourself. But I, what shall I do, who can no more imagine who should write those boremes, than who I shall love next, if I break off with Charmante?
FLORINDA. If he be a man of honor, cousin, when a maid protests her innocence—
BELLEMANTE. Aye, but he's a man of wit too, cousin, and knows when women protest most, they likely lie most.
ELARIA. Most commonly, for truth needs no asseveration.[86]
BELLEMANTE. That's according to the disposition of your lover, for some believe you most, when you most abuse and cheat 'em; some are so obstinate, they would damn a woman with protesting, before she can convince 'em.
ELARIA. Such a one is not worth convincing; I would not make the world wise at the expense of a virtue.
BELLEMANTE. Nay, he shall e'en remain as heaven made him for me, since there are men enough for all uses.

Enter Charmante and Cinthio, dressed in their gothic habits; Scaramouch, Harlequin and music. Charmante and Cinthio kneel.

CINTHIO. Can you forgive us? (*Elaria takes him up.*)
BELLEMANTE. That, Cinthio, you're convinced, I do not wonder; but how Charmante's goodness is inspired, I know not. (*Takes him up.*)
CHARMANTE. Let it suffice, I'm satisfied, my Bellemante.
ELARIA. Pray know my Cousin Florinda. (*They salute the lady.*)

---

85   Bellemante's faux French pronunciation of "uncommon."
86   Solemn declaration.

BELLEMANTE. Come, let us not lose time, since we are all friends.

CHARMANTE. The best use we can make of it, is to talk of love.

BELLEMANTE. Oh! We shall have time enough for that hereafter. Besides, you may make love in dancing as well as in sitting; you may gaze, sigh—and press the hand, and now and then receive a kiss. What would you more?

CHARMANTE. Yes, wish a little more.

BELLEMANTE. We were unreasonable to forbid you that cold joy, nor shall you wish long in vain, if you bring matters so about, to get us with my uncle's consent.

ELARIA. Our fortunes depending solely on his pleasure, which is too considerable to lose.

CINTHIO. All things are ordered as I have written you at large: our scenes and all our properties are ready. We have no more to do but to banter the old gentleman into a little more faith, which the next visit of our new cabalist, Charmante, will complete.

The music plays. Enter some antics, and dance. They all sit the while.

ELARIA. Your dancers have performed well, but 'twere fit we knew whom we trusted with this evening's intrigue.

CINTHIO. Those, madam, who are to assist us in carrying on a greater intrigue, the gaining of you. They are our kinsmen.

ELARIA. Then they are doubly welcome.

Here is a song in dialogue, with flute doux and harpsicals,[87] *shepherd and shepherdess, which ended, they all dance a figure dance.*

CINTHIO. Hark, what noise is that? Sure 'tis in the next room.

DOCTOR. (*Within.*) Scaramouch, Scaramouch!

Scaramouch runs to the door, and holds it fast.

SCARAMOUCH. Ha! The devil in the likeness of my old master's voice, for 'tis impossible it should be he himself.

CHARMANTE. If it be he, how got he in? Did you not secure the doors?

ELARIA. He always has a key to open 'em. Oh! What shall we do? There's no escaping him; he's in the next room, through which you are to pass.

DOCTOR. Scaramouch, knave, where are you?

---

87   Harpsichord

SCARAMOUCH. 'Tis he, 'tis he, follow me all—

He goes with all the company behind the front curtain.

DOCTOR. (*Without.*) I tell you, sirrah, I heard the noise of fiddles.
PETER. (*Without.*) No surely, sir, 'twas a mistake.

Knocking at the door.

Scaramouch having placed them all in the hanging,[88] *in which they make the figures, where they stand without motion in postures. He comes out. He opens the door with a candle in his hand.*

Enter the doctor and Peter with a light.

SCARAMOUCH. Bless me, sir! Is it you—or your ghost?
DOCTOR. 'Twere good for you, sir, if I were a thing of air; but, as I am a substantial mortal, I will lay it on as substantially— (*Canes him. He cries.*)
SCARAMOUCH. What d'ye mean, sir? What d'ye mean?
DOCTOR. Sirrah, must I stand waiting your leisure, while you are roguing here? I will reward ye. (*Beats him.*)
SCARAMOUCH. Aye, and I shall deserve it richly, sir, when you know all.
DOCTOR. I guess all, sirrah, and I heard all, and you shall be rewarded for all. Where have you hid the fiddles, you rogue?
SCARAMOUCH. Fiddles, sir!
DOCTOR. Aye, fiddles, knave.
SCARAMOUCH. Fiddles, sir! Where?
DOCTOR. Here, here I heard 'em, thou false steward of thy master's treasure.
SCARAMOUCH. Fiddles, sir! Sure 'twas wind got into your head, and whistled in your ears, riding so late, sir.
DOCTOR. Aye, thou false varlet,[89] there's another debt I owe thee, for bringing me so damnable a lie. My brother's well: I met his valet but a league from town, and found thy roguery out. (*Beats him. He cries.*)
SCARAMOUCH. Is this the reward I have for being so diligent since you went?
DOCTOR. In what, thou villain? In what?

---

88   I.e., the curtain.
89   Rascal.

The curtain is drawn up, and discovers the hangings where all of them stand.

SCARAMOUCH. Why, look you, sir, I have, to surprise you with pleasure, against you came home, been putting up this piece of tapestry, the best in Italy, for the rareness of the figures, sir.

DOCTOR. Ha! Hum, it is indeed a stately piece of work; how came I by 'em?

SCARAMOUCH. 'Twas sent your reverence from the virtuoso,[90] or some of the cabalists.

DOCTOR. I must confess, the workmanship is excellent; but still I do insist I heard the music.

SCARAMOUCH. 'Twas then the tuning of the spheres:[91] some serenade, sir, from the inhabitants of the moon.

DOCTOR. Hum, from the moon—and that may be—

SCARAMOUCH. Lord, d'ye think I would deceive your reverence?

DOCTOR. (*Aside.*) From the moon, a serenade—I see no signs on't here; indeed it must be so—I'll think on't more at leisure.—Prithee what story's this? (*Looks on the hangings.*)

SCARAMOUCH. Why, sir. 'Tis—

DOCTOR. Hold up the candles higher, and nearer.

Peter and Scaramouch hold candles near. He takes a perspective,[92] and looks through it; and coming nearer, Harlequin, who is placed on a tree in the hangings, hits him on the head with his truncheon. He starts and looks about. [Harlequin] sits still.

SCARAMOUCH. Sir—

DOCTOR. What was that struck me?

SCARAMOUCH. Struck you, sir? Imagination.

DOCTOR. Can my imagination feel, sirrah?

SCARAMOUCH. Oh, the most tenderly of any part about one, sir!

DOCTOR. Hum—that may be.

SCARAMOUCH. Are you a great philosopher, and know not that, sir?

DOCTOR. (*Aside.*) This fellow has a glimpse of profundity. (*Looks again.*) —I like the figures well.

SCARAMOUCH. You will, when you see 'em by daylight, sir.

---

90   Student of antiquities or natural curiosities; often a term of mockery.
91   Astronomers once believed that transparent globes revolved around the earth, carrying with them heavenly bodies and emitting divine music when they moved in harmony.
92   Some type of magnifying glass or telescope.

Harlequin hits him again. The doctor sees him.

DOCTOR. Ha—is that imagination too? Betrayed, betrayed, undone! Run for my pistols. Call up my servants, Peter—a plot upon my daughter and my niece!

Runs out with Peter. Scaramouch puts out the candle; they come out of the hanging, which is drawn away. He places 'em in a row just at the entrance.

SCARAMOUCH. Here, here, fear nothing, hold by each other, that when I go out, all may go; that is, slip out, when you hear the doctor is come in again, which he will certainly do, and all depart to your respective lodgings.
CINTHIO. And leave thee to bear the brunt?
SCARAMOUCH. Take you no care for that; I'll put it into my bill of charges, and be paid all together.

Enter the doctor with pistols, and Peter.

DOCTOR. What, by dark? That shall not save you, villains, traitors to my glory and repose.—Peter, hold fast the door; let none escape. (*They all slip out.*)
PETER. I'll warrant you, sir. (*Doctor gropes about, then stamps and calls.*)
DOCTOR. Lights there—lights—I'm sure they could not 'scape.
PETER. Impossible, sir.

Enter Scaramouch undressed in his shirt,[93] *with a light. Starts.*

SCARAMOUCH. Bless me! What's here?
DOCTOR. Ha! Who art thou? (*Amazed to see him enter so.*)
SCARAMOUCH. I? Who the devil are you, and you go to that? (*Rubs his eyes, and brings the candle nearer. Looks on him.*) Mercy upon us! Why, what, is't you, sir, returned so soon?
DOCTOR. Returned! (*Looking sometimes on him, sometimes about.*)
SCARAMOUCH. Aye, sir, did you not go out of town last night, to your brother the advocate?
DOCTOR. Thou villain, thou question'st me, as if thou knew'st not that I was returned.

---

93   I.e., nightshirt.

SCARAMOUCH. I know, sir! How should I know? I'm sure I am but just
waked from the sweetest dream.

DOCTOR. You dream still, sirrah, but I shall wake your rogueship. Were
you not here but now, showing me a piece of tapestry, you villain?

SCARAMOUCH. Tapestry! (*Mopsophil listening all the while.*)

DOCTOR. Yes, rogue, yes, for which I'll have thy life— (*Offering a pistol.*)

SCARAMOUCH. Are you stark mad, sir? Or do I dream still?

DOCTOR. Tell me, and tell me quickly, rogue, who were those traitors
that were hid but now in the disguise of a piece of hangings? (*Holds the
pistol to his breast.*)

SCARAMOUCH. Bless me! You amaze me, sir. What conformity has every
word you say, to my rare dream! Pray let me [feel] you, sir. Are you
human?

DOCTOR. You shall feel I am, sirrah, if thou confess not.

SCARAMOUCH. Confess, sir! What should I confess? I understand not
your cabalistical language; but in mine, I confess that you have waked
me from the rarest dream, where methought the emperor of the
moon world was in our house, dancing and reveling, and methoughts
his grace was fallen desperately in love with Mistress Elaria, and that
his brother, the prince, sir, of Thunderland, was also in love with
Mistress Bellemante, and methoughts they descended to court 'em in
your absence. And that at last you surprised 'em, and that they transformed themselves into a suit of hangings to deceive you. But at last,
methought you grew angry at something, and they all fled to heaven
again; and, after a deal of thunder and lightning, I waked, sir, and
hearing human voices here, came to see what the matter was.

*This while the Doctor lessens his signs of rage by degrees, and at last stands in
deep contemplation.*

DOCTOR. May I credit this?

SCARAMOUCH. Credit it! By all the honor of your house, by my insepa-
rable veneration for the mathematics, 'tis true, sir.

DOCTOR. (*Aside.*) That famous Rosicrucian, who yesterday visited me,
told me—the emperor of the moon was in love with a fair mortal. This
dream is inspiration in this fellow. He must have wondrous virtue
in him, to be worthy of these divine intelligences. But if that mortal
should be Elaria! But no more, I dare not yet suppose it—perhaps
the thing was real and no dream, for oftentimes the grosser part is
hurried away in sleep by the force of imagination, and is wonder-
fully agitated. This fellow might be present in his sleep: of this we've

frequent instances.—I'll to my daughter and my niece, and hear what knowledge they may have of this.

MOPSOPHIL. [*Aside.*] Will you so? I'll secure you; the frolic shall go round.

DOCTOR. Scaramouch, if you have not deceived me in this matter, time will convince me farther; if it rest here, I shall believe you false.

SCARAMOUCH. Good sir, suspend your judgment and your anger then.

DOCTOR. I'll do't, go back to bed.

SCARAMOUCH. No, sir, 'tis morning now, and I'm up for all day. (*Exeunt doctor and Peter.*) —This madness is a pretty sort of pleasant disease, when it tickles but in one vein. Why, here's my master now, as great a scholar, as grave and wise a man, in all argument and discourse, as can be met with. Yet name but the moon, and he runs into ridicule, and grows as mad as the wind.

Well, doctor, if thou canst be madder yet,
We'll find a medicine that shall cure your fit,
—Better than all Galenists.[94] (*Goes out.*)

Scene draws off. Discovers Elaria, Bellemante and Mopsophil in nightgowns.

MOPSOPHIL. You have your lessons; stand to it bravely, and the town's our own, madam.

They put themselves in postures of sleeping, leaning on the table, Mopsophil lying at their feet. Enter doctor softly.

DOCTOR. Ha, not in bed! This gives me mortal fears.

BELLEMANTE. Ah, prince— (*She speaks as in her sleep.*)

DOCTOR. Ha, prince! (*Goes nearer, and listens.*)

BELLEMANTE. (*In a feigned voice.*) How little faith I give to all your courtship, who leaves our orb so soon.

DOCTOR. Ha, said she orb? (*Goes nearer.*)

BELLEMANTE. But since you are of a celestial race,
And easily can penetrate
Into the utmost limits of the thought,
Why should I fear to tell you of your conquest?
—And thus implore your aid.

---

94   Followers of Galen, second-century Greek physician, writer, and philosopher who influenced medical theory and practice in Europe from the Middle Ages until the mid-seventeenth century.

Rises and runs to the Doctor. Kneels, and holds him fast. He shows signs of joy.

DOCTOR. I am ravished!

BELLEMANTE. Ah, prince divine, take pity on a mortal—

DOCTOR. I am rapt!

BELLEMANTE. And take me with you to the world above!

DOCTOR. (*Leaping and jumping from her hands. She seems to wake.*) The moon, the moon she means; I am transported, overjoyed, and ecstasied!

BELLEMANTE. Ha, my uncle come again to interrupt us!

DOCTOR. Hide nothing from me, my dear Bellemante, since all already is discovered to me—and more.

ELARIA. Oh, why have you waked me from the softest dream that ever maid was blest with?

DOCTOR. (*With over-joy.*) What—what, my best Elaria?

ELARIA. Methought I entertained a demigod, one of the gay inhabitants of the moon.

BELLEMANTE. I'm sure mine was no dream: I waked, I heard, I saw, I spoke—and danced to the music of the spheres; and methought my glorious lover tied a diamond chain about my arm—and see 'tis all substantial. (*Shows her arm.*)

ELARIA. And mine a ring, of more than mortal luster.

DOCTOR. Heaven keep me moderate lest excess of joy should make my virtue less! (*Stifling his joy.*)
There is a wondrous mystery in this,
A mighty blessing does attend your fates.
Go in, and pray to the chaste powers above
To give you virtue for such rewards. (*They go in.*)
—How this agrees with what the learned cabalist informed me of last night! He said, that great Iredonozar, the emperor of the moon, was enamored on a fair mortal. It must be so—and either he descended to court my daughter personally, which for the rareness of the novelty, she takes to be a dream; or else, what they and I beheld, was visionary, by way of a sublime intelligence—and possibly, 'tis only thus the people of that world converse with mortals. I must be satisfied in this main point of deep philosophy.
I'll to my study, for I cannot rest,
Till I this weighty mystery have discussed. (*Exit very gravely.*)

Scene. The garden.

Enter Scaramouch with a ladder.

SCARAMOUCH. Though I am come off *en cavalier*[95] with my master, I am
  not with my mistress, whom I promised to console this night, and is
  but just I should make good this morning; 'twill be rude to surprise
  her sleeping, and more gallant to wake her with a serenade at her window. (*Sets the ladder to her window, fetches his lute, and goes up the ladder.*)

He plays and sings this song.

When maidens are young and in their spring
Of pleasure, of pleasure, let 'em take their full swing,
Full swing, full swing,
And love, and dance, and play, and sing.
For Silvia, believe it, when youth is done,
There's naught but hum drum, hum drum, hum drum;
There's naught but hum drum, hum drum, hum drum.

Then Silvia be wise, be wise, be wise,
Though painting and dressing for a while are supplies,
And may—surprise—
But when the fire's going out in your eyes,
It twinkles, it twinkles, it twinkles, and dies.
And then to hear love, to hear love from you,
I'd as lief[96] hear an owl cry—wit to woo,
Wit to woo, wit to woo.

Enter Mopsophil above.

MOPSOPHIL. What woeful ditty-making mortal's this?
  That ere the lark her early note has sung,
  Does doleful love beneath my casement thrum?
  —Ah, Seignior Scaramouch, is it you?
SCARAMOUCH. Who should it be that takes such pains to sue!
MOPSOPHIL. Ah, lover most true blue.

---

95   Like a cavalier (French); gallantly or gracefully.
96   I'd as willingly.

Enter Harlequin in woman's clothes.

HARLEQUIN. If I can now but get admittance, I shall not only deliver the young ladies their letters from their lovers, but get some opportunity, in this disguise, to slip this billet-doux into Mopsophil's hand, and bob[97] my comrade Scaramouch. Ha! What do I see? My mistress at the window, courting my rival! Ah gipsy!

SCARAMOUCH. But we lose precious time, since you design me a kind hour in your chamber.

HARLEQUIN. Ah traitor!

MOPSOPHIL. You'll be sure to keep it from Harlequin.

HARLEQUIN. Ah yes, he, hang him, fool, he takes you for a saint.

SCARAMOUCH. Harlequin! Hang him, shotten herring.[98]

HARLEQUIN. Aye, a cully,[99] a noddy.[100]

MOPSOPHIL. A meer zany.[101]

HARLEQUIN. Ah, hard-hearted Turk.

MOPSOPHIL. Fit for nothing but a cuckold.

HARLEQUIN. Monster of ingratitude! How shall I be revenged? (*Scaramouch, going over the balcony.*) —Hold, hold, thou perjured traitor. (*Cries out in a woman's voice.*)

MOPSOPHIL. Ha, discovered! —A woman in the garden!

HARLEQUIN. Come down, come down, thou false perfidious wretch.

SCARAMOUCH. Who in the devil's name, art thou? And to whom dost thou speak?

HARLEQUIN. (*Bawling out.*) To thee, thou false deceiver, that hast broke thy vows, thy lawful vows of wedlock. Oh, oh, that I should live to see the day (*crying*).

SCARAMOUCH. Who mean you, woman?

HARLEQUIN. Whom should I mean but thou—my lawful spouse?

MOPSOPHIL. Oh villain! Lawful spouse! Let me come to her.

Scaramouch comes down, as Mopsophil flings out of the balcony.

SCARAMOUCH. The woman's mad! Hark ye, jade—how long have you been thus distracted?

---

97   Cheat.
98   Emaciated, or worthless.
99   Dupe.
100   Simpleton.
101   Buffoon.

HARLEQUIN. E'er since I loved and trusted thee, false varlet. See here, the witness of my love and shame. (*Bawls, and points to her belly.*)

Just then Mopsophil enters.

MOPSOPHIL. How! With child! Out, villain! Was I made a property?
SCARAMOUCH. Hear me.
HARLEQUIN. Oh, thou heathen Christian! Was not one woman enough?
MOPSOPHIL. Aye, sirrah, answer to that.
SCARAMOUCH. I shall be sacrificed.
MOPSOPHIL. I am resolved to marry tomorrow—either to the apothecary[102] or the farmer, men I never saw, to be revenged on thee, thou termagant[103] infidel.

Enter the doctor.

DOCTOR. What noise, what outcry, what tumult's this?
HARLEQUIN. Ha, the doctor! What shall I do? (*Gets to the door; Scaramouch pulls her in.*)
DOCTOR. A woman! Some bawd I am sure. Woman, what's your business here? Ha.
HARLEQUIN. I came, an't like your seigniorship, to madam the governante here, to serve her in the quality of a *fille de chambre*[104] to the young ladies.
DOCTOR. A *fille de chambre*! 'Tis so, a she-pimp.
HARLEQUIN. Ah, seignior— (*Makes his little dapper leg,*[105] *instead of a curtsy.*)
DOCTOR. How now, what, do you mock me?
HARLEQUIN. Oh seignior! (*Gets nearer the door.*)
MOPSOPHIL. Stay, stay, mistress; and what service are you able to do the seignior's daughters?
HARLEQUIN. Is this seignior Doctor Baliardo, madam?
MOPSOPHIL. Yes.
HARLEQUIN. Oh! He's a very handsome gentleman, indeed.
DOCTOR. Aye, aye, what service can you do, mistress?
HARLEQUIN. Why, seignior, I can tie a cravat the best of any person in Naples, and I can comb a periwig—and I can—

---

102   Shop keeper of non-perishable commodities such as spices, drugs, and preserves.
103   Shrewish.
104   Chamber maid (French).
105   A neat bow.

DOCTOR. Very proper service for young ladies; you, I believe, have been *fille de chambre* to some young cavaliers?

HARLEQUIN. Most true, seignior; why should not the cavaliers keep *filles de chambre*, as well as great ladies *valets de chambre*?[106]

DOCTOR. Indeed 'tis equally reasonable.—'Tis a bawd (*aside*). —But have you never served ladies?

HARLEQUIN. Oh yes! I served a parson's wife.

DOCTOR. Is that a great lady?

HARLEQUIN. Aye, surely, sir, what is she else? For she wore her mantuas[107] of *brocade d'or*,[108] petticoats laced up to the gathers, her points, her patches, paints and perfumes, and sat in the uppermost place in the church too.

MOPSOPHIL. But have you never served countesses and duchesses?

HARLEQUIN. Oh, yes, madam; the last I served, was an alderman's wife in the city.

MOPSOPHIL. Was that a countess or a duchess?

HARLEQUIN. Aye, certainly—for they have all the money; and then for clothes, jewels, and rich furniture, and eating, they outdo the very *vice-reine*[109] herself.

DOCTOR. This is a very ignorant running bawd; therefore first search her for *billets-doux*, and then have her pumped.[110]

HARLEQUIN. Ah, seignior, seignior. (*Scaramouch searches him; finds letters.*)

SCARAMOUCH. Ha, to Elaria—and Bellemante! (*Reads the outside, pops them into his bosom.*) These are from their lovers. Ha, a note to Mopsophil. Oh, rogue! Have I found you?

HARLEQUIN. If you have, 'tis but trick for your trick, seignior Scaramouch, and you may spare the pumping.

SCARAMOUCH. For once, sirrah, I'll bring you off, and deliver your letters.—Sir, do you not know who this is? Why, 'tis a rival of mine, who put on this disguise to cheat me of Mistress Mopsophil. See, here's a billet to her.

DOCTOR. What is he?

SCARAMOUCH. A mongrel dancing-master; therefore, sir, since all the injury's mine, I'll pardon him for a dance, and let the agility of his heels save his bones, with your permission, sir.

---

106   Male attendants of the bed chamber (French).
107   Loose gowns.
108   Gold brocade (French).
109   Literally "vice-queen" (French): wife of the viceroy, or a woman representing a queen.
110   Interrogated.

DOCTOR. With all my heart, and am glad he comes off so comically. (*Harlequin dances.*)

A knocking at the gate. Scaramouch goes and returns.

SCARAMOUCH. Sir, sir, here's the rare philosopher who was here yesterday.
DOCTOR. Give him entrance, and all depart.

Enter Charmante.

CHARMANTE. Blest be those stars that first conducted me to so much worth and virtue; you are their darling, sir, for whom they wear their brightest luster. Your fortune is established; you are made, sir.
DOCTOR. Let me contain my joy. (*Keeping in an impatient joy.*) May I be worthy, sir, to apprehend you?
CHARMANTE. After long searching, watching, fasting, praying, and using all the virtuous means in nature, whereby we solely do attain the highest knowledge in philosophy, it was resolved, by strong intelligence— you were the happy sire of that bright nymph, that had effascinated, charmed, and conquered the mighty emperor Iredonozor, the monarch of the moon.
DOCTOR. (*Aside.*) I am—undone with joy! Ruined with transport.—Can it—can it, sir,—be possible? (*Stifling his joy, which breaks out.*)
CHARMANTE. Receive the blessing, sir, with moderation.
DOCTOR. I do, sir, I do.
CHARMANTE. This very night, by their great art, they find,
He will descend, and show himself in glory.
An honor, sir, no mortal has received
This sixty hundred years.
DOCTOR. Hum—say you so, sir? No emperor ever descend this sixty hundred years? (*Looks sad.*) —Was I deceived last night? (*aside*).
CHARMANTE. Oh! Yes, sir, often in disguise, in several shapes and forms, which did of old occasion so many fabulous tales of all the shapes of Jupiter—but never in their proper glory, sir, as emperors. This is an honor only designed to you.
DOCTOR. (*Joyful.*) And will his grace—be here in person, sir?
CHARMANTE. In person—and with him, a man of mighty quality, sir— 'tis thought—the prince of Thunderland. But that's but whispered, sir, in the cabal, and that he loves your niece.

DOCTOR. [*Aside.*] Miraculous! How this agrees with all I've seen and
heard.—Tonight, say you, sir?

CHARMANTE. So 'tis conjectured, sir. Some of the cabalists are of opinion, that last night there was some sally from the moon.

DOCTOR. About what hour, sir?

CHARMANTE. The meridian of the night, sir, about the hours of twelve or
one; but who descended, or in what shape, is yet uncertain.

DOCTOR. This I believe, sir.

CHARMANTE. Why, sir?

DOCTOR. May I communicate a secret of that nature?

CHARMANTE. To any of the cabalists, but none else.

DOCTOR. Then know—last night, my daughter and my niece were entertained by those illustrious heroes.

CHARMANTE. Who, sir? The emperor and prince, his cousin?

DOCTOR. Most certain, sir. But whether they appeared in solid bodies,
or phantomical, is yet a question; for at my unlucky approach, they all
transformed themselves into a piece of hangings.

CHARMANTE. 'Tis frequent, sir; their shapes are numerous, and 'tis
also in their power to transform all they touch, by virtue of a certain
stone—they call the ebula.

DOCTOR. That wondrous ebula, which Gonzales had?

CHARMANTE. The same, by virtue of which, all weight was taken from
him, and then with ease the lofty traveler flew from Parnassus
Hill,[111] and from Hymettus Mount,[112] and high Gerania,[113] and
Acrocorinthus,[114] thence to Taygetus,[115] so to Olympus's top,[116] from
whence he had but one step to the moon. Dizzy he grants he was.

DOCTOR. No wonder, sir. Oh happy great Gonzales!

CHARMANTE. Your virtue, sir, will render you as happy. But I must haste.
This night, prepare your daughter and your niece, and let your house
be dressed, perfumed, and clean.

DOCTOR. It shall be all performed, sir.

CHARMANTE. Be modest, sir, and humble in your elevation; for nothing
shows the wit so poor, as wonder, nor birth so mean, as pride.

DOCTOR. I humbly thank your admonition, sir, and shall, in all I can,
struggle with human frailty. (*Brings Charmante to the door bare. Exeunt.*)

---

111   Mountain in central Greece; in legend sacred to Apollo and home of the muses.
112   Mountain in Greece, near Athens, famous for its honey.
113   Mountain range in Greece.
114   Citadel of Corinth, site of a temple of Aphrodite.
115   Mountain range of the Peloponnesus.
116   Highest mountain in Greece, mythical abode of the gods.

Enter Scaramouch, peeping at the other door.

SCARAMOUCH. So, so, all things go gloriously forward, but my own
amour, and there is no convincing this obstinate woman, that 'twas
that rogue Harlequin in disguise that claimed me; so that I cannot
so much as come to deliver the young ladies their letters from their
lovers. I must get in with this damned mistress of mine, or all our plot
will be spoiled for want of intelligence. Hum, the devil does not use
to fail me at a dead lift. I must deliver these letters, and I must have
this wench, though but to be revenged on her for abusing me. Let me
see—she is resolved for the apothecary or the farmer. Well, say no
more, honest Scaramouch; thou shalt find a friend at need of me—
and if I do not fit you with a spouse, say that a woman has outwitted
me. (*Exit.*)

The End of the Second Act.

ACT III

Scene 1. The street, with the town gate, where an officer stands with a
staff like a London constable.

*Enter Harlequin riding in a calash, comes through the gate towards the stage,
dressed like a gentleman, sitting in it. The officer lays hold [of] his horse.*

OFFICER. Hold, hold, sir. You, I suppose, know the customs that are due
to this city of Naples, from all persons that pass the gates in coach,
chariot, calash, or *siege voglant*.117
HARLEQUIN. I am not ignorant of the custom, sir, but what's that to me.
OFFICER. Not to you, sir! Why, what privilege have you above the rest?
HARLEQUIN. Privilege, for what, sir?
OFFICER. Why, for passing, sir, with any of the before-named carriages.
HARLEQUIN. Art mad? Dost not see I am a plain baker, and this my cart,
that comes to carry bread for the viceroy's and the city's use? Ha.
OFFICER. Are you mad, sir, to think I cannot see a gentleman farmer and
a calash, from a baker and a cart?

---

117   I.e., *siege volant*: a light two-wheeled carriage.

HARLEQUIN. Drunk by this day—and so early too? Oh, you're a special officer! Unhand my horse, sirrah, or you shall pay for all the damage you do me.

OFFICER. Hey day! Here's a fine cheat upon the viceroy. Sir, pay me, or I'll seize your horse. (*Harlequin strikes him. They scuffle a little.*) Nay, and you be so brisk, I'll call the clerk from his office. (*Calls.*) —Mr. Clerk, Mr. Clerk. (*Goes to the entrance to call the clerk; the meantime Harlequin whips a frock over himself, and puts down the hind part of the chariot, and then 'tis a cart.*)

Enter clerk.

CLERK. What's the matter here?

OFFICER. Here's a fellow, sir, will persuade me, his calash is a cart, and refuses the customs for passing the gate.

CLERK. A calash? Where? I see only a carter and his cart. (*The officer looks on him.*)

OFFICER. Ha, what a devil! Was I blind?

HARLEQUIN. Mr. Clerk, I am a baker, that came with bread to sell, and this fellow here has stopped me this hour, and made me lose the sale of my ware—and being drunk, will outface me[118] I am a farmer, and this cart a calash.

CLERK. He's in an error, friend; pass on—

HARLEQUIN. No, sir, I'll have satisfaction first, or the viceroy shall know how he's served by drunken officers, that nuisance to a civil government.

CLERK. What do you demand, friend?

HARLEQUIN. Demand! I demand a crown, sir.

OFFICER. This is very hard, Mr. Clerk. If ever I saw in my life, I thought I saw a gentleman and a calash.

CLERK. Come, come, gratify him, and see better hereafter.

OFFICER. Here, sir, if I must, I must. (*Gives him a crown.*)

CLERK. Pass on, friend. (*Exit clerk.*)

Harlequin, unseen, puts up the back of his calash, and whips off his frock, and goes to drive on. The officer looks on him, and stops him again.

OFFICER. Hum, I'll swear it is a calash—Mr. Clerk—Mr. Clerk, come back, come back. (*Runs out to call him. He changes as before.*)

---

118   Boldly maintain to me.

Enter officer and clerk.

—Come, sir, let your own eyes convince you, sir.
CLERK. Convince me, of what, you sot?
OFFICER. That this is a gentleman, and that a—ha— (*Looks about on Harlequin.*)
CLERK. Stark drunk! Sirrah, if you trouble me at every mistake of yours thus, you shall quit your office.
OFFICER. I beg your pardon, sir, I am a little in drink I confess, a little blind and mad, sir.—This must be the devil, that's certain [*aside*].

The clerk goes out. Harlequin puts up his calash again, and pulls off his frock and drives out.

—Well, now to my thinking, 'tis as plain a calash again as ever I saw in my life, and yet I'm satisfied 'tis nothing but a cart. (*Exit.*)

Scene 2. Changes to the doctor's house. The hall.

Enter Scaramouch in a chair, which set down and opened on all sides and on the top, represents an apothecary's shop, the inside being painted with shelves and rows of pots and bottles; Scaramouch sitting in it dressed in black, with a short black cloak, a ruff, and little hat.

SCARAMOUCH. The devil's in't, if either the doctor, my master, or Mopsophil, know me in this disguise—and thus I may not only gain my mistress, and outwit Harlequin, but deliver the ladies those letters from their lovers, which I took out of his pocket this morning; and who would suspect an apothecary for a pimp? Nor can the jade Mopsophil, in honor, refuse a person of my gravity, and (*pointing to his shop*) so well set up.—Hum, the doctor here first; this is not so well, but I'm prepared with impudence for all encounters.

Enter the Doctor. Scaramouch salutes him gravely.

—Most Reverend Doctor Baliardo. (*Bows.*)
DOCTOR. Seignior— (*Bows.*)
SCARAMOUCH. I might, through great pusillanimity, blush—to give you this anxiety, did I not opine you were as gracious as communitive and eminent; and though you have no cognizance of me, your humble servant, yet I have of you—you being so greatly famed for your

admirable skill both in Galenical and Paracelsian phenomenas,[119] and other approved felicities in vulnerary emetics,[120] and purgative experiences.

DOCTOR. Seignior, your opinion honors me—a rare man this [*aside*].

SCARAMOUCH. And though I am at present busied in writing (those few observations I have accumulated in my peregrinations, sir), yet the ambition I aspired to, of being an ocular and aurial[121] witness of your singularity, made me trespass on your sublimer affairs.

DOCTOR. Seignior—

SCARAMOUCH. Besides a violent inclination, sir, of being initiated into the denomination of your learned family, by the conjugal circumference of a matrimonial tie, with that singularly accomplished person—madam, the governante of your hostel—

DOCTOR. (*Aside.*) Hum—a sweet-heart for Mopsophil!

SCARAMOUCH. And if I may obtain your condescension to my hymenæal[122] propositions, I doubt not my operation with the fair one.

DOCTOR. Seignior, she's much honored in the overture, and my abilities shall not be wanting to fix the concord. But have you been a traveler, sir?

SCARAMOUCH. Without circumlocutions, sir, I have seen all the regions beneath the sun and moon.

DOCTOR. Moon, sir! You never traveled thither, sir?

SCARAMOUCH. Not *in propria persona*,[123] seignior, but by speculation, I have, and made most considerable remarks on that incomparable *terra firma*,[124] of which I have the completest map in Christendom—and which Gonzales himself omitted in his *Cosmographia* of the *Lunar Mundus*.[125]

DOCTOR. A map of the *Lunar Mundus*, sir! May I crave the honor of seeing it?

SCARAMOUCH. You shall, sir, together with a map of *Terra Incognita*:[126] a great rarity, indeed, sir.

---

119   Paracelsus was an influential sixteenth-century Swiss physician.
120   Medicines to induce vomiting.
121   Using the eyes and the ears.
122   Marriage.
123   In person (Latin).
124   Firm earth (Latin); ground.
125   Map of the moon world (Latin).
126   Unknown land (Latin); a part of the world that has not been explored.

Enter Bellemante.

DOCTOR. Jewels, sir, worth a king's ransom!
BELLEMANTE. Ha! What figure of a thing have we here, bantering my
   credulous uncle? This must be some scout sent from our forlorn
   hope,[127] to discover the enemy, and bring in fresh intelligence. Hum,
   that wink tipped me some tidings, and she deserves not a good look,
   who understands not the language of the eyes.—Sir, dinner's on the
   table.
DOCTOR. Let it wait, I am employed—

She creeps to the other side of Scaramouch, who makes signs with his hand to her.

BELLEMANTE. Ha, 'tis so: this fellow has some novel for us: some letter
   or instructions. But how to get it—

*As Scaramouch talks to the doctor, he takes the letters by degrees out of his pocket,
and unseen, gives 'em to Bellemante behind him.*

DOCTOR. But this map, seignior; I protest you have filled me with curiosity. Has it signified all things so exactly, say you?
SCARAMOUCH. Omitted nothing, seignior: no city, town, village, or villa;
   no castle, river, bridge, lake, spring, or mineral.
DOCTOR. Are any, sir, of those admirable mineral waters there, so frequent in our world?
SCARAMOUCH. In abundance, sir: the famous Garamanteen, a young
   Italian, sir, lately come from thence, gives an account of an excellent
   scaturigo,[128] that has lately made an ebulation[129] there, in great reputation with the lunary ladies.
DOCTOR. Indeed, sir! Be pleased, seignior, to 'solve me some queries that
   may enode[130] some appearances of the virtue of the water you speak
   of.
SCARAMOUCH. [*Aside.*] Pox upon him, what questions he asks—but
   I must on.—Why, sir, you must know, the tincture of this water
   upon stagnation ceruberates,[131] and the crocus[132] upon the stones

---

127   Band of soldiers sent ahead, often on a perilous mission.
128   *Scaturrigo* (Latin): a bubbling spring.
129   Ebullition: a state of bubbling or fizzing over.
130   Explain (as in a riddle).
131   He means "ceruleates": turns cerulean or blue.
132   Alchemical term for yellow or red powders obtained from metals by calcination.

flaveces;[133] this he observes—to be, sir, the indication of a generous
water.

DOCTOR. Hum— (*Gravely nodding.*)

SCARAMOUCH. Now, sir, be pleased to observe the three regions: if they
be bright, without doubt Mars is powerful; if the middle region, or
camera, be palled, *filia solis*[134] is breeding.

DOCTOR. Hum.

SCARAMOUCH. And then the third region: if the faeces be volatile, the
birth will soon come *in balneo*.[135] This I observed also in the laboratory of that ingenious chemist Lysidono, and with much pleasure
animadverted that mineral of the same zenith and nadir, of that now
so famous water in England, near that famous metropolis, called
Islington.[136]

DOCTOR. Seignior—

SCARAMOUCH. For, sir, upon the infusion, the crow's head immediately
procures the seal of Hermes; and had not *lac virginis*[137] been too
soon sucked up, I believe we might have seen the consummation of
Amalgena.[138]

*Bellemante having got her letters, goes off. She makes signs to him to stay a little.
He nods.*

DOCTOR. Most likely, sir.

SCARAMOUCH. But, sir, this Garamanteen relates the strangest operation of a mineral in the lunar world, that ever I heard of.

DOCTOR. As how, I pray, sir?

SCARAMOUCH. Why, sir, a water impregnated to a circulation with *fema
materia*;[139] upon my honor, sir, the strongest I ever drank of.

DOCTOR. How, sir! Did you drink of it?

SCARAMOUCH. I only speak the words of Garamanteen, sir.—Pox on
him, I shall be trapped (*aside*).

DOCTOR. Cry mercy, sir. (*Bows.*)

---

133   Turns yellow (*flavus* is Latin for "yellow")
134   Daughter of the sun (Latin).
135   In the bath (of water).
136   In the seventeenth century, a popular resort, north of London, known for its springs
and spas.
137   Milk of the virgin (Latin).
138   Eighteenth-century editions have "Amalgama"; Scaramouch's language throughout this scene reflects Paracelsus's description of how to change iron into copper in his
Tincture of the Nature of Things, which was widely read in the seventeenth century.
139   He means *prima materia* (Latin): original matter.

SCARAMOUCH. The lunary physicians, sir, call it *urinam Vulcani*;[140] it calibrates everyone's excrements more or less according to the *gradus*[141] of the natural *calor*.[142] To my knowledge, sir, a smith of a very fiery constitution is grown very opulent by drinking these waters.

DOCTOR. How, sir, grown rich by drinking the waters, and to your knowledge?

SCARAMOUCH. The devil's in my tongue, to my knowledge, sir; for what a man of honor relates, I may safely affirm.

DOCTOR. Excuse me, seignior— (*Puts off his hat again gravely.*)

SCARAMOUCH. For, sir, conceive me how he grew rich! Since he drank those waters, he never buys any iron, but hammers it out of *stercus proprius*.[143]

Enter Bellemante with a billet.

BELLEMANTE. Sir, 'tis three o'clock, and dinner will be cold.

Goes behind Scaramouch, and gives him the note and goes out.

DOCTOR. I come, sweetheart. But this is wonderful.

SCARAMOUCH. Aye, sir, and if at any time nature be too infirm, and he prove costive,[144] he has no more to do, but apply a lodestone *ad anum*.[145]

DOCTOR. Is't possible?

SCARAMOUCH. Most true, sir, and that facilitates the journey *per viscera*.[146] But I detain you, sir—another time, sir. I will now only beg the honor of a word or two with the governante, before I go.

DOCTOR. Sir, she shall wait on you, and I shall be proud of the honor of your conversation. (*They bow. Exit doctor.*)

Enter to him Harlequin, dressed like a farmer, as before.

HARLEQUIN. Hum! What have we here? A tailor or a tumbler?

---

140 Urine of Vulcan (Latin); Vulcan was god of fire and metal work.
141 Degree (Latin).
142 Heat (Latin).
143 His own excrement (Latin).
144 Constipated.
145 To the anus (Latin).
146 Through the bowels (Latin).

SCARAMOUCH. Ha! Who's this? Hum! What if it should be the farmer that the doctor has promised Mopsophil to? My heart misgives me. (*They look at each other a while.*) Who would you speak with, friend?

HARLEQUIN. This is, perhaps, my rival, the apothecary. Speak with, sir! Why, what's that to you?

SCARAMOUCH. Have you affairs with seignor doctor, sir?

HARLEQUIN. It may be I have; it may be I have not. What then, sir?

While they seem in angry dispute, enter Mopsophil.

MOPSOPHIL. Seignior doctor tells me I have a lover waits me; sure it must be the farmer or the apothecary. No matter which, so a lover, that welcomest man alive. I am resolved to take the first good offer, though but in revenge of Harlequin and Scaramouch, for putting tricks upon me. Ha! Two of 'em!

SCARAMOUCH. My mistress here! (*They both bow, and advance, putting each other by.*)

MOPSOPHIL. Hold, gentlemen—do not worry me. Which of you would speak with me?

BOTH. I, I, I, madam—

MOPSOPHIL. Both of you?

BOTH. No, madam, I, I.

MOPSOPHIL. If both lovers, you are both welcome; but let's have fair play, and take your turns to speak.

HARLEQUIN. Aye, seignior, 'tis most uncivil to interrupt me.

SCARAMOUCH. And disingenuous, sir, to intrude on me. (*Putting one another by.*)

MOPSOPHIL. Let me then speak first.

HARLEQUIN. I'm dumb.

SCARAMOUCH. I acquiesce.

MOPSOPHIL. I was informed there was a person here had propositions of marriage to make me.

HARLEQUIN. That's I, that's I— (*Shoves Scaramouch away.*)

SCARAMOUCH. And I attend to that consequential *finis*.[147] (*Shoves Harlequin away.*)

HARLEQUIN. I know not what you mean by your *finis*, seignior; but I am come to offer myself this gentlewoman's servant, her lover, her husband, her dog in a halter, or anything.

---

147 Conclusion (Latin).

SCARAMOUCH. (*In rage.*) Him I pronounce a poltroon, and an ignomini-
ous utensil, that dares lay claim to the renowned lady of my *primum
mobile*;[148] that is, my best affections.

HARLEQUIN. I fear not your hard words, sir, but dare aloud pronounce,
if Donna Mopsophil like me, the farmer, as well as I like her, 'tis a
match, and my chariot's ready at the gate to bear her off, d'ye see.

MOPSOPHIL. (*Aside.*) Ah, how that chariot pleads.

SCARAMOUCH. And I pronounce, that being intoxicated with the sweet
eyes of this refulgent lady, I come to tender her my noblest particulars,
being already most advantageously set up with the circumstantial
implements of my occupation. (*Points to the shop.*)

MOPSOPHIL. A city apothecary, a most genteel calling—. Which shall I
choose? Seignior apothecary, I'll not expostulate the circumstantial
reasons that have occasioned me this honor.

SCARAMOUCH. Incomparable lady, the elegancy of your repartees most
excellently denote the profundity of your capacity.

HARLEQUIN. What the devil's all this? Good Mr. Conjurer, stand by—
and don't fright the gentlewoman with your elegant profundities.
(*Puts him by.*)

SCARAMOUCH. (*In rage.*) How, a conjurer! I will chastise thy vulgar ignorance, that yclepes[149] a philosopher a conjurer.

HARLEQUIN. 'Losophers!—Prithee, if thou be'st a man, speak like a man,
then.

SCARAMOUCH. Why, what do I speak like? What do I speak like?

HARLEQUIN. What do you speak like! Why you speak like a wheelbarrow.

SCARAMOUCH. How!

HARLEQUIN. And how.

*They come up close together at half sword, parry, stare on each other for a while,
then put up and bow to each other civilly.*

MOPSOPHIL. That's well, gentlemen. Let's have all peace, while I survey
you both, and see which likes me best. (*She goes between 'em, and surveys
'em both, they making ridiculous bows on both sides, and grimaces the while.*)
—Ha, now on my conscience, my two foolish lovers, Harlequin and
Scaramouch; how are my hopes defeated? But, faith, I'll fit you both.
(*She views them both.*)

---

148   Prime mover (Latin): the outer sphere that moves the others in Ptolemaic astronomy.
149   Calls.

SCARAMOUCH. (*Aside.*) So she's considering still; I shall be the happy dog.

HARLEQUIN. (*Aside.*) She's taking aim; she cannot choose but like me best.

SCARAMOUCH. (*Bowing and smiling.*) Well, madam, how does my person propagate?

MOPSOPHIL. Faith, seignior, now I look better on you, I do not like your phisnomy[150] so well as your intellects; you discovering some circumstantial symptoms that ever denote a villainous inconstancy.

SCARAMOUCH. Ah, you are pleased, madam—

MOPSOPHIL. You are mistaken, seignior. I am displeased at your gray eyes, and black eyebrows and beard; I never knew a man with those signs, true to his mistress or his friend. And I would sooner wed that scoundrel Scaramouch, that very civil pimp, that mere pair of chemical bellows that blow the doctor's projecting fires, that deputy-urinal shaker, that very guzman of Salamanca[151] than a fellow of your infallible *signum mallis.*[152]

HARLEQUIN. Ha, ha, ha—you have your answer, Seignior Friskin[153]— and may shut up your shop and be gone. Ha, ha, ha.

SCARAMOUCH. (*Aside.*) Hum, sure the jade knows me.

MOPSOPHIL. And as for you, seignior—

HARLEQUIN. (*Bowing and smiling.*) Ha, madam.

MOPSOPHIL. Those lanthorn[154] jaws of yours, with that most villainous sneer and grin, and a certain fierce air of your eyes, looks altogether most fanatically—which with your notorious whey beard, are certain signs of knavery and cowardice; therefore I'd rather wed that spider Harlequin, that skeleton buffoon, that ape of man, that Jack of Lent,[155] that very top, that's of no use, but when 'tis whipped and lashed, that piteous property I'd rather wed than thee.

HARLEQUIN. A very fair declaration.

MOPSOPHIL. You understand me—and so adieu, sweet Glisterpipe, and Seignior Dirty-Boots, Ha, ha, ha. (*Runs out.*)

They stand looking simply on each other, without speaking a while.

---

150 She means "physiognomy."
151 Rogue of Salamanca, home of Spain's oldest university.
152 Probably a corruption of *signum mali*, "sign of evil" (Latin); possibly with a pun on "malice."
153 The name suggests a playful character.
154 Lantern.
155 Puppet that boys set up to pelt with sticks and burn before Easter.

SCARAMOUCH. (*Aside.*) That I should not know that rogue, Harlequin.

HARLEQUIN. (*Aside.*) That I should take this fool for a physician.—How long have you commenced apothecary, seignior?

SCARAMOUCH. Ever since you turned farmer. Are not you a damned rogue to put these tricks upon me, and most dishonorably break all articles between us?

HARLEQUIN. And are not you a damned son of a—something—to break articles with me?

SCARAMOUCH. No more words, sir; no more words. I find it must come to action. Draw! (*Draws.*)

HARLEQUIN. Draw! So I can draw, sir. (*Draws.*)

They make a ridiculous cowardly fight. Enter the doctor, which they seeing, come on with more courage. He runs between 'em, and with his cane beats the swords down.

DOCTOR. Hold, hold! What mean you, gentlemen?

SCARAMOUCH. Let me go, sir. I am provoked beyond measure, sir.

DOCTOR. You must excuse me, seignior. (*Parleys with Harlequin.*)

SCARAMOUCH. (*Aside.*) I dare not discover the fool for his master's sake, and it may spoil our intrigue anon; besides, he'll then discover me, and I shall be discarded for bantering the doctor.—A man of honor to be so basely affronted here.

The doctor comes to appease Scaramouch.

HARLEQUIN. Should I discover this rascal, he would tell the old gentleman I was the same that attempted his house today in woman's clothes, and I should be kicked and beaten most unsatiably.

SCARAMOUCH. What, seignior, for a man of parts to be imposed upon— and whipped through the lungs here like a mountebank's[156] zany for sham cures! Mr. Doctor, I must tell you 'tis not civil.

DOCTOR. I am extremely sorry for it, sir—and you shall see how I will have this fellow handled for the affront to a person of your gravity, and in my house. Here, Pedro— (*Enter Pedro.*) Take this intruder, or bring some of your fellows hither, and toss him in a blanket. (*Exit Pedro.*)

Harlequin going to creep away; Scaramouch holds him.

---

156   An itinerant charlatan who sold supposed medicines and remedies (OED).

HARLEQUIN. (*Aside to him.*) Hark ye, bring me off, or I'll discover all your intrigue.

SCARAMOUCH. Let me alone.

DOCTOR. I'll warrant you some rogue that has some plot on my niece and daughter.

SCARAMOUCH. No, no, sir, he comes to impose the grossest lie upon you that ever was heard of.

Enter Pedro with others, with a blanket. They put Harlequin into it, and toss him.

HARLEQUIN. Hold, hold—I'll confess all, rather than endure it.

DOCTOR. Hold—what will you confess, sir? (*He comes out, makes sick faces.*)

SCARAMOUCH. That he's the greatest impostor in nature. Would you think it, sir? He pretends to be no less than an ambassador from the emperor of the moon, sir.

DOCTOR. Ha! Ambassador from the emperor of the moon! (*Pulls off his hat.*)

SCARAMOUCH. Aye, sir, thereupon I laughed, thereupon he grew angry—I laughed at his resentment, and thereupon we drew, and this was the high quarrel, sir.

DOCTOR. Hum—ambassador from the moon. (*Pauses.*)

SCARAMOUCH. I have brought you off; manage him as well as you can.

HARLEQUIN. (*Aside.*) Brought me off, yes! Out of the frying pan into the fire. Why, how the devil shall I act an ambassador?

DOCTOR. [*Aside.*] It must be so, for how should either of these know I expected that honor? (*He addresses him with profound civility to Harlequin.*) —Sir, if the figure you make, approaching so near ours of this world, have made us commit any indecent indignity to your high character, you ought to pardon the frailty of our mortal education and ignorance, having never before been blessed with the descension of any from your world.

HARLEQUIN. (*Aside.*) What the devil shall I say now?—I confess I am, as you may see by my garb, sir, a little *incognito*,[157] because the public message I bring is very private—which is, that the mighty Iredonozar, emperor of the moon, with his most worthy brother, the prince of Thunderland, intend to sup with you tonight. Therefore be sure you

---

157   With identity concealed (Latin).

get good wine—though by the way let me tell you, 'tis for the sake of
your fair daughter.

SCARAMOUCH. I'll leave the rogue to his own management.—I presume,
by your whispering, sir, you would be private, and humbly begging
pardon, take my leave. (*Exit.*)

HARLEQUIN. You have it, friend.—Does your niece and daughter drink,
sir?

DOCTOR. Drink, sir?

HARLEQUIN. Aye, sir, drink hard?

DOCTOR. Do the women of your world drink hard, sir?

HARLEQUIN. According to their quality, sir, more or less; the greater the
quality, the more profuse the quantity.

DOCTOR. Why, that's just as 'tis here; but your men of quality, your
statesmen, sir, I presume they are sober, learned, and wise.

HARLEQUIN. Faith, no, sir, but they are, for the most part, what's as
good, very proud and promising, sir, most liberal of their word to
every fawning suitor, to purchase the state of long attendance, and
cringing as they pass. But the devil of a performance, without you get
the knack of bribing in the right place and time, but yet they all defy it,
sir—

DOCTOR. Just, just, as 'tis here. But pray, sir, how do these great men live
with their wives?

HARLEQUIN. Most nobly, sir: my lord keeps his coach, my lady hers;
my lord his bed, my lady hers; and very rarely see one another, unless
they chance to meet in a visit, in the park, the mall, the tour, or at the
basset-table,[158] where they civilly salute and part, he to his mistress,
she to play.

DOCTOR. Good lack![159] Just as 'tis here.

HARLEQUIN.—Where, if she chance to lose her money, rather than
give out, she borrows of the next amorous coxcomb, who, from that
minute, hopes, and is sure to be paid again one way or other, the next
kind opportunity.

DOCTOR. Just as 'tis here.

HARLEQUIN. As for the young fellows that have money, they have no
mercy upon their own persons, but wearing nature off as fast as they
can, swear, and whore, and drink, and borrow as long as any rooking
citizen will lend till, having dearly purchased the heroic title of a bully

---

158   Basset was a popular card game, usually involving gambling.
159   An exclamation of surprise.

or a sharper, they live pitied of their friends, and despised by their whores, and depart this transitory world, diverse and sundry ways.

DOCTOR. Just, just as 'tis here!

HARLEQUIN. As for the citizen, sir, the courtier lies with his wife; he, in revenge, cheats him of his estate, till rich enough to marry his daughter to a courtier, again gives him all—unless his wife's over-gallantry break him; and thus the world runs round.

DOCTOR. The very same 'tis here. Is there no preferment, sir, for men of parts and merit?

HARLEQUIN. Parts and merit! What's that? A livery, or the handsome tying a cravat, for the great men prefer none but their footmen and valets.

DOCTOR. By my troth, just as 'tis here. Sir, I find you are a person of most profound intelligence—under favor, sir, are you a native of the moon, or this world?

HARLEQUIN. [*Aside.*] The devil's in him for hard questions.—I am a Neapolitan, sir.

DOCTOR. Sir, I honor you. Good luck, my countryman! How got you to the region of the moon, sir?

HARLEQUIN. [*Aside.*] A plaguy inquisitive old fool!—Why, sir—pox on't, what shall I say? [*aside*] —I being—one day in a musing melancholy, walking by the seaside—there arose, sir, a great mist, by the sun's exhaling of the vapors of the earth, sir.

DOCTOR. Right, sir.

HARLEQUIN. In this fog, or mist, sir, I was exhaled.

DOCTOR. The exhalations of the sun draw you to the moon, sir?

HARLEQUIN. [*Aside.*] I am condemned to the blanket again.—I say, sir, I was exhaled up, but in my way, being too heavy, was dropped into the sea.

DOCTOR. How, sir, into the sea?

HARLEQUIN. The sea, sir, where the emperor's fisherman casting his nets, drew me up, and took me for a strange and monstrous fish, sir— and as such, presented me to his mightiness—who going to have me spitchcocked[160] for his own eating—

DOCTOR. How, sir, eating?

HARLEQUIN. What did me I, sir (life being sweet) but fall on my knees, and besought his gloriousness not to eat me, for I was no fish, but a man. He asked me of what country; I told him of Naples, whereupon the emperor, overjoyed, asked me if I knew that most reverend

---

160   Prepared like an eel for the table.

and learned Doctor Baliardo, and his fair daughter. I told him I did, whereupon he made me his bedfellow, and the confidant to his amour to Seigniora Elaria.

DOCTOR. Bless me, sir! How came the emperor to know my daughter?

HARLEQUIN. [*Aside.*] There he is again with his damned hard questions.—Know her, sir? Why, you were walking abroad one day—

DOCTOR. My daughter never goes abroad, sir, farther than our garden.

HARLEQUIN. Aye, there it was indeed, sir—and as his highness was taking a survey of this lower world—through a long perspective, sir—he saw you and your daughter and niece, and from that very moment fell most desperately in love. But hark, the sound of timbrels,[161] kettledrums and trumpets. The emperor, sir, is on his way; prepare for his reception.

A strange noise is heard of brass kettles, and pans, and bells, and many tinkling things.

DOCTOR. I'm in a rapture—how shall I pay my gratitude for this great negotiation? But as I may, I humbly offer, sir— (*Presents him with a rich ring and a purse of gold.*)

HARLEQUIN. Sir, as an honor done the emperor, I take your ring and gold. I must go meet his highness. (*Takes leave.*)

Enter to him Scaramouch, as himself.

SCARAMOUCH. Oh, sir! We are astonished with the dreadful sound of the sweetest music that ever mortal heard, but know not whence it comes. Have you not heard it, sir?

DOCTOR. Heard it? Yes, fool! 'Tis the music of the spheres: the emperor of the moon world is descending.

SCARAMOUCH. How, sir? No marvel then, that looking towards the south, I saw such splendid glories in the air.

DOCTOR. Ha! Saw'st thou aught descending in the air?

SCARAMOUCH. Oh, yes, sir, wonders! Haste to the old gallery, whence, with the help of your telescope, you may discover all.

DOCTOR. I would not lose a moment for the lower universe.

Enter Elaria, Bellemante, Mopsophil, dressed in rich antique habits.

---

161 Tambourines.

ELARIA. Sir, we are dressed as you commanded us. What is your farther pleasure?

DOCTOR. It well becomes the honor you're designed for, this night, to wed two princes. Come with me and know your happy fates. (*Exeunt doctor and Scaramouch.*)

ELARIA. Bless me! My father, in all the rest of his discourse, shows so much sense and reason, I cannot think him mad, but feigns all this to try us.

BELLEMANTE. Not mad! Marry, heaven forbid, thou art always creating fears to startle one. Why, if he be not mad, his want of sleep this eight and forty hours, the noise of strange unheard-of instruments, with the fantastic splendor of the unusual sight, will so turn his brain and dazzle him, that in grace and goodness, he may be mad, if he be not. Come, let's after him to the gallery, for I long to see in what showing equipage our princely lovers will address to us. (*Exeunt.*)

Scene the last.

The gallery richly adorned with scenes and lights.

Enter doctor, Elaria, Bellemante, and Mopsophil. Soft music is heard.

BELLEMANTE. Ha! Heavens! What's here? What palace is this? No part of our house, I'm sure.

ELARIA. 'Tis rather the apartment of some monarch.

DOCTOR. [*Aside.*] I'm all amazement too, but must not show my ignorance.—Yes, Elaria, this is prepared to entertain two princes.

BELLEMANTE. Are you sure on't, sir? Are we not, think you, in that world above, I often heard you speak of? In the moon, sir?

DOCTOR. (*Aside.*) How shall I resolve her?—For aught I know, we are.

ELARIA. Sure, sir, 'tis some enchantment.

DOCTOR. Let not thy female ignorance profane the highest mysteries of natural philosophy. To fools it seems enchantment—but I've a sense can reach it. Sit and expect the event.—Hark, I am amazed, but must conceal my wonder—that joy of fools—and appear wise in gravity [*aside*].

BELLEMANTE. Whence comes this charming sound, sir?

DOCTOR. From the spheres—it is familiar to me.

The scene in the front draws off, and shows the hill of Parnassus, a noble large walk of trees leading to it, with eight or ten negroes upon pedestals, ranged on each side of the walks. Next Kepler and Galileus descend on each side, opposite to each other, in chariots, with perspectives in their hands, as viewing the machine of the zodiac. Soft music plays still.

DOCTOR. Methought I saw the figure of two men descend from yonder cloud, on yonder hill.

ELARIA. I thought so too, but they are disappeared, and the winged chariot's fled.

Enter Kepler and Galileus.

BELLEMANTE. See, sir, they approach.

The doctor rises and bows.

KEPLER. Most reverend sir, we, from the upper world, thus low salute you—Kepler and Galileus we are called, sent as interpreters to Great Iredonozar, the emperor of the moon, who is descending.

DOCTOR. Most reverend bards, profound philosophers, thus low I bow to pay my humble gratitude.

KEPLER. The emperor, sir, salutes you, and your fair daughter.

GALILEUS. And, sir, the prince of Thunderland salutes you, and your fair niece.

DOCTOR. Thus low I fall to thank their royal goodness. (*Kneels. They take him up.*)

BELLEMANTE. Came you, most reverend bards, from the moon world?

KEPLER. Most lovely maid, we did.

DOCTOR. May I presume to ask the manner how?

KEPLER. By cloud, sir, through the regions of the air, down to the famed Parnassus; thence by water, along the river Helicon,[162] the rest by post[163] upon two winged eagles.

DOCTOR. Sir, are there store of our world inhabiting the moon?

KEPLER. Oh, of all nations, sir, that lie beneath it; in the emperor's train, sir, you will behold abundance. Look up and see the orbal world descending. Observe the zodiac, sir, with her twelve signs.

162　Legendary river flowing from Parnassus.
163　By courier.

Next the zodiac descends, a symphony playing all the while; when it is landed, it delivers the twelve signs. Then the song, the persons of the Zodiac being the singers. After which, the negroes dance and mingle in the chorus.

A Song for the Zodiac.

Let murmuring lovers no longer repine,
But their hearts and their voices advance;
Let the nymphs and the swains in the kind chorus join,
And the satyrs and fauns in a dance.
Let nature put on her beauty of May,
And the fields and the meadows adorn;
Let the woods and the mountains resound with the joy,
And the echoes their triumph return.

Chorus.
For since love wore his darts,
And virgins grew coy;
Since these wounded hearts,
And those could destroy,
There ne'er was more cause for your triumphs and joy.

Hark, hark, the music of the spheres,
Some wonder approaching declares;
Such, such, as has not blessed your eyes and ears
This thousand, thousand, thousand years.
See, see what the force of love can make,
Who rules in heaven, in earth, and sea;
Behold how he commands the zodiac,
While the fixed signs unhinging all obey.
Not one of which, but represents
The attributes of Love,
Who governs all the elements
In harmony above.

Chorus.
For since Love wore his darts
And virgins grew coy;
Since these wounded hearts,
And those could destroy,
There ne'er was more cause for your triumphs and joy.

The wanton Aries first descends,
To show the vigor and the play,
Beginning Love, beginning Love attends,
When the young passion is all over joy,
He bleats his soft pain to the fair curled throng,
And he leaps, and he bounds, and loves all the day long.

At once Love's courage and his slavery
In Taurus is expressed,
Though o'er the plains he conqueror be,
The generous beast
Does to the yoke submit his noble breast;
While Gemini, smiling and twining of arms,
Shows Love's soft endearments and charms.
And Cancer's slow motion the degrees do express,
Respectful Love arrives to happiness.
Leo his strength and majesty,
Virgo his blushing modesty,
And Libra all his equity.
His subtlety does Scorpio show,
And Sagittarius all his loose desire,
By Capricorn his forward humor know,
And Aqua, lovers' tears that raise his fire,
While Pisces, which entwined do move,
Show the soft play, and wanton arts of love.

Chorus.
For since Love wore his darts,
And virgins grew coy;
Since these wounded hearts,
And those could destroy,
There ne'er was more cause for your triumphs and joy.

KEPLER. See how she turns, and sends her signs to earth. Behold the
    ram, Aries; see Taurus next descends; then Gemini—see how the
    boys embrace. Next Cancer, then Leo, then the Virgin; next to her
    Libra, Scorpio, Sagittary, Capricorn, Aquarius, Pisces. This eight
    thousand years no emperor has descended, but *incognito*; but when
    he does, to make his journey more magnificent, the zodiac, sir,
    attends him.
DOCTOR. 'Tis all amazing, sir.

KEPLER. Now, sir, behold the globic world descends two thousand leagues below its wonted station, to show obedience to its proper monarch.

After which, the globe of the moon appears, first like a new moon; as it moves forward, it increases till it comes to the full. When it is descended, it opens and shows the emperor and the prince. They come forth with all their train, the flutes playing a symphony before him, which prepares the song, which ended, the dancers mingle as before.

A song.

All joy to mortals, joy and mirth,
Eternal Io's sing;[164]
The gods of love descend to earth,
Their darts have lost the sting.
The youth shall now complain no more
On Sylvia's[165] needless scorn,
But she shall love, if he adore,
And melt when he shall burn.

The nymph no longer shall be shy,
But leave the jilting road;
And Daphne now no more shall fly
The wounded panting god;
But all shall be serene and fair,
No sad complaints of love
Shall fill the gentle whispering air,
No echoing sighs the grove.
Beneath the shades young Strephon lies,
Of all his wish possessed;
Gazing on Sylvia's charming eyes,
Whose soul is there confessed.
All soft and sweet the maid appears,
With looks that know no art,
And though she yields with trembling fears,
She yields with all her heart.

---

164   Greek and Latin exclamation of joy or triumph (OED).
165   Sylvia, like Daphne and Strephon that follow, are conventional names for pastoral characters.

KEPLER. See, sir, the cloud of foreigners appears: French, English, Spaniards, Danes, Turks, Russians, Indians, and the nearer climes of Christendom; and lastly, sir, behold the mighty emperor—

A chariot appears, made like a half-moon, in which is Cinthio for the emperor, richly dressed, and Charmante for the prince, rich, with a good many heroes attending. Cinthio's train borne by four Cupids. The song continues while they descend and land. They address themselves to Elaria and Bellemante. Doctor falls on his face; the rest bow very low as they pass. They make signs to Kepler.

KEPLER. The emperor would have you rise, sir; he will expect no ceremony from the father of his mistress. (*Takes him up.*)
DOCTOR. I cannot, sir, behold his mightiness—the splendor of his majesty confounds me.
KEPLER. You must be moderate, sir; it is expected.

The two lovers make all the signs of love in dumb show to the ladies, while the soft music plays again from the end of the song.

DOCTOR. Shall I not have the joy to hear their heavenly voices, sir?
KEPLER. They never speak to any subject, sir, when they appear in royalty, but by interpreters, and that by way of stentraphon,[166] in manner of the Delphic oracles.[167]
DOCTOR. Any way, so I may hear the sense of what they would say.
KEPLER. No doubt you will. But see the emperor commands by signs his foreigners to dance.
(*Soft music changes.*)

A very antic dance. The dance ended, the front scene draws off, and shows a temple, with an altar, one speaking through a stentraphon from behind it. Soft music plays the while.

KEPLER. Most learned sir, the emperor now is going to declare himself, according to his custom, to his subjects. Listen—
STENTRAPHON. Most reverend sir, whose virtue did incite us,
  Whose daughter's charms did more invite us;
  We come to grace her with that honor,
  That never mortal yet had done her;

---

166 Device for augmenting the human voice.
167 The oracle of Apollo at Delphi, on the slopes of Mt. Parnassus.

Once only, Jove was known in story,
To visit Semele[168] in glory.
But fatal 'twas; he so enjoyed her,
Her own ambitious flame destroyed her.
His charms too fierce for flesh and blood,
She died embracing of her god.
We gentler marks of passion give,
The maid we love, shall love and live;
Whom visibly we thus will grace,
Above the rest of human race.
Say, is't your will that we should wed her,
And nightly in disguises bed her?

DOCTOR. The glory is too great for mortal wife. (*Kneels with transport.*)
STENTRAPHON. What then remains, but that we consummate
    This happy marriage in our splendid state?
DOCTOR. Thus low I kneel, in thanks for this great blessing.

Cinthio takes Elaria by the hand, Charmante [takes] Bellemante; two of the singers in white being priests, they lead 'em to the altar, the whole company dividing on either side. Where, while a hymeneal song is sung, the priest joins their hands. The song ended, and they married, they come forth; but before they come forward, two chariots descend, one on one side above, and the other on the other side, in which is Harlequin dressed like a mock hero, with others, and Scaramouch, in the other, dressed so in helmets.

SCARAMOUCH. Stay, mighty emperor, and vouchsafe to be the umpire of
    our difference. (*Cinthio signs to Kepler.*)
KEPLER. What are you?
SCARAMOUCH. Two neighboring princes to your vast dominion.
HARLEQUIN. Knights of the sun, our honorable titles,
    And fight for that fair mortal, Mopsophil.
MOPSOPHIL. Bless us! My two precious lovers, I'll warrant; well, I had
    better take up with one of them, than lie alone tonight.
SCARAMOUCH. Long as two rivals we have loved and hoped,
Both equally endeavored, and both failed.
At last by joint consent, we both agreed
To try our titles by the dint of lance,
And chose your mightiness for arbitrator.

---

168   The mortal mother of Dionysus.

KEPLER. The emperor gives consent.

They both all armed with gilded lances and shields of black, with golden suns painted. The music plays a fighting tune. They fight at barriers, to the tune. Harlequin is often foiled, but advances still; at last Scaramouch throws him, and is conqueror. All give judgment for him.

KEPLER. (*To Scaramouch.*) The emperor pronounces you are victor.
DOCTOR. Receive your mistress, sir, as the reward of your undoubted
  valor. (*Presents Mopsophil.*)
SCARAMOUCH. Your humble servant, sir, and Scaramouch returns you
  humble thanks. (*Puts off his helmet.*)
DOCTOR. Ha! Scaramouch! (*Bawls out, and falls in a chair. They all go to
  him.*) My heart misgives me. Oh, I am undone and cheated every way.
  (*Bawling out.*)
KEPLER. Be patient, sir, and call up all your virtue,
  You're only cured, sir, of a disease
  That long has reigned over your nobler faculties.
  Sir, I am your physician, friend and counselor;
  It was not in the power of herbs or minerals,
  Of reason, common sense, and right religion,
  To draw you from an error that unmanned you.
DOCTOR. I will be patient, gentlemen, and hear you.—Are not you
  Ferdinand?
KEPLER. I am—and these are gentlemen of quality,
  That long have loved your daughter and your niece;
  Don Cinthio this, and this Don Charmante,
  The viceroy's nephews both.
  Who found as men, 'twas impossible to enjoy 'em,
  And therefore tried this stratagem.
CINTHIO. Sir, I beseech you, mitigate your grief,
  Although indeed we are but mortal men,
  Yet we shall love you, serve you, and obey you.
DOCTOR. Are not you then the emperor of the moon?
  And you the prince of Thunderland?
CINTHIO. There's no such person, sir.
  These stories are the phantoms of mad brains,
  To puzzle fools withal—the wise laugh at 'em—
  Come, sir, you shall no longer be imposed upon.
DOCTOR. No emperor of the moon—and no moon world!
CHARMANTE. Ridiculous inventions.

If we'd not loved you, you'd been still imposed on;
We had brought a scandal on your learned name,
And all succeeding ages had despised it.
DOCTOR. (*He leaps up.*) Burn all my books and let my study blaze,
Burn all to ashes, and be sure the wind
Scatter the vile contagious monstrous lies.
—Most noble youths, you've honored me with your alliance, and
you, and all your friends, assistances in this glorious miracle, I invite
tonight to revel with me. Come all and see my happy recantation of
all the follies fables have inspired till now. Be pleasant to repeat your
story, to tell me by what kind degrees you cozened me. I see there's
nothing in philosophy— (*gravely to himself*). Of all that writ, he was the
wisest bard, who spoke this mighty truth—

"He that knew all that ever learning writ,
  Knew only this—that he knew nothing yet." (*Exeunt.*)

EPILOGUE

To be spoken by Mrs. Cooke.
With our old plays, as with dull wife it fares,
To whom you have been married tedious years.
You cry—she's wondrous good, it is confessed,
But still 'tis *Chapon Boüillé*[169] at the best;
That constant dish can never make a feast:
Yet the palled pleasure you must still pursue,
You give so small encouragement for new;
And who would drudge for such a wretched age,
Who want the bravery to support one stage?
The wiser wits have now new measures set,
And taken up new trades that they may eat.
No more your nice fantastic pleasures serve,
Your pimps you pay, but let your poets starve,
They long in vain for better usage hoped,
Till quite undone and tired, they dropped and dropped;
Not one is left will write for thin third day,
Like desperate pickeroons,[170] no prize no pay;

169 Boiled capon (French), meaning homely fare.
170 Pirates or outlaws.

And when they have done their best, the recompense
Is, "Damn the sot, his play wants common sense."
Ill-natured wits, who can so ill requite
The drudging slaves, who for your pleasure write.
Look back on flourishing Rome, ye proud ingrates,
And see how she her thriving poets treats:
Wisely she prized 'em at the noblest rate,
As necessary ministers of state,
And contributions raised to make 'em great.
They from the public bank she did maintain,
And freed from want, they only writ for fame;
And were as useful in a city held,
As formidable armies in the field.
They but a conquest over men pursued,
While these by gentle force the soul subdued.
Not Rome in all her happiest pomp could show
A greater Caesar than we boast of now;
Augustus reigns, but poets still are low.
May Caesar live, and while his mighty hand
Is scattering plenty over all the land;
With god-like bounty recompensing all,
Some fruitful drops may on the muses fall;
Since honest pens do his just cause afford
Equal advantage with the useful sword.

FINIS.

NOTE ON THE TEXT

Two quarto editions of the play were published in the seventeenth century, one in 1687 (Q1) and one in 1688 (Q2). I have used the latter as copy text because, as Jane Spencer observes, it "corrects numerous errors and introduces relatively few new ones" (xxiii). Behn probably oversaw these corrections herself. While Q2 is the copy text, I have used the date of the first edition at the top of the play.

TEXTUAL VARIATIONS

Prologue
Q1, Q2: Jevern

Q2: noon ninny
Q1: nown ninny

I.I

(p. 40)

Q2: Then she that constancy

Q1: Than she that constancy

(p. 41)

Q2: weapon-salve

Q1: weapon

(p. 43)

Q2: *Dialogue of Icaromenipus*

Q1: *Dialogue of the Lofty Traveller*

(p. 44)

Q2: Marrois charé

Q1: Ma tres chear

(p. 44)

Q2: plumees

Q1: plumeys

(p. 45)

Q1, Q2: *Chivalier a chevave blond*

Q2: But heaven be praised

Q1: But thanks be praised

(p. 45)

Q1, Q2: billet deux

I.2

(p. 47)

Q2: Imagination itself, imagination is not half so

Q1: Fancy, imagination is not half

Q2: admitted into that society

Q1: admitted to that society

Q2: the optics of your sight

Q1: the opticles of your sight

(p. 48)

Q2: Saw you no figure?

Q1: Saw you no fuger?

(p. 49)

Q2: Aquinas

Q1: Aquinius

(p. 51)

Q2: there are better things

Q1: there's better things

Q2: I have somewhere read in an author

Q1: I have somewhere read an author

(p. 52)

Q2: the common loss

Q1: the mutual loss

I.3

(p. 52)

Q1, Q2: Scene II [should be Scene III]

(p. 57)

Q1, Q2: fleut deux

Q1, Q2: He my Bone Ame

(p. 57)

Q2: taking mule

Q1: taking horse

(P. 59)

Q1, Q2: *Exit doctor, and all with him*

II.I

(p. 61)

Q2: your cousin Florinda, with a lady, is come to visit you

Q1: your cousin Florinda, with a lady, are come to visit you.

II.3

(p. 64)

Q1, Q2: fleut deux

(p. 68)

Q2: let me fell you

Q1: let me feel you

(p. 69)

Q2: Better than all Galenists

Q1: Better than all Gallanicus

II.5

(p. 72)

Q2: I'd as lief

Q1: I'd as live
(p. 72)
Q1, Q2: billet deux
(p. 74)
Q2: billet deux
Q1: bellet deux
(p. 75)
Q2: effascinated
Q1: infascinated
(p. 76)
Q2: Hymettus
Q1: Hymethus

III.I
(p. 77)
Q2: *on his horse*
Q1: *of his horse*

III.2
(p. 85)
Q2: 'Losophers!
Q1: 'Losaphers
(p. 87)
Q2: He runs between 'em
Q1: He runs between
(p. 89)
Q2: indecent indignity
Q1: undecent indignity
(p. 90)
Q2: as long as any rooking citizen
Q1: as long any rooking citizen
(p. 90)
Q2: walking be
Q1: walking by

THE
GAMESTER:
A Comedy.

As it is Acted at the New-Theatre

I N

LINCOLNS-INN-FIELDS,

B Y

Her Majesty's
SERVANTS.

LONDON:

Printed for *William Turner*, at the *Angel* at *Lincolns-Inn Back-Gate*, and *William Davis* at the *Black-Bull* in *Cornhill.* **1705.**

PRICE 1 s. 6d.

Lately Publiſhed
Ariſtotle's Art of Poetry. Tranſlated from the Original Greek, according to Mr. *Theodore Goulſton's* Edition, together with Mr. *D'Acier's* Notes Tranſlated from the *French.* By *William Maundij*, M. D. Sold by *William Turner.* Price 6 s.

DEDICATION

To the Right Honorable George, Earl of Huntingdon

The kind reception this play has met with from the Town, gives me some hopes of your Lordship's acceptance, since amongst our English noblemen none is more conspicuously graced with those qualifications that render a soul truly generous, than your Lordship's. You have given the world sufficient proof that you prefer the service of your country to any pleasure whatsoever. In you, the peer is shown without the vanity, and the inherent virtue without the common vice; the actions of your life file the teeth of satire, as much as others give 'em an edge; strangers admire, while friends adore your conduct.

The design of this piece were to divert without that vicious strain which usually attends the comic muse; and, according to the first intent of plays, recommend morality, and I hope have, in some measure, performed it. I dare affirm there is nothing immodest, nor immoral in it. Part of it, I own myself obliged to the French for, particularly the character of the Gamester; but he is entirely ruined in the French. Whereas I, in complaisance to the many fine gentlemen that play in England, have reclaimed him, after I have discovered the ill consequence of gaming, that very often happen to those, who are too passionately fond of it. I shall not enlarge upon the alterations, but refer your Lordship to the original, who are a perfect master in that tongue.

I heartily wish all men of rank and quality as indifferent to this bewitching diversion of gaming as your Lordship; then, would the distressed be relieved, the poor supported, and the virtuous encouraged, which would distinguish our nobility as much above our neighbors, as their heroic deeds have done.

But you, my Lord, pursue a nobler end, and have chose rather to stain the field with the blood of your nation's enemies, than increase your fortune by another's ruin, or expose your own to the hazardous die—a resolution worthy of your birth and fortune. And that you may live to be a terror to our foes, and a succor to your country, in perfect health and happiness, till your dearest friends consent to part with you, are the humble wishes of,

My Lord,
Your Lordship's most obedient and most devoted servant.

DRAMATIS PERSONAE

MEN

Sir Thomas Valere, father to Valere, the gamester	Mr. Freeman
Dorante, his brother, in love with Angelica	Mr. Corey
Young Valere, a gentleman much in love with Angelica	Mr. Verbruggen
Mr. Lovewell, in love with Lady Wealthy	Mr. Betterton
Marquis of Hazard, a supposed French Marquis	Mr. Fieldhouse
Hector, Valet to Valere	Mr. Pack
Mr. Galoon, a tailor	Mr. Smeaton
Count Cogdie	Mr. Dickins
First Gentleman	Mr. Weller
Second Gentleman	Mr. Knap
Box Keeper	Mr. Lee

} three gamesters (Mr. Dickins, Mr. Weller, Mr. Knap)

WOMEN

Lady Wealthy, a very vain coquettish widow, very rich, sister to Angelica	Mrs. Barry
Angelica, in love with Valere	Mrs. Bracegirdle
Betty, woman to the Lady Wealthy	Mrs. Parsons
Favorite, woman to Angelica	Mrs. Hunt
Mrs. Security, one that lends money upon pawns	Mrs. Willis
Mrs. Topknot, a milliner	Mrs. Fieldhouse

PROLOGUE

Written by Mr. N. Rowe, Esq.
Spoke by Mr. Betterton.

If humble wives that drag the marriage chain,
With cursed dogged husbands may complain,
If turned at large to starve, as we by you,
They may, at least, for alimony sue.
Know, we resolve to make the case our own,

Between the plaintiff-stage and the defendant-town.
When first you took us from our father's house,
And lovingly our interest did espouse,
You kept us fine, caressed, and lodged us here,
And honeymoon held out above three year.
At length, for pleasures known do seldom last,
Frequent enjoyment palled your sprightly taste,
And though, at first, you did not quite neglect,
We found your love was dwindled to respect;
Sometimes, indeed, as in your way it fell,
You stopped, and called to see if we were well.
Now, quite estranged, this wretched place you shun,
Like bad wine, business, duels, or a dun.¹
Have we for this increased Apollo's race?
Been often pregnant with your wit's embrace?
And borne you many chopping² babes of grace?
Some ugly toads we had, and that's the curse,
They were so like you, that they fared the worse.
For this tonight we are not much in pain.
Look on't, and if you like it, entertain;
If all the midwife says of it be true,
There are some features too like some of you.
For us, if you this fitting to forsake it,
We mean to run away, and let the parish take it.

ACT I

The curtain draws up and discovers Hector in an armed-chair just waking,
yawning.

HECTOR. Bless me! 'Tis broad daylight! Who the devil would serve a
   gamester? 'Tis a cursed life, this that I lead. Oh, my dear bed, how seldom do I visit thee! When shall I be lapped in the fold of thy embraces
   and snore forth my thanks? I, that could enjoy the four and twenty
   hours together, am grown a perfect stranger to thy charms. Oh, my
   precious master! Now, ten to one, will he come home with an empty
   pocket, and then will he be confoundedly out of humor. Then shan't I

---

1   Debt collector.
2   Big, strapping.

dare to ask him for any dinner. Thus am I robbed of the two chiefest
pleasures of my life: eating and sleeping.

Enter Mrs. Favorite.

FAVORITE. Good morrow, Monsieur Hector. Where is your sweet
master?

HECTOR. Asleep.

FAVORITE. I must see him.

HECTOR. My master sees nobody when he's asleep.

FAVORITE. I must speak with him.

HECTOR. Indeed, sweet Mrs. Favorite, but you cannot.

FAVORITE. Pshaw, I tell you I must, and will speak with him.

HECTOR. With who, child?

FAVORITE. With who? Why, with Valere.

HECTOR. Heark'ee, would you speak with my master in *propria persona*,[3]
or with his picture?

FAVORITE. Leave fooling, for I come not upon so merry a message as you
imagine.

HECTOR. Why, then, to be serious, my master is not come in. He's a man
of business, child, and neglects his ease to follow that.

FAVORITE. Yes, yes, I guess the business; he is at shaking his elbows over
a table, saying his prayers backwards, courting the dice like a mistress, and cursing them when he is disappointed. Between you and I,
Angelica knows his extravagance, and, finding he breaks all the oaths
he made against play, resolves to see him no more.

HECTOR. If he has lost his money, this news will break his heart.

FAVORITE. Tell him that I say he has deceived more women than he has
played games at Hazard,[4] and—

HECTOR. You say! Aye, I find Dorante, my master's uncle, has given you
a retaining fee. What should she do with that old fellow?

FAVORITE. Oh! He's a lover ripe with discretion.

HECTOR. Aye, but women generally love green fruit best; besides, my
master's handsome.

FAVORITE. He handsome! Behold his picture just as he'll appear this
morning, with arms across, downcast eyes, no powder in his periwig,
a steenkirk[5] tucked in to hide the dirt, swordknot untied,[6] no gloves,

---

3   In person (Latin).
4   A dice game.
5   Neck cloth.
6   A ribbon or tassel tied to the hilt of a sword.

and hands and face as dirty as a tinker. This is the very figure of your beautiful master.

HECTOR. The jade has hit it.

FAVORITE. And pocket as empty as a Capuchin.7

HECTOR. Hold, hold, this is spite, mere spite and burning envy.

FAVORITE. Aye, 'tis no matter for that. I'll take care he shan't deceive my mistress; for, she that marries a gamester that plays upon the square, as the fool your master does, can expect nothing but an almshouse for a jointure. Once more, I tell you, that Dorante has both reason and Favorite of his side.

HECTOR. And we have love on our side, and love never fails to conquer reason. For your part, you are like the Swiss8—take any side for pay.

FAVORITE. Is not Valere ashamed, the only son of such a family, to leave his father's house and sneak up and down in lodgings?

HECTOR. You're mistaken, Mrs. Favorite. He did not leave his father's house, but his father, who is as obstinate as the devil, and as ill natured as a Dutchman, turned him out.

FAVORITE. He was a dutiful child in the meantime. Well, you may take my word; he will have small welcome at our house. I shall let my lady know he is a-gaming; so, sweet Mr. Hector, adieu.

HECTOR. Farewell, Mrs. Fripry.9 I am glad I know my master's enemy, however. Ho! Here he comes.

Enter Valere in disorder.

VALERE. Sirrah, what's o'clock?

HECTOR. It is—in troth, sir, I have been up so long, I have forgot.

VALERE. Away! I am weary of your fooleries. My nightgown! Quick, quick, the devil, the devil!

HECTOR. Ah! I find whereabout he is; he swears between his teeth.

VALERE. So hey! What, must I wait all day? My gown here! (*Valere still walks about, and Hector still following him with the gown.*)

HECTOR. 'Tis ready, sir.

VALERE. What a dog am I? I know I have no luck, yet, can't forebear playing. Oh, Fortune, Fortune! But why do I exclaim against her? I'll

---

7   A Franciscan friar.

8   Swiss mercenary soldiers were popular with European armies throughout the medieval and early modern periods.

9   I.e., "frippery": frivolity or ostentatiousness.

be even with her I warrant her; she has made me lose, but I defy her to make me pay, for the devil a souse[10] have I.

HECTOR. Sir, sir, please to put on your gown, sir.

VALERE. Get you to bed, you dog, and don't trouble me.

HECTOR. With all my heart, sir. (*Exit.*)

Valere sits down in the armed-chair.

VALERE. I think I am sleepy. Death! 'Tis impossible to sleep. (*Rises.*) For I can no sooner shut my eyes, but methinks my evil genius slings Amm's ace[11] before me. Why, Hector, sirrah! That rogue sleeps happy. Why, Hector!

HECTOR. Sir— (*From the bottom of the stage, unbuttoned.*)

VALERE. Sir, you sot! Are you never tired with sleeping?

HECTOR. Tired? Why, sir, I han't had time to unbutton my coat yet.

VALERE. Was anybody here to ask for me?

HECTOR. Yes, sir! Here was your music master and your dancing master.

VALERE. Aye, they want their quarteridge,[12] I suppose.

HECTOR. They'll call again, sir.

VALERE. Then I'm not at home, sir.

HECTOR. Oh! I know that, sir. But, sir, here was a kind of a—kind of shabby-looked fellow. He said his name was Cogdie. He'll call again too.

VALERE. I know him not. None else?

HECTOR. Yes, sir, a back-friend[13] of yours. Sir, may I be so bold as to ask you one question? Do you love charming Angelica?

VALERE. Love her! I adore her!

HECTOR. [*Aside.*] Ah! That's an ill sign. Now do I know he has not a penny in his pocket.—Ah, sir, your fob,[14] like a barometer, shows the temper of your heart, as that does the weather.

VALERE. Don't you imagine, whatever passion I have for play, that I have power to forget that amiable creature?

HECTOR. Ah, sir, but if that amiable creature should have banished you—

VALERE. Impossible!

HECTOR. Talk not of impossibilities, good sir, for pert Mrs. Favorite is just gone, who, I find, hates you, and swears her lady has declared for

---

10   A French coin.
11   Two aces thrown on the dice; nowadays called "snake eyes."
12   Payment made quarterly.
13   False friend.
14   Contents of the fob, a small waistcoat pocket; i.e., cash.

your uncle. Ah, sir—what she says is not altogether false; (*shaking his head*) for notwithstanding you have sworn heartily to Angelica never to play again, you do throw away a merry main;[15] or see, sir—

VALERE. Cease your impertinence. I give you leave to jest upon my losses, but my mistress touches my heart, sirrah.

HECTOR. (*Aside.*) Ah! Love's fever is always highest when cash is at an ebb. But, sir, be not cast down; I have heard 'em say, a new passion is the only thing to cure an old one. There's the charming widow of my Lord Wealthy, her sister richer than Angelica. Ah, sir! Had you made your addresses there.

VALERE. There! She's the only woman I would avoid. She's a coquette of the first rate, addresses all, and cares for none. How did she tyrannize over my friend Lovewell before she married my lord, though he is a gentleman without exception? And now she's playing the same game over again, for the good-natured fellow is in love still.

HECTOR. Truly, sir, I believe the French Marquis will carry it.

VALERE. No, he is too much of her temper. Heark! Who's there?

HECTOR. A dun, I warrant.

VALERE. I am not within, sirrah.

HECTOR. Oh, sir! Your father.

VALERE. Ah! That's worse. Now will he rail as heartily against gaming, as the Whigs against plays.

Enter Sir Thomas Valere.

SIR THOMAS. What, are you up? This is not a gamester's hour; or have you not been in bed all night? That's most likely.

HECTOR. (*Aside.*) He's the devil of a guesser.—Indeed my master keeps as early hours as any man, I'll say that for him.

SIR THOMAS. Hold your tongue, sirrah, or I shall break your head. Your freedom will not pass on me.

HECTOR. Your most humble servant, sir. I've done, sir; I've done.

SIR THOMAS. I am come to make the last trial of you, sir. Your course of life is so very scandalous, that unless I see a speedy and sincere reformation, I have resolved to disinherit you. Then try if what has ruined you will maintain you. But, do you hear, quit the name of your ancestors, who never yet produced such a profligate. The estate has not been reserved so long in the family to be thrown away at Hazard.

HECTOR. (*Aside.*) Short and pithy. We are in a hopeful way.

---

15   To throw a merry main is to play a game a dice (in particular, the game Hazard).

VALERE. Sir, I have been revolving in my mind all my acts of folly, and am ashamed that I harbored them so long and am now armed with manly resolution. Forgive my past faults and try my future conduct.

SIR THOMAS. If I could believe thee real, my joys would be complete.

HECTOR. (*Aside.*) Ah! I smoke[16] the design; a little money is wanting.

VALERE. My cruel uncle, who was never a friend to you, now endeavors to supplant me in Angelica's heart; you know I live but in her.

SIR THOMAS. I know your love, and the only thing I like in you. She's a virtuous lady and her fortune's large; 'tis base and most unfit my brother's years to become your rival.

HECTOR. Ah, sir! If my master loses her, I dare swear it will break his heart. In my conscience, I believe it is love keeps him awake, and puts gaming into his head.

SIR THOMAS. Well, son, if you obtain her, I'll forgive your faults and pay your debts once more.

VALERE. Sir, I don't doubt it, but I'm a little out of money at present.

HECTOR. Humph!

VALERE. Money, sir, is an ingredient absolutely necessary in a lover. A hundred guineas would accomplish my design.

HECTOR. [*Aside.*] As I guessed.

SIR THOMAS. At your old trick again. No, no! I have been too often cozened with your fair promises.

VALERE. Try me this time. Lend me but fifty.

SIR THOMAS. No.

VALERE. Twenty.

SIR THOMAS. No.

VALERE. Ten.

SIR THOMAS. No.

HECTOR. [*Aside.*] Hard-hearted Jew.

VALERE. Five, sir. For I can't go without some money.

SIR THOMAS. Not a souse from me.

HECTOR. One, sir, that we may dine. For I am sure my master has not a groat[17] by his humility.

SIR THOMAS. No, if you are hungry, go fling a merry main for your dinner.

HECTOR. Ah, sir, I never was so well bred. Besides, I hate to trusting to chance for my food.

---

16   Smell, suspect.
17   A coin of small value.

SIR THOMAS. I admire you have lived so long with your master. Then, look'ee, Valere, get you to Angelica: out with your uncle, and you shan't want money. In the meantime, sirrah, do you get me a list of his debts.

HECTOR. Yes, sir.—There's some hopes I may come in for my wages (*aside*).

VALERE. Sir, I obey you in everything—and fly to Angelica.—Heark'ee, rascal, get me some money or I will cut your ears off (*aside to Hector*). (*Exit.*)

HECTOR. Money! Mercy on me! Where shall I get it? Well I think I am bewitched to him. (*Exit.*)

SIR THOMAS. If I can but reclaim my child and match him to Angelica, I shall date the happiest part of my life from this moment.

Enter Cogdie.

COGDIE. Sir, your most humble servant. Is not your name Valere?

SIR THOMAS. It is, sir.

COGDIE. Sir, I come to offer you my best service.

SIR THOMAS. In what, pray, sir?

COGDIE. Sir, I am master of all sorts of games, and live by that noble art. My name is Cogdie, called by some Count Cogdie.

SIR THOMAS. (*Aside.*) He takes me for my son; I'll humor it, and hear what the rogue has to say—Well, sir, what then?

COGDIE. Hearing of your ill fortune at play, I came out of pure generosity to teach you the management of the die.

SIR THOMAS. The management of the die? Why, is that to be taught?

COGDIE. Oh! Aye, sir. To learn to cog a die nicely requires as good a genius as the study of mathematics. Now, sir, here's your true dice; a man seldom gets anything by them. Here's your false, sir; hey, how they run. Now, sir, these we generally call doctors.

SIR THOMAS. (*Aside.*) The consumption, rather. Mercy upon me! What is our world come to?

COGDIE. Come, throw a main, sir, then I'll instruct you how to nick[18] it; he is very dull. I tell you, sir, in this age, 'tis necessary that children learn to play before they learn to read.

SIR THOMAS. I tell you, sir, that I am amazed the government never preferred you to the pillory for your wondrous skill.

---

18   Win.

COGDIE. (*Aside.*) I find his ill fortune has put him horridly out of
humor.—I say again that learning to play is of more use than *fa, la, mi,
sol,*[19] or cutting a caper.
SIR THOMAS. I'll *fa, la,* caper, you dog. Know I am his father and hate
gaming, and all such rascals are you are. But stay, I'll pay you your
wages for the care you took of my son.
COGDIE. Sir, your humble servant, sir! Not a penny, sir.
SIR THOMAS. No, sir, a cane.
COGDIE. Not in the least, sir. I, I, I would not give you the trouble by no
means, sir. What a sot was I, to mistake the father for the son. (*Exit
running.*)

Enter Hector running.

HECTOR. Oh, sir! Undone! Undone! Undone!
SIR THOMAS. Undone! When wert thou otherwise?
HECTOR. Ah, sir, but my master, my master—
SIR THOMAS. What of him? Surely he was given me for a curse.
HECTOR. Ah, sir! As my master was just stepping into Angelica's lodgings, so nicely dressed—his wig, I believe, had a pound of hair and
two pound of powder in't; he looked so pretty, that had she but seen
him, she must have loved him, though her heart had been made of
brass. But just as he was stepping in—
SIR THOMAS. She ordered her footman to shut the door upon him, I
suppose, hearing his continued extravagance.
HECTOR. No, no, sir, worse than that: a slovenly filthy fellow whipped
his sword from his side, whilst another, as bluff as a midnight constable, slapped him on the back with an action of forty pounds.
SIR THOMAS. Ha! And did Angelica see it?
HECTOR. No, no, sir. We, being cunning, wheedled 'em to the tavern;
and 'tis but giving 'em a lusty bottle, sir, and I warrant we get it off for
ten guineas.
SIR THOMAS. [*Aside.*] How's this? An action of forty pounds got off for
ten guineas? I suspect a trick.—Come, show me the way to this tavern.
HECTOR. [*Aside.*] What shall I do now?—Sir, I, I, I, came in such haste
that I never thought to look up at the sign.
SIR THOMAS. Then you are likely to carry the money, sirrah. Sirrah, this
sham won't take; the next time, rascal, lay your lies closer, rogue.
(*Slaps him. Exit*)

---

19 I.e., singing.

HECTOR. Ah, Hector, Hector! Thou art no good, plotter. Well, I draw comfort from it, however; I shall never dread the gallows for plotting.

Enter Valere.

VALERE. Well, I have overheard all; I thought what your projects would come to.

HECTOR. Why, sir, the wisest men sometimes fail; and you must own, that I study as hard as a starving poet for your interest. But if my plots, like their poetry, miscarry, 'tis no fault of mine.

VALERE. You'll still be witty out of season. But prithee, what's to be done now?

HECTOR. Oh, sir, yonder goes Mrs. Security, who lent you once a hundred guineas upon your diamond ring that you lost at play.

VALERE. I remember I gave her fifty for the use of it. But, however, call her in this extremity, and bring up a bottle of sack with you. (*Exit Hector.*) Now for the art of persuasion to squeeze this old sponge of fifty guineas that may make me master of a thousand before night.

Enter Hector and Mrs. Security.

VALERE. Mrs. Security, good morrow.

MRS. SECURITY. Mr. Valere, your humble servant.

VALERE. A chair there, quickly. Mrs. Security, let us renew our old acquaintance, and cement it with a glass of sack.

MRS. SECURITY. Oh, dear Mr. Valere! I never drink in a morning.

VALERE. What! Not a glass of sack? Come, Hector, fill. My service to you.

MRS. SECURITY. Pray, young man, give me but a little.

VALERE. Fill it up, I say.

MRS. SECURITY. Oh, dear sir! Your health. (*Drinks half.*)

VALERE. What! My health by halves? I'll not bate you a drop.

MRS. SECURITY. Well, I profess, it will be too strong for me.

VALERE. Hector, does not Mrs. Security look very handsome?

HECTOR. Truly, sir, I think she grows younger and younger.

MRS. SECURITY. Away, you make me blush.

HECTOR. Ah! She'll have another husband; I see by those roguish eyes.

MRS. SECURITY. Fie, fie, Mr. Hector. These eyes have done nothing but wept since my good husband, Zekiel Security, died, and the more because he died suddenly. (*Weeps.*)

HECTOR. Suddenly! Good lack! Good lack! It e'en makes me weep to think on't.

MRS. SECURITY. He died in his vocation, just sealing of a bond.

VALERE. (*Aside.*) Ah! Would thou wert with him, so I had a little of thy money.—Hector, fill t'other glass to Mrs. Security, to wash away sorrow.

MRS. SECURITY. Oh! Dear sir, I thank you for your civility, and you shall find me always ready to serve you.

VALERE. I do believe you, Mrs. Security, and have occasion to try your kindness.

HECTOR. Aye, my master pitched upon you.

MRS. SECURITY. He knows he may command me.

VALERE. I would borrow fifty guineas, Mrs. Security, which shall be repaid.

MRS. SECURITY. I don't doubt it sir, in the least, for you know my way: a pledge. If it be not quite double the value, I won't stand with a friend. And it shall be as safe as my eyes—that I assure you.

VALERE. Humph!

HECTOR. Ah, deuce on't!²⁰ Here's the sack lost.

MRS. SECURITY. You had your ring again, Mr. Valere, and I hope you don't mistrust me now.

VALERE. Mistrust you! No, no, madam. Hector, fetch Mrs. Security a pledge.

HECTOR. A pledge, sir?—Bless me! What does he mean now? (*aside*). —A pen and ink, sir?

VALERE. Aye, aye, Mrs. Security shall have my note.

HECTOR. As good as any pledge in England.

MRS. SECURITY. It may be so—but I promised good Zekiel to be wary of the money he left me. Yea, and I will be very wary.

HECTOR. And very wicked—

VALERE. Refuse my note? I scorn your money.

HECTOR. I'd have you to know, my master's note is as good as a banker's—sometimes, when the dice run well (*aside*).

MRS. SECURITY. Nay, if you are angry for my fair dealing, good morrow to you.

HECTOR. Oh impudence! She calls *cent per cent* fair dealing! Go thy ways, but take my curse along with thee. May some town sharper persuade that sanctified face into matrimony, and in one night empty all thy bags at Hazard.

MRS. SECURITY. Your wishes hurt not me, ill-mannered fellow. I'd have you know, if I would marry again, I could have a—

---

20   A curse.

VALERE. Nay, nay, mistress, if we must have none of your money, let's have none of your impertinence.

HECTOR. Be gone, be gone, woman, be gone. (*Pushes her off.*)

VALERE. Oh, deep reflection! Would I could avoid thee. To become the scoff of mercenary wretches—and, through my own mismanagement, reduced to base necessity. Oh, Angelica! I'll cast a real penitent beneath thy feet.

> And if once more thy pardon I obtain,
> Love in my heart shall the sole monarch reign.

ACT II

Enter Angelica and Favorite.

ANGELICA. After all his solemn promises to quit that scandalous vice, when he can hold my love upon no other terms, does he still pursue that certain ruin to his fame and fortune? But I resolve to banish him my heart, which he has justly lost by his perfidious dealing. I feel, I feel my liberty return; and I charge thee, Favorite, speak of him no more.

FAVORITE. No, no, madam, fear not me. I hate him for your sake, madam. Was he like his uncle! There's the man for my money.

ANGELICA. Because you have a large share of his, I suppose. Old men must bribe high. Name neither to me. I hate mankind. (*Exit Favorite.*)

Enter Lady Wealthy.

LADY WEALTHY. Well said, sister. I hate mankind too, and yet the fellows will follow me. But who is the man that has put you out of conceit with the whole sex? Valere?

ANGELICA. The same. No other had ever power to shock my quiet—nor shall he! For this moment I'll raze him from my thoughts.

LADY WEALTHY (*Aside.*) If she holds her resolution, I am happy.—That task may prove more difficult than you imagine, sister. Come, come, this is a flight of sudden passion that would fall upon the sight of Valere.

ANGELICA. You mistake, sister; my resentment is grounded upon reason.

LADY WEALTHY. I know he has given you cause enough. But love is blind. Had a man used me so, I should have suspected his reality sooner.

ANGELICA. Why, do you think he loves me not?

LADY WEALTHY. It looks with such a face—

ANGELICA. Why, then, did he take such pains to be reconciled?

LADY WEALTHY. Gallantry, mere gallantry; and she that cannot distinguish, often mistakes it for a real amour. Ah, Angelica! You are but a novice yet, and don't understand the beau monde. A woman should always speak more than she thinks, and think more than she writes, or she'll ne'er be upon the square with men.

ANGELICA. I shall neither write nor speak to any of 'em for the future, I assure you.

LADY WEALTHY. And do you positively think you could resist Valere, if he should come in this minute?

ANGELICA. I do, positively.

LADY WEALTHY. What, in his most moving air? For you know he is master of a false insinuating tongue. Should he, I say, throw himself at your feet in a tone of tragedy, cry "Forgive me, Angelica, or kill me if you please; I'll not oppose the blow, nor strive to save my life by one poor word. I love you, and only you. Does not your soul tell you so in my behalf? Will you not answer me?" Then, rising from his knees, "Will then," says he, "nothing but my death wipe out my fault? Give it me then, cruel Fair, for now to live is pain. If I have lost you, I have lost all that's worth my care." Then offers to draw his sword, at the sight of which you are melted into pity, and once again betrayed. Is not this true, Angelica? Ha, ha, ha.

ANGELICA. I confess, I have too often been deceived—but now he shall find I am upon my guard. And were he the only one remaining of all his sex, I would not—if I know my heart—marry him.

LADY WEALTHY. I am pleased to hear your resolution, and doubly pleased to find you mistress of your passion. 'Tis a point of wisdom to cashier[21] such follies as blind our sense and make our judgments err.

ANGELICA. 'Tis very true.

LADY WEALTHY. Believe me, sister, I had rather see you marry to age, avarice, or a fool than to Valere—for can there be a greater misfortune than to marry a gamester?

ANGELICA. I know 'tis the high road to beggary.

LADY WEALTHY. And your fortune being all ready money will be thrown off with expedition—were it as mine is indeed. But are you sure your heart is disengaged?

ANGELICA. Why do you doubt it?

---

21   Cast off.

LADY WEALTHY. I have a reason, sister, that when you have satisfied me, you shall know.

ANGELICA. Then be satisfied: I shall never see him more. Now the secret.

LADY WEALTHY. Why, then know I love him.

ANGELICA. How! You!

LADY WEALTHY. Yes, I! Where's the wonder?

ANGELICA. You that advised against the gamester.

LADY WEALTHY. That was for your good, sister. Our circumstances are different. My estate's entailed[22] enough to supply his riots, and why should I not bestow it upon the man I like?

ANGELICA. What, in that mourning weed resolved on matrimony, and is your lord forgot already? Did I take such pains in rubbing your temples, whilst Favorite applied the hartshorn[23] to your nose, when the fainting fits came thicker and thicker, and was it all but affectation? And does your dead husband's picture that dangles at your watch there, serve only to put you in mind of another?

LADY WEALTHY. And where's the crime? I loved him living as much as any wife, or rather more. And did what decency required when he died. But being free, I'm free to choose.

ANGELICA. Then who so fit as Lovewell for your choice, whose honorable love has long pursued you.

LADY WEALTHY. You are not to direct my inclinations.

ANGELICA. Nor you mine.—Favorite! (*Enter Favorite.*) If Valere comes, I will see him—that good you have done, sister.

FAVORITE. See him, madam!

ANGELICA. Yes, impertinence. (*Exit [Angelica and] Favorite.*)

LADY WEALTHY. Aye, see him, if thou wilt, but to little purpose.—I doubt not his return, when once he finds encouragement; 'tis his awe that has kept him silent, not that I care much for him neither. But it is the greatest mortification in nature to see a handsome fellow make love to another before one's face. (*Enter footman.*)

FOOTMAN. Madam, the Marquis of Hazard to wait on Your Honor.

LADY WEALTHY. Pugh, that fool. (*Enter Marquis.*)

MARQUIS. Hey, let my three footmen wait with my chair there. The rascals have come such a high trot they've jolted me worse than a hackney coach[24]—and I'm in as much disorder—as if I had not been

---

22   A common term of estate transactions of the time, this means that her estate is settled on designated successors and cannot be touched by any would-be possessor.
23   Salt of hartshorn; smelling salts.
24   Coach for hire.

dressed today. Pardon me, madam, I took the liberty to adjust myself, ere I approached you.

LADY WEALTHY. You are the exact model of dress! But, Monsieur Mareque, methinks you are grown perfect in our tongue.

MARQUIS. The value I have for the English ladies, made me take particular pains in the study.—Deuce on't I shall be discovered if I forget my French tone [*aside*]. —Ah, madam, *vous parles Francois mienque I parlez l'Englais*.[25]

LADY WEALTHY. Ah, *ponit de ton't*, monsieur.[26]

MARQUIS. But there's no language like the eyes, madam—and yours would set the world on fire.

LADY WEALTHY. Oh, gallant.

A song. Sung to the widow.

In vain you sable weeds put on;
Clouds cannot long eclipse the sun.
Nature has placed you in a sphere,
To give us daylight all the year;
'Tis well for those
Of Cupid's foes,
That your beauties thus shrouded lie;
For when that night
Puts on the light,
What crowds of martyred slaves will die.

A song. Sung to the gamester, when he has won money.

Fair Caelia, she is nice and coy,
While she hold the lucky lure;
Her repartees are pish and fie,
And you in vain pursue her.
Stay but till her hand be out,
And she become your debtor;
Address her then, and without doubt,
You'll speed a great deal better.
'Tis the only way

---

25   The Marquis's "French" is corrupt throughout; here he is probably trying to say "Your French is better than my English."

26   Also not a correct French phrase: possibly she means "*point du tout*" or "*pas du tout*"—"Not at all!"

When she has lost at play,
To purchase the courted favor;
Forgive the score,
And offer her more,
I'll lay my life you have her.

MARQUIS. I had liked to have fought last night, for asserting your prerogative of beauty.

LADY WEALTHY. With whom, pray?

MARQUIS. With Valere, whose continual toast was your sister. I must
confess it has given me a passionate desire of seeing her, that I may
hereafter with greater assurance maintain your cause.

LADY WEALTHY. [*Aside.*] What, would the fellow have me introduce
him?—My cause don't want your sword.

MARQUIS. [*Aside.*] She's jealous already; if my footmen observe my
orders, she'll secure me here for fear of losing the prize.

LADY WEALTHY. [*Aside.*] This fool's doubly my aversion. Now he has
named my sister, would I were rid of him.

MARQUIS. Has your ladyship played at court this winter?

LADY WEALTHY. In my weed?27

MARQUIS. I ask pardon, madam, but that beauty and gaiety nothing can
eclipse. Who can look on you and mind your dress?

LADY WEALTHY. [*Aside.*] That's well enough expressed—but nothing he
says can please me now.

Enter footman; gives a letter.

FOOTMAN. A footman in green, monsieur, waits for an answer. (*Exit
footman.*)

MARQUIS. Is this a time? Let him wait at the chocolate house at St.
James's an hour hence.—Oh, madam, did you know how I languish
for you!

LADY WEALTHY. When did I give you leave to make a declaration of your
love, monsieur? Pray, read your letter and give the lady an answer.

MARQUIS. I confess it comes from a lady—but if—

Enter another footman.

FOOTMAN. My Lady Gamewell has sent three times for you, and will not
begin play till you come.

---

27   Widow's weeds: mourning clothes

MARQUIS. *Allez vous en cocquin*²⁸—Let her stay. (*Exit footman.*)

LADY WEALTHY. Insolence! What does the fellow mean?

MARQUIS. 'Tis the greatest fatigue in nature to hold a correspondence with impertinence—but your ladyship is the reverse of— (*Enter another footman.*)

FOOTMAN. Sir, the Lady Amorous begs the honor of your company this minute; Sir Credulous is just gone out of town.

MARQUIS. *La diable t'omport*²⁹—out of my sight! Am I not engaged?

LADY WEALTHY. Engaged? Upon my word you are not. What house is the place you appoint to receive your assignations in?

MARQUIS. No, upon my honor, madam. But I presume they have searched the whole town—and seeing my equipage at your door were so audacious to send in their message. But I'll turn away my footmen for this embarrassment.

LADY WEALTHY. Pray, let not my house be distinguished by you, nor your equipage, for the future—I am not to be used so (*angrily*). —Now for a set and grave face to put me more out of humor, if possible [*aside*]. (*Enter Lovewell.*)

LOVEWELL. You seem in disorder, madam.

LADY WEALTHY. Who can be otherwise, when people take liberty beyond the bounds of good manners—

LOVEWELL. Who dares in my Lady Wealthy's house? (*Looking angrily at the Marquis.*)

MARQUIS. Upon my soul, sir, she takes it quite wrong. Or she's—confoundedly jealous.

LOVEWELL. Sir, I am positive that lady cannot be in the wrong. And read it in her looks; your absence would please her—

MARQUIS. Sir—

LOVEWELL. No words here, sir. If you would dispute it, I'll meet you when and where you please—

MARQUIS. Your most humble servant—(*in a low voice*) you shall hear from me!—Hey, hey, who's there? My servants—Madam, as your ladyship said, I'm not to be used thus— (*Exit.*)

LADY WEALTHY. Monsieur—he's gone! I would not lose the fop neither—

LOVEWELL. Gone, madam! So you would have him, I suppose.

---

28   There is no such verb as "cocquin"; he seems to be cursing the footman as he tells him to "Get lost," and he incorrectly uses the formal rather than the informal second person pronoun and verb form in "*allez vous*"
29   Probably he means to say, "The devil away with you!"

LADY WEALTHY. You suppose! How dare you suppose my thoughts—and
who gave you this privilege in my house? Shortly I shall be wished
joy,[30] for this is a prerogative above a depending lover—

LOVEWELL. I plead no merit, and my long successless love assures me I
have no power—but I understood—

LADY WEALTHY. You understood! Aye, you always understand wrong, Mr.
Lovewell.

LOVEWELL. I do confess, I wander in the mazes—and still pursue a
brightness, which I cannot fix. To please you has been my long and
only study; witness the many years of awful servitude I paid your virgin beauty, and the pains I felt when I beheld you wedded to another.
I could not bear the sight, but in a cruel banishment past my unlucky
hours 'till fate, in pity, set you free, but all in vain, for still my portion
is despair.

LADY WEALTHY. Nay, if you are running into that grave stuff, I must
leave you, though in my own house, for I have got the spleen[31] intoler-
ably and cannot endure it.

LOVEWELL. No, madam, I'll retire—I love too much to disobey. Only,
when you reflect on your admiring slaves, think on my fidelity. (*Exit.*)

LADY WEALTHY. Thou art a poor constant fool, that's the truth on't. And
thou hast merit too, I'll say that for thee—but we women don't always
mind that. (*Enter Valere.*) —Here comes the present ascendant of my
heart [*aside*].

VALERE. [*Aside.*] Ha! The widow here. Now could I make her my friend:
now, for a serious face—and an heroic style.—Madam—

LADY WEALTHY. Sir—

VALERE. My stars shed their kindest influence today and blessed me
with the opportunity of finding you alone. Pity is essential to the fair,
and ought to be extended to those that sink beneath the rigor of their
chains—

LADY WEALTHY. 'Tis the diversion of your sex to complain; I believe Mr.
Valere finds few barbarous in ours—

VALERE. None more unfortunate in love than I, and though my heart is
breaking, I'm forbid to tell my pain.

LADY WEALTHY. I hope 'tis to my wish.—It may be me he means, else
why this address? (*aside*). —She must be very cruel, that lets you sigh
without return. Is it in my power to assist you?

VALERE. Oh, madam, all, all's in your power. You rule my fate.

---

30   I.e., congratulated on my engagement, evidently meant sarcastically.
31   Thought to be the source of melancholy and other negative feelings—here irritability.

LADY WEALTHY. Then you shall be happy, 'tis so—

VALERE. On my knees let me receive the confirmation of your promise—
and seal it here— (*Kneels and kisses her hand.*)

Enter Angelica.

ANGELICA. Ha! Kneeling to my sister, faithless man—

VALERE. There, madam, there's the angry brow that darts distraction to
my peace. Your aid to that storm is what I sued for—

LADY WEALTHY. Insufferable, ill-breeding—

VALERE. Oh, Angelica! I cast me at your feet.

ANGELICA. No! Back to my sister's; there I found you.

VALERE. Only to intercede to you—

LADY WEALTHY. False by my honor! He was making violent love.—I'll
tease her, however [*aside*].

VALERE. [*Aside.*] Making love! What does she mean?

ANGELICA. And you received it, I suppose.

LADY WEALTHY. You interrupted me, ere I could give my answer.

VALERE. Why, madam, my design, you know—

LADY WEALTHY. Yes, yes, Mr. Valere, I know your design. I have not had
so many sighing, dying lovers, but I can guess their design—

VALERE. But mine was—

LADY WEALTHY. [*Aside.*] Oh, fie, don't declare it here.—You know my
sister has a passion for you, and I would not tyrannize—

ANGELICA. 'Tis not in your power—

VALERE. [*Aside.*] Oh, the devil!—Madam, I own 'tis an offence to a lady
of your beauty and merit to make a declaration of love—

LADY WEALTHY. Not at all, sir—when one likes the person. I'll—consider on't. But, heark'ee, do not deceive my sister too far. It may be
dangerous—

ANGELICA. 'Tis not in your power, or his, to deceive me; I see through
your shallow artifices, and despise it—

LADY WEALTHY. Those that rely upon their own judgment are soonest
caught, sister—remember I have given you fair warning! (*Exit.*)

VALERE. I'm in amaze—

ANGELICA. You need not. I know my sister's design, but that's not my
quarrel to you. Quarrel, did I say? No, I am grown to a perfect state of
indifference. Quarrels may be reconciled, but a man that basely breaks
his word and forfeits faith and honor, is not worth our anger but
deserves to be despised.

VALERE. I do confess I am a wretch below your scorn; I own my faults,
and have no refuge but your mercy.

FAVORITE. [*Aside.*] In the old strain again—

VALERE. If you abandon me, I'm lost forever—for you and only you are mistress of my fate.

ANGELICA. Your daily actions contradict your words—and shows I have no such power in your heart. Did you not promise, nay, swear, you'd never game again?

VALERE. I did, and for the perjured crime, merit your endless hate. But you, in pity, may forgive me. Oh, Angelica, see at your feet an humble penitent kneel, who, if not by your goodness raised, will grow forever to his native soil.

ANGELICA. You would be pardoned only to offend again.

VALERE. Never, never. Here on this beauteous hand I swear, whose touch runs thrilling through my heart—and by those lovely eyes that dart their fire into my soul, never to disoblige you more.

FAVORITE. [*Aside.*] That oath hath done the business, I see by her looks.

ANGELICA. Rise, Valere! I differ from my sex in this; I would not change where once I've given my heart, if possible. Therefore, resolve to make this last trial—banish your love for play and rest secured of mine.

VALERE. Oh transport! Let me kiss those soft forgiving lips, the memory of whose sweetness shall arm me against temptation.

FAVORITE. (*Aside.*) So, now my old man may go hang himself.

VALERE. Could you but know the anxious pains I felt, the jealous racking cares that preyed upon my soul. When I heard my uncle was allowed to tell his suit, you'd then have found out how dear Valere had prized you.

ANGELICA. What I did was to revenge your falsehood; though love's my witness, Dorante's my aversion—and let this present show who 'tis that reigns triumphant in my heart.

VALERE. Your picture! Oh, give it me, that in the absence of the dear original, I may feast my eyes on that.

ANGELICA. But mark, Valere, the injunction I shall lay: whilst you keep safe this picture, my heart is yours, but if, though avarice, carelessness, or falsehood, you ever part with it, you lose me from that moment. (*Gives him the picture.*)

VALERE. I agree. And when I do (*kissing it*), except to yourself, may all the curses, ranked with your disdain, pursue me. This, when I look on't, will correct my folly, and strike a sacred awe upon my actions—

FAVORITE. (*Aside.*) 'Tis worth two hundred pounds: a good moveable, when cash runs low.

ANGELICA. Well, I am convinced. Let a woman make what resolutions she will when alone, the sight of her lover will break 'em.

FAVORITE. Madam, Mr. Dorante is coming up.

ANGELICA. I'll not be seen, adieu. (*Exit.*)

VALERE. My charming love, adieu! Take care to welcome your benefactor, Mrs. Favorite; he's a lover ripe with discretion. Ha, ha, ha. (*Enter Dorante.*) Your servant, uncle, ha, ha, ha— (*Holds up the picture to the nose. Exit.*)

DORANTE. [*Aside.*] This young rake's presence bodes me no good, I fear.— Mrs. Favorite, your servant. Is your lady to be spoke with?

FAVORITE. I doubt not, sir! I don't know what she is. I'm sure I'm almost wild; our business is all spoiled—Valere is reconciled again.

DORANTE. Ah, that insinuating young dog.

FAVORITE. She has just now given him her picture set round with diamonds.

DORANTE. I thought, indeed, something sparkled in my eyes. But what's to be done?

FAVORITE. I know not! He has promised her to play no more. If he keeps his word we have no hopes. But if he breaks it, as I doubt not but he will, pride and revenge may work her to our ends. You may be certain, sir, I'll let slip no opportunity to serve you.

DORANTE. I do believe it—and to encourage you to believe me grateful, accept of this ring.

FAVORITE. Oh, dear sir, you are too generous. I don't merit it. Pray, excuse me.

DORANTE. Nay, I will not be denied.

FAVORITE. Well, sir, since you will have it so, I'll not fail to move your suit. I'll do my best endeavors, I'll assure you. Write, sir, write, and I'll deliver the letter—then let me alone to back it.

DORANTE. You must urge the largeness of my fortune, the staidness of my temper, and withal tell her I am not above two and forty—I was gray at thirty.

FAVORITE. I warrant you, sir. Be sure you exclaim against your nephew's gaming.

DORANTE. Aye, aye, I'll go write it this moment—and send it presently.

FAVORITE. I'll be in the way to receive it. (*Exeunt severally.*)

Scene: Changes to Sir Thomas Valere's house.

Enter Sir Thomas and Hector, with several papers.

HECTOR. Sir, I have brought you a complete account of the debts of my master. I think I have not forgot one farthing; for, if I mistake not, you desired to know 'em all, sir—

SIR THOMAS. Aye, aye, come read 'em over.

HECTOR. That I will, sir, in two words: a true list of the debts of Mr. James Valere, which was by him contracted within the City of London and Liberty of Westminster, which his father, Sir Thomas Valere, has promised to discharge.

SIR THOMAS. If I discharge them, or not, is not your business. Go on—

HECTOR. 'Tis my design, sir. In the first place, then, item due to Richard Scrape, fifty-five pounds, nine shillings, and ten pence, half-penny— for five years wages and money disbursed for necessaries.

SIR THOMAS. Richard Scrape? Who's he?

HECTOR. Your most humble servant, sir— (*Bows*.)

SIR THOMAS. You? Why, is not your name Hector?

HECTOR. Aye, sir, that is my name *de novo*.[32] My master thought Richard sounded too clumsy for a gentleman's valet and a gamester—so, sir, he gave me the name of Hector, from the knave of diamonds.

SIR THOMAS. A very pretty name. I admire he don't call his mistress Pallas, from the Queen of Spades. But how came you so rich, sirrah, to be able to lend your master money?

HECTOR. Why, when the dice has run well, my master would now and then tip me a guinea, sir.

SIR THOMAS. And so you supplied him, when he wanted, with his own money. Oh, extravagance!

HECTOR. 'Tis what many an honest gentleman is drove to sometimes, sir.

SIR THOMAS. More shame for 'em! Go on.

HECTOR. Secondly, sir, here is due to Jeremy Aron, usurer by profession—and Jew by religion.

SIR THOMAS. Never trouble yourself about that; I shall pay no usurer's debts, I assure you.

HECTOR. Then, sir, here is two hundred guineas lost to my Lord Lovegame, upon honor.[33]

SIR THOMAS. That's another debt I shall not pay.

HECTOR. How not pay it, sir? Why, sir, among gentlemen, that debt is looked upon as the most just of any. You may cheat widows, orphans, tradesmen without a blush, but a debt of honor, sir, must be paid. I could name you some noblemen that pays nobody—yet a debt of honor, sir, is as sure as their ready money.

SIR THOMAS. He that makes no conscience of wronging the man, whose goods have been delivered for his use, can have no pretence to honor— whatever title he may wear. But to the next—

---

32   Beginning anew (Latin).

33   A debt owed upon one's word.

HECTOR. Here is the tailor's bill, the milliner's, hosier's, shoemaker's, tavern, and eating house—in all £300.

SIR THOMAS. A fine sum, truly.

HECTOR. Ah, sir, I have not named the barber, periwig maker and perfumer, which is £100 more; besides, he is in arrears to Mademoiselle Margret de la Plant, lately arrived from France, with whom he covenanted for four guineas a week.

SIR THOMAS. For four guineas a week? For what?

HECTOR. Oh, sir, pardon me there; I never betray the secrets of my master.

SIR THOMAS. Four guineas a week—

HECTOR. Aye, sir, and very cheap—considering he made his bargain in the winter, and truly I don't know but the woman lost by it.

SIR THOMAS. You don't—take that, sirrah. You shan't lose by it, however! Go, rascal, pay your whores and debts of honor out of that.

HECTOR. Aye, sir, they'll never take this money of me. If you please, sir, I'll send 'em to your levee,[34] and you may pay 'em yourself.

SIR THOMAS. Sirrah, I shall break your head—go, get you to the rake, your master. Play, hang, or starve together; I care not. Debts, with a pox, gaming, drinking, wenching, rare debts to bring into a court of chancery. You, I, I, I, I, I—bring me such a bill of debts, rogue. Mercy on me, that there can be such impudence in the world. Oh, oh, I have much ado to forbear thee—me such a bill of debts. (*Exit.*)

HECTOR. So our affairs goes backwards, I find, honest Richard; patient, I say, go seek thy master out.

Fortune may change, and give a lucky main;
And what undid us, set us up again.

ACT III

Hector solus.

HECTOR. Where can my master be now? I should suspect he were at play, but that I know he has no money. Sure this old dad of his will open his purse strings once more, if he is reconciled to Angelica. I long to know what success he meets with. Oh, here he comes. (*Enter Valere with his hat under his arm, full of money, he counting it.*)— I waited on your father, according to order, sir, with a list of your

---

34   A nobleman's formal reception of visitors while rising from bed.

debts. And the generous old gentleman (I think him) gave me more than I expected.—Hey day, he minds me not. Ah, I doubt we are all untwisted. No hopes of Angelica— [*aside*].

VALERE. Five hundred fifty seven guineas and a half.

HECTOR. Ha! What do I see? The plate fleet's arrived. By what miracle fell these galleons into our power? I hope, sir, since fortune has been so kind—

VALERE. A curse of ill-luck! (*Stamps.*) Had I but held in the last hand, I should have had 300 guineas more of my lord duke's—besides what I betted. (*Walks about.*)

HECTOR. I am overjoyed, sir, at your good fortune. But, as I was saying, sir—

VALERE. But hold, my Lord Lovegame owes me 200 upon honor. 'Tis pretty well; I have not made an ill morning's work on't.

HECTOR. There's no speaking to him—

VALERE. Ah! There's no music like the chink of gold. By Jove, this sound is sweeter in my ear, than all the margarites[35] in Europe. Ha! Hector, where come you from sirrah?

HECTOR. Came, sir? Why I was here before you, but Fortune's golden mist concealed me from your sight. Sir, I congratulate your good success. But how—

VALERE. Aye, 'tis success indeed if thou know'st all. Honest Jack Sharper lent me five guineas, that I should pay him ten if luck ran on my side. I have discharged my promise and brought off a thousand clear.

HECTOR. Huzza! Why, you are a made man!

VALERE. And we meet again at five, where I design to win a thousand more, boy.

HECTOR. Aye, but if you should lose all back, sir?

VALERE. Impossible! This is a lucky day: Angelica and I are reconciled, my faults forgiven, and all my wishes crowned, Hector— (*Showing the picture.*)

HECTOR. Bless my eyesight! A picture set with diamonds!—Nay, then, Hector, cheer up, for now the bad times will mend [*aside*]. —Why now a fig for your father's kindness. You are able to pay your debts yourself, sir—

VALERE. A pox on thee for naming 'em. Thou hast given me the spleen. Pay my debts, quotha! The bare word is enough to turn all my luck.

HECTOR. Say you so, sir! Is paying debts unlucky?

VALERE. Aye, certainly; the most unlucky thing in the world!

---

35   Precious stones.

HECTOR. [*Aside.*] Humph! I now find the reason why quality hate to pay their debts. A deuce on't! I wish I had known as much this morning; I would not have paid the cobbler for heel-piecing my shoes.[36] For aught I know, it may be a guinea out of my way, for my master does not use to be so slow.—Sir, now you are in stock, sir, if you please to put my wages into my hands, it shall be very safe in bank, against you want it.

VALERE. The devil's in the fellow [*aside*]. —Speak one word more of pay-ing debts, sirrah, and I'll cut your ears off. I shall have no occasion to borrow—and my father will pay your debt amongst the rest.   .

HECTOR. He won't pay a souse, sir. He broke my head at the very sight of the list.

VALERE. Aye, that was in his passion. There's a plaster for that wound. (*Gives him a guinea.*)

HECTOR. Sir, your humble servant!—I find we middling people are out of the quality's latitude; paying debts are only unlucky to gentlemen [*aside*]. —Sir, pray, sir, give me leave to offer one thing to your serious consideration.

VALERE. I bar debts—

HECTOR. Not a word of that, sir.

VALERE. Out with it then.

HECTOR. That you'd lay by £500 of that money against a rainy day.

VALERE. But suppose I should have more set me than I can answer.

HECTOR. 'Tis but sending for it, at worst, sir.

VALERE. So balk my hand in the mean time and lose the winning of a thousand. No, no, there's nothing like ready money to nick Fortune.

HECTOR. Ah, sir, but you know she has often jilted you, and would it not be better to have a little pocket money secure? Put by but £200, sir.

VALERE. Well, I'll consider on't. Ha! See who knocks.

HECTOR. A dun, I warrant.

VALERE. I have not a farthing of money; remember that, sirrah! (*Puts up his money hastily.*)

HECTOR. Lying is a thriving vocation.

Enter Galloon, a tailor, and Mrs. Topknot, a milliner.

VALERE. Ha! Good morrow to you—and good morrow to you, Mrs. Topknot. Mrs. Topknot, you are a great stranger. Why don't you call and see me sometimes?

---

36   Putting a piece of leather on a shoe heel (Samuel Johnson's *Dictionary*).

MRS. TOPKNOT. Indeed, sir, I call very often, though I have not had the good fortune to see you, for you was still asleep or gone abroad.

VALERE. I am sorry it fell out so; well, have you brought your bill?

MRS. TOPKNOT. Yes, sir. (*Gives him bill.*) I hope you liked your last linen sir.

VALERE. Very well.

GALLOON. Sir, I beg the favor of you—

HECTOR. [*Aside.*] I must not let two fasten upon him at once—Mr. Galloon, a word with you! You always make my clothes too little for me.

GALLOON. I am sorry for that.

HECTOR. My breeches are seam-rent in three or four places.

GALLOON. I'll take care—

HECTOR. You sew most abominably slight.

MRS. TOPKNOT. We are about marrying our daughter.

VALERE. I hope you have provided a good match, for she is very handsome, faith!

MRS. TOPKNOT. The girl is not despisable; the man is very well to pass in the world, but the small fortune we design for her must be paid down upon the nail. Therefore, sir, I entreat you to help me to my money if possible.

VALERE. If it was possible, I would, Mrs. Topknot, and I am heartily sorry that it is not in my power.

MRS. TOPKNOT. It is a debt of long standing, Mr. Valere, and I must not be said nay.

VALERE. I know it is, but, upon my honor, I can't pay you now.

MRS. TOPKNOT. Let me have some, if you can't pay me all; ten guineas at present would do me singular service.

VALERE. May I sink if I have seen five these six months.

HECTOR. That he has not to my knowledge.

GALLOON. Pray, sir, consider me, if it be never so small; my wife is ready to lie in,[37] and coals are very dear and journeymen's wages must be paid.

HECTOR. Why, the devil's in the fellow! Would you have a man pay what he has not? What business have you to get children, without you had cabbage enough to maintain 'em?

VALERE. (*Aside to Hector.*) Hector—no invention?

GALLOON. When will you be pleased that I call again, sir?

VALERE. When you please.

---

37   Is ready to give birth.

GALLOON. I'll call tomorrow, sir.

VALERE. With all my heart.

GALLOON. Do you think, sir, you can let me have some if I come?

VALERE. Not that I know of.

HECTOR. No, nor I neither. Heark ye, when he has money, I'll bring you word.

MRS. TOPKNOT. Don't tell me; I won't go out of the house without money.

VALERE. With all my heart.—Hector! No stratagem to save me from these leeches (*aside to Hector*)?

HECTOR. Then you must e'en lie with my master or me, for here are no spare beds. Let me advise you to make no noise; you'll have your money sooner than you think for—your ear. (*Whispers.*)

MRS. TOPKNOT. To be married, say you?

GALLOON. And to madam Angelica, the great fortune?

HECTOR. The same.

MRS. TOPKNOT. I wish you joy, sir. Pray, recommend me to you lady for gloves, fans, and ribbons.

GALLOON. I hope, sir, I shall have the honor to make your wedding suit.

VALERE. That you shall, I promise you—the rogue has hit on't (*aside*).

MRS. TOPKNOT. But will this match be speedy, sir?

VALERE. I hope so.

GALLOON. Tomorrow, sir?

HECTOR. Or next day—but we must entreat your absence at present, for my master expects his father with the lady's trustees in order to settle the affair, and if you are seen, it may spoil the business.

MRS. TOPKNOT. Well, well, well; I go, I go. (*Runs a little way and turns.*) You'll put your master in mind of me?

HECTOR. Aye, aye.

GALLOON. And me too, pray.

HECTOR. I'll do your business, I warrant you. Go, go, go—be gone, be gone, be gone. (*Pushes 'em out.*) There, sir, I have brought you off once more. Here's two or three days' respite, however.

VALERE. Why, then, there's two or three days of peace, for these are the most disagreeable companions a gentleman can meet with. I dine at the Rummer, where you'll find me if you want me. I promised to visit Angelica again tonight, but fear I shall break my word.

HECTOR. And will you prefer play before that charming lady?

VALERE. Not before her—but I have given my parole to some men of quality, and I can't in honor disappoint 'em.

HECTOR. [*Aside.*] Ah, what a juggler's box is this word, honor! It is a kind
of Knight of the Post[38] that will swear on either side for interest, I
find.—But, sir, had you not better make sure work on't. Marry the
lady whilst she's in the mind, lest Fortune wheel about and throw you
back again.

VALERE. Marry her, say'st thou? I am not resolved if I shall marry or not.

HECTOR. High day! Why I thought it had been what you desired above
all things. But I find your pocket and your heart still runs counter.

VALERE. No, sirrah! I love the charming maid as much as ever: love her
from my soul. But then I love liberty.

HECTOR. And what should hinder you from enjoying it?

VALERE. Ah, Hector! If I marry her, I must forsake my dear diversion
(*pulling out a box and dice*), which to me is the very soul of living; 'tis
the genteelest way of passing one's time. Every day produces something new. Who is happier than a gamester? Who more respected—I
mean those that make any figure in the world? Who more caressed
by lords and dukes? Or whose conversation more agreeable? Whose
coach finer in the ring? Or finger in the side box[39] produce more
luster? Who has more attendance from the drawers, or better wine
from the master? Or nicer served by the cook? In short, there is an air
of magnificence in't. A gamester's hand is the philosopher's stone that
turns all it touches into gold.

HECTOR. And gold into nothing!

VALERE. A gentleman that plays is admitted everywhere; women of the
strictest virtue will converse with him, for gaming is as much in fashion here as 'tis in France, and our ladies look upon it as the height of
ill breeding, not to have a passion for play. Oh, the charming company
of half a dozen ladies, with each a dish of tea—to behold their lan-
guishing ogles with their eyes, their ravishing white hand, to hear the
delicious scandal, which they vent between each sip, just piping hot
from the invention's mint, wherein they spare none from the states-
man to the cit—and damn plays before they are acted, especially if the
author be unknown. This ended, the cards are called for.

HECTOR. And open war proclaimed—and every cock boat[40] proves a
privateer.

---

38   A notorious perjurer.
39   The side boxes at the theatre were the most expensive seating.
40   A small ship's boat, often towed behind.

VALERE. Our engagements are not so terrible. With us revenge reaches no farther than the pocket.

HECTOR. No more don't a highwayman—and yet the world thinks both lives equally immoral.

VALERE. None of your similes, sirrah, do you hear? Where is the immorality of gaming? Now, I think there can be nothing more moral: it unites men of all ranks, the lord and the peasant; the haughty duchess and the city dame; the marquis and the footman, all without distinction play together.
And sure that life can ne'er offensive prove,
That teacheth men such peaceful ways of love.

HECTOR. The Marquis of Hazard, sir!

VALERE. The Marquis of Hazard? What wants he?

Enter Marquis.

MARQUIS. Do you hear? Do you wait with my chair at the corner of the street, for I would be incognito.

HECTOR. What does he pretend to?

MARQUIS. I presume, sir, your name is Valere.

VALERE. I don't remember I ever had any other, sir.

MARQUIS. Sir, I should take it as an extraordinary favor, if you'll be pleased to command the absence of your *valet de chambre*.

VALERE. Be gone. (*Exit Hector.*)

MARQUIS. Now, sir, do you know who I am?

VALERE. I think, sir, I never had the honor of your acquaintance.

MARQUIS. (*Aside.*) *Allom Courage!*[41] Push him home; he seems daunted already.—Sir, I have made the Tour of Europe, and have had the respect paid to me in all courts, that became my quality. In Spain, I kept company with none but archdukes; in France with princes of the blood—and since I have been here, I have had the honor to sup or dine with most of the great people at court.

VALERE. Why so hot sir?

MARQUIS. And, sir, my person is not more known than my valor; I have fought a hundred duels, and never failed to kill or wound—without receiving the least hurt myself.

---

41   Later editions have "*Allons Courage*," which would literally mean "Let us go, courage!"; he seems to be plucking up the courage to go on with his masquerade.

VALERE. You had very good luck truly, sir.—What does the blockhead aim at (*aside*)?

MARQUIS. Sir, Fortune owes my life protection, for the sake of the noble race from whence I sprung: my father's grandfather's great grandfather was viceroy of Naples.

VALERE. Oh, one may see that in your air, sir.

MARQUIS. Now, sir, there is a certain lady that has a passion for my person, not that I am in love with her—only gratitude—and I am informed by her woman, that you make your addresses there. Now, sir, I suffer no man beneath my quality to mix his pretensions with mine.

VALERE. The lady's name, sir?

MARQUIS. The Lady Wealthy.

VALERE. You are misinformed, upon my word, sir; that lady is at your service for me.

MARQUIS. That declaration comes not from your heart: your encomiums on Angelica last night, served only to conceal your love from me.

VALERE. So far from that, I did not know you till you had left the room.

MARQUIS. Sir, I say you must not pretend to vie with quality!

VALERE. I know the distance Fortune has put between us, sir.

MARQUIS. Then pray, observe it, sir. Don't think every fellow we condescend to play with, fit companions for us men of quality.

VALERE. (*Cocking his hat.*) Fellow sir— (*Laying his hand on his sword.*)

MARQUIS. Yes, fellow sir!—He has a heart, I find; I'll moderate my passion (*aside*).

VALERE. You will have it, then, I see. (*Draws.*)

MARQUIS. No, upon my word, sir; I was in jest all the while.

VALERE. But I am in earnest, sir—and, therefore, draw! What, does the courage of your royal ancestors, viceroys of Naples, fail you?

MARQUIS. Sir, I made a vow never to kill another man—and therefore, pray, put up; you have given me as much satisfaction as I desired. I thirst for no revenge.

VALERE. Sir, I am not to be trifled with; the wine is drawn and you shall drink. (*Slaps him.*)

Enter Hector.

HECTOR.
Hey, what's the matter? (*Lays hold of the marquis, who draws.*)

MARQUIS. Ha, company! Nay, then, sir, this is too much to bear.

HECTOR. Hold, hold, sir, hold. What do you do?

MARQUIS. Let me go; let me go.

VALERE. Aye, aye, prithee, let him go. He's not so dangerous as thou imagin'st, Hector—ha, ha, ha.

HECTOR. Why, then, let him go—there, sir, I have done.

MARQUIS. I shall find a time, sir.

VALERE. To be kicked. You have been used too civilly here.

HECTOR. A time! For what? For what the devil do you come into our nation to crow over us? I believe we shall find a time this campaign to teach you better manners. Your capering country are fitter for dancing masters than soldiers, ha, ha, ha.

MARQUIS. It suits not with my quality, to answer the impertinency of a valet. Monsieur, adieu; *previs gard uns aut'ne fois.*[42] (*Exit.*)

VALERE. Coxcomb below resentment. (*Looking on his watch.*) I have out-stayed my time.

      Now Fortune be my friend; I'll ask no more,
      One lucky hour may double all my store.

HECTOR. Or make you bankrupt as you was before. (*Exeunt.*)

      Scene changes: A table; pen, ink, paper set out.

Enter Lady Wealthy sola.

LADY WEALTHY. Which way shall I contrive to disappoint my sister's wishes? Now would I give half my estate to feed my vanity. Oh, that I could once bring Valere within my power; I'd use him as his ill breeding deserves. I'd teach him to be particular. He has promised Angelica to play no more; I fancy that proceeds from his want of money rather than inclination. If I could be sure of that—I'll try, however. If my project takes, I shall again break their union—and if I can't serve my pride, I shall at least disturb their peace, and either brings me pleasure. (*Sits down and writes.*) Now, how shall I convey this to his hands? It is not proper to send any of my own servants.— Who's there?

Enter Mrs. Betty.

BETTY. Did your ladyship call, madam?

LADY WEALTHY. Aye, get me a porter.

---

42   He seems to be saying "Watch out for me another time."

BETTY. A porter! Madam, Robin, John, and Nicholas are all within.

LADY WEALTHY. And what then? Do as I bid you.

BETTY. [*Aside.*] What, can she want with a porter! I am resolved to watch. (*Exit.*)

LADY WEALTHY. 'Tis better being confined to a desert where one never sees the face of man, than not to be admired by all. (*Enter porter.*) Here carry this to Mr. Valere. Do you know him?

PORTER. Yes, and please your Honor, very well.

LADY WEALTHY. Go, bring me an answer then. (*Exit Porter.*)

Enter Lovewell.

LADY WEALTHY. [*Aside.*] Ha, Lovewell! I must avoid his presence lest he discover this intrigue. He'll be alarmed at the sight of a porter in my lodgings; besides, my soul resents the ill treatment I have given him. He indeed merits better usage, but I know not how—I cannot resolve on matrimony. (*Exit*)

LOVEWELL. Gone! Am I then shunned like pestilential air, yet doomed to dote upon her cold indifference? Oh, give me patience or I burst with rage. There must be more than her bare temper in't. She loves—aye, there's the cause. Oh, the racking thought! By all the powers it fires each vital part, and with a double warmth strikes every active sense. Hear me ye powers—and if you e'er design
To make this dear, this scornful beauty mine,
Grant in the lieu, I may my rival meet,
And throw him gasping at his lady's feet. (*Exit.*)

Enter Angelica and Favorite with a letter in her hand.

ANGELICA. I shall not open it, indeed. If you venture to receive letters again, without my leave, I shall discharge you from your attendance, Mrs. Favorite.

FAVORITE. I do it for your good, madam.

ANGELICA. For my good! Impertinence! Am I to be governed by those I may command?

FAVORITE. (*Aside.*) In spite of all that I can do, I shall lose my salary, for when he finds the cause go backwards, he'll fee no more.

Enter Dorante.

ANGELICA. So, he's here too, by your appointment, I suppose.

DORANTE. May I venture to approach the rays of that divinity, which dart into my soul an impetuous flame?

ANGELICA. Oh dear, sir, there's a fire in the next room, whose flames will warm you better than my beauty, I believe.

FAVORITE. Well really, madam, I think Valere could not have expressed himself finer.

ANGELICA. Cease your odious comparisons. Mr. Dorante, might I advise you, make your addresses to my woman—I'm sure you'll meet a kind reception. Ha, ha, ha.

DORANTE. Your woman, madam! I thought a person of your rank knew how to treat a gentleman better.

ANGELICA. And I thought a person of your years might have understood better, than to make love to one of mine.

DORANTE. My years, madam! I'm not so old. Can I help being in love with you?

ANGELICA. No more can Favorite being in love with you.

FAVORITE. You are always witty upon me, madam.—I'd have her to know I love a young fellow as well as herself (*aside*).

DORANTE. 'Tis for my extravagant nephew that I am despised, that complicated piece of vice, whose headstrong courses and luxurious life will ruin both your peace and fortune. I saw him a little while ago enter one of those schools of poverty, a gaming house in St. Martin's Lane.

ANGELICA. 'Tis false.

FAVORITE. Nay, madam, I dare say 'tis true. Yonder goes his man; I'll call him and convince you. (*Exit and re-enters with Hector.*)

ANGELICA. [*Aside.*] He cannot be so ungrateful after my last favors.— Hector, where's your master?

HECTOR. Where'er his person is—his heart is with your ladyship, madam. I dare answer for him.

ANGELICA. That's foreign to my question. Where is he?

DORANTE. Yes, yes, he's a fit person to inquire of truly.

HECTOR. So I am, sir, for nobody knows my master's outgoings and his incomings better than myself.

ANGELICA. Come, you shall tell me. Dorante says he saw him go into a gaming house.

HECTOR. [*Aside.*] Discovered! Nay I must bring him off.—Why that's true, madam.

ANGELICA. Perfidious.

HECTOR. But, madam, it is to take his leave, upon my word. He's gone to play, with a design to play no more.

FAVORITE. Now, madam, who was in the right?

ANGELICA. Is it possible a man can be so base?

DORANTE. There are men, madam, that never was guilty of such crimes.

HECTOR. But, madam, you won't hear me? My master is making all the speed he can to put himself in a condition to keep his word with you; he is shaking his elbows, rattling the box, and breaking his knuckle for haste. He has sent me post for his last auxiliary guineas, which when he has thrown off, he'll lay himself at your feet, with full resolution never to touch box or dice more.

ANGELICA. A likely matter, truly.

HECTOR. So it is, madam—for he'll put it out of his power to offend again.

DORANTE. Till he has a new recruit.

HECTOR. Madam, your ladyship's most humble servant. I must fly, for my master will think every hour seven till he's here. (*Exit.*)

DORANTE. Now, madam, are you convinced? Will you yet accept a heart devoted only to your charms?

ANGELICA. No more of your fustian; 'tis unseasonable. Don't provoke me to use you worse than good manners will allow. I respect your age, but hate your—

DORANTE. Well, scornful maid. Take up with your gamester, do. You'll be the first that repents it. And so, farewell. (*Exit.*)

ANGELICA. Oh! My too constant heart. Can'st thou still hold the image of this faithless man. And yet methinks I'd fain reclaim him. I'll try the last extremity.

For when from ill a proselyte we gain,
The goodness of the act rewards the pain;
But if my honest arts successless prove,
To make the vices of his soul remove.
I'll die—or rid me from this tyrant love.

ACT IV

Enter Valere with a box and dice in his hand, as from play, to a porter. Betty listening.

BETTY. So, thus far I have followed this porter. Here I'll observe who he wants—I'm sure 'tis against the interest of Mr. Lovewell.

VALERE. From a lady, say'st thou? And must be delivered into my own hand?

BETTY. As I imagined.

VALERE. Prithee, fellow, do'st know what 'tis to interrupt a gamester when his fortune's at stake. Seven or eleven have more charms now than the brightest lady in the kingdom. (*Opens the letter. Reads.*) — Humph! "Pursuant to what I told you before Angelica, that a declaration of love would not be disagreeable, I confirm my words in a golden shower—'tis what I believe most acceptable to a man in your circumstances"—well guessed, i' faith. A bill for one hundred pounds, payable at sight! Monsieur La Porter, your very humble servant, tell the lady I am hers most obediently. It requires no other answer till I fly myself to return my thanks.

PORTER. Yes, sir. (*Exit porter.*)

VALERE. What must I do now—prove a rogue and betray my friend, Lovewell. If I accept this present, I must make my returns in love; for when a widow parts with money, 'tis easy to read the valuable consideration she expects. But then Angelica, the dear, the faithful maid— but then a hundred guineas, the dear tempting sight. Ha! Lovewell, thou com'st in good time, for my virtue's staggering.

Enter Lovewell.

LOVEWELL. I have been seeking you all the town over.

VALERE. And what news? Thou hast a very lovesick countenance; the widow has used thee scurvily I know.

LOVEWELL. Beyond all bearing. Valere, thou ever wert my friend; prithee, instruct me—help to find the cursed rival out. 'Tis not the fool marquis, I'm convinced, but some lurking villain, some wretch unworthy of her charms—else her vanity would ne'er conceal him.

VALERE. Hold, hold, friend; you run on a little too fast. What would your mightiness do now, supposing you discovered the detested rival?

LOVEWELL. I'd force him to renounce her, or lose my life and leave her free.

VALERE. Why, then, I have such a respect for this gentleman, that I must preserve him from your lion-like fury.

LOVEWELL. Ha! Dost thou know him then? Oh! I charge thee by our past years of friendship and by my peace of mind, which this cruel woman takes eternally away, tell me but who he is; describe him to me. Is he a gentleman?

VALERE. Yes, faith.

LOVEWELL. And handsome?

VALERE. The ladies think so.

LOVEWELL. Tell but his name, that my revenge may reach him. Hast
thou a friend more dear than I? No, no, thy companions are no
friends: gamesters and profligates, whom in thy reflecting hours I
know thou hates. She is not fit for one of these.

VALERE. The spark is a little given to gaming, I confess—yet holds his
nose as high as your widow, I can tell you that.

LOVEWELL. Prithee, trifle no longer with me—nor do not jest with pains
like mine.

VALERE. Do you know her hand?

LOVEWELL. Death, does she write to him?

VALERE. These credentials will confirm she does. (*Gives him her letter with
the bill.*)

LOVEWELL. Confusion to thee—and a bill for money. Away, it cannot
be—by hell, the company thou keeps has taught thee to be a villain.
Thou hast abused her honor, which I will justify. Draw.

VALERE. Here's a rogue, now—when I have withstood a temptation
would have shook a hermit, he'd cut my throat for not taking his
mistress from him. Well, these romantic lovers are whimsical things.
Heark ye, Charles, I believe you know I am no coward, and if your
fighting fit remains on you till tomorrow morning, I'll meet you
when and where you please. But I am engaged now—as you may see.
Farewell! (*Showing him box etc. Exit.*)

LOVEWELL. What man, but would forever scorn, despite this false
ingrate. But I'm a slave to love, and bound with such a chain no injuries can break. Something must be done, but what I know not. (*Exit.*)

Mrs. Betty comes forward.

BETTY. So, my lady has brought herself into a fine premunire.[43] Well,
I'm glad I heard all this, and hope to make it turn to Mr. Lovewell's
advantage, who is a generous man and deserves a countess. (*Exit.*)

Scene changes to Lady Wealthy's lodgings.

Lady Wealthy, sola.

LADY WEALTHY. So, thus far I'm successful; the porter says he was transported with the letter and will instantly be here—who's there? (*Enter
footman.*) Bid my woman come hither.

---

43   Predicament.

FOOTMAN. She's not within, madam.
LADY WEALTHY. How, not within?
FOOTMAN. Here she comes.

Enter Betty.

LADY WEALTHY. Hey! Where have you been to put yourself in this heat?
BETTY. Speaking to a relation, madam.
LADY WEALTHY. A relation! Sure 'twas a warm conference has set such
    sign on't in your cheeks. Set my toilet. I'll throw these mournful
    blacks away—adorned in cheerful white receive and charm my hero.
BETTY. Mr. Lovewell, madam?
LADY WEALTHY. No, fool. When did you ever see me dress at an old
    lover? He's mine, securely mine. But Valere, the gay, the rover, the
    unconquered rambler; he, he alone deserves my care.
BETTY. Madam, might I presume to speak?
LADY WEALTHY. Your nonsense freely. I am in a good humor, and can
    bear it all.
BETTY. Then Valere is the most ungrateful—and Mr. Lovewell the most
    accomplished of any man breathing.
LADY WEALTHY. Ha, ha, ha, and this is your speech? Lovewell is
    beholden to you truly and Mr. Valere shall know his friend.
BETTY. I hate him, madam, and you have reason.
LADY WEALTHY. Peace! I find I gave you too much liberty.

Enter a footman.

FOOTMAN. Madam, a letter for your ladyship.
LADY WEALTHY. Humph! From Lovewell! I know the hand: some com-
    pliment, some dismal madrigal, or tedious ditty in worse prose, I am
    sure. (*Opens it.*) Ha! My own bill. What means this?—"Madam, you
    have bestowed your favors unworthily; notwithstanding this proof, I
    would have fought, defended you beyond demonstration, but your
    new choice declined the sword—and that love I so long languished for.
    Your neglected, injured, but still faithful, Lovewell."—Base traitor! Is
    this a man of honor? This the return of my advances? It is impossible.
    — He has waylaid the porter, bribed him, and deceived me.
BETTY. Indeed, he has not, madam.
LADY WEALTHY. Why, know you ought of this?
BETTY. Yes, I can tell you—if you will promise to interpret for the good
    of him who loves you truly.

LADY WEALTHY. Come in, and let me hear the story. If Valere has tri-
umphed o'er my weakness, and exposed my unrequested bounty—
Such a repulse may fix this wand'ring heart;
And constant love may meet its due depart. (*Going.*)

Enter the Marquis.

MARQUIS. Turn back, bright fair, and listen to an action as glorious as
Conde, Luxenburg, or Hess, or any he that ever graced the field.
LADY WEALTHY. More plagues!—I begin to grow weary of this train of
fools [*aside*]. —Pray, make your story short, sir.
MARQUIS. I'll be as concise as the heroic deed—*veni, vidi, vici*, as Caesar
said.[44]
LADY WEALTHY. Over whom were this conquest? Your footman and your
tailor?
MARQUIS. No, madam, over my rival, Valere.
LADY WEALTHY. Ha! Where meet you that report?
MARQUIS. Everywhere—the world says you are in love with him. 'Tis all
the discourse at the chocolate house.
LADY WEALTHY. Confusion! I am become so wretched—I shall be sung
in ballads shortly.
MARQUIS. Having a profound respect for your ladyship, away flew I to
his lodgings, where I had no sooner entered, but the memory of your
wrongs—set the stormy marks of anger on my brow. "Sir," said I. "Sir,"
said he. "Your most humble servant—sir," said I. "Here is a rumor
spread abroad, prejudicial to the reputation of a lady, whom I have
honored with my esteem."
LADY WEALTHY. Honored! Oh, audacious!
MARQUIS. "And report says you are the author—" "Who, I?" said he, in
the meekest, humblest tone, that ever lover begged in, frightened out
of his wits. "Her name, I pray!" Which, when I had told him, and bid
him draw, he poorly disclaimed his passion, and said, I might take you
with all his heart, for he would not fight. At which I stepped up to him,
saying, "Seavez vous,[45] Monsieur du Lansquenet." That is as much
as to say, in English, a flip of the nose, madam—at which the good
gentleman pulled off his hat, and made me the lowest bow, and I, in
triumph, left. Now my reward—my reward, madam.

---

44   "I came, I saw, I conquered" (Latin), a phrase famously attributed to Julius Caesar.
45   He may mean "Savez-vous?" ("Do you know Monsieur du Lansquenet?") but as well
as corrupting it, he has the wrong verb.

LADY WEALTHY. Your reward: never to see me more. For, though I [love] valor, I know this story false—and you made up of cowardice, d'ye hear. (*Enter three footmen.*)—If ever my doors are open to this bold intruder more, I'll have your liveries pulled over your ears. (*Exit.*)

MARQUIS. Gone! I durst have sworn she would have married me for the news. Now here's a good invention lost. Ah, poor Monsieur Markee, thou'lt never thrive with these women of quality. I must to some rich, toothless, city dame—
On them my courage, and my shame may pass,
These court and wits, discover me an ass. (*Exit.*)

Scene: The street. Hector solus.

HECTOR. Well, I have not patience any longer to see this master of mine play: I find which way he is going. Od'so here's his father. How shall I send him away? For, if he should see his son coming out of the gaming house, we shall be undone again. (*Enter Sir Thomas Valere.*) Oh, sir, I have been all over the town to look you—

SIR THOMAS. For what, pray? Did my last greeting please you so well, you have a mind to more on't? Where's the rake, your master?

HECTOR. Oh sir, happy, happy beyond expression. He's with Angelica, who has presented him with her picture, set round with gems of inestimable fortune.

SIR THOMAS. Ha! Say'st thou so boy? And is he likely to carry Angelica?

HECTOR. Carry her, sir? Why the business is done and nothing wanting but your presence with a lawyer to fit 'em for the priest. Good sir, make haste—

SIR THOMAS. I'll be there in an instant. And shall I be a grandfather adod;[46] I could find in my heart to give thee sixpence for thy news. And I will too—there Hector, drink your young master and lady's health, sirrah. Ah, my dear boy, Jemmy, I forgive thee all—I am so transported I think an age till I embrace thee. (*Exit.*)

HECTOR. 'Fore George if this old fellow finds me in a lie, as he most certainly will! For if Angelica hears my master is at play again, she'll never have him; that's sure too. I must let him know what I have done, and get him in the mind to go this hour to Angelica—or Hector's bones will pay for it.
To serve my master, I a lie may tell
But would not suffer, when I mean it well. (*Exit.*)

---

46   An exclamation.

Scene: Discovers a gaming table with Valere, Count Cogdie, and other gentlemen at Hazard, with several rakes and sharpers waiting round the table. A box-keeper and attendance.

COGDIE. Come, seven—what do you set, gentlemen?
BOX-KEEPER. Seven's the main.
FIRST GENTLEMAN. That.
SECOND GENTLEMAN. Ten pieces.
VALERE. The devil's in the dice.—There, sir, a hundred guineas (*angrily*).

Cogdie rattling the dice and considering where to throw.

BOX-KEEPER. Knock where you are, sir.
COGDIE. (*Throws out the dice.*) I am at the fairest only. Come, and that little silver too.
BOX-KEEPER. Four to seven.
FIRST RAKE. Mr. Cogdie, to three a crown, shall I?
SECOND RAKE. To three, and eleven guineas, if you please.
FIRST SHARPER. Here's three crowns to eleven, and if I lose, by all that's good, I know not where to eat.
COGDIE. (*To first rake.*) You go to three a crown; (*to second rake*) you to three, and eleven guineas; (*to sharper*) you shall go yours to eleven Jack.
BOX-KEEPER. Pray, sir, throw away; don't hold the box all night.
COGDIE. There (*shakes the box and throws three*); you're in once, gentlemen.
BOTH RAKES. We go again.
COGDIE. With all my heart. (*Shakes the box again and throws four.*)
BOX-KEEPER. Four, trae-ace.[47]
COGDIE. (*To the rakes.*) There, gentlemen; I have brought you off again.
VALERE. You did not throw out your dice fair, and I'll not yield it.
COGDIE. Judgment, gentlemen.
FIRST GENTLEMAN. I think 'twas fair enough.
SECOND GENTLEMAN. Aye, aye, a man may throw his dice how he pleases.
VALERE. (*In a passion.*) Sir, I say this hat's white.
COGDIE. I say so too.
VALERE. 'Tis false; 'tis black.
COGDIE. As you say; I think it is black.
VALERE. No, sir; 'tis neither black nor white.

---

47   The pips, or spots, on dice were numbered in an approximation to French (ace, deuce, trey, quattor).

COGDIE. Nay, very likely, sir!—He has lost his money and now he grows mutinous (*aside*).

BOX-KEEPER. Come, pray, gentleman, don't quarrel, and I'll ask it round.

COGDIE. Ask what, you blockhead? Whether his hat's black or white? (*Tosses a pair of dice in his face.*)

BOX-KEEPER. No, master, whether you won the money or not.

SECOND GENTLEMAN. He won it fairly. Come, Valere, I'll lend thee ten pieces. Set boldly; I'll warrant thee luck, boy.

FIRST GENTLEMAN. Aye, aye, come, whose is the box?

COGDIE. 'Tis mine—

SECOND GENTLEMAN. Throw a main then.

COGDIE. Five.

BOX-KEEPER. Five's the main.

VALERE. There—take all.

FIRST GENTLEMAN. That—

SECOND GENTLEMAN. That—

COGDIE. Where I was last. Now little dice.

VALERE. Shake your dice.

COGDIE. There, sir! (*Shakes the dice and throws deuce, ace*). Oh, burn 'em.

BOX-KEEPER. Deuce, ace!

VALERE. Out! Give me the box—six.

BOX-KEEPER. Six is the main.

COGDIE. There, sir, if you dare throw at it.

FIRST GENTLEMAN. That—

SECOND GENTLEMAN. That—

VALERE. At you all— (*Shakes the box and throws quattor deuce.*)

BOX-KEEPER. Six, quattor deuce; you've won it, sir.

COGDIE. Um! (*Seems disordered.*)

VALERE. Come, seven. (*Throws*).

BOX-KEEPER. Seven's the main.

COGDIE. A hundred guineas.

VALERE. Now little dice—

COGDIE. Not another nick, sure. (*Speaks as Valere is going to throw the dice.*)

VALERE. Nick, by Juno—

BOX-KEEPER. Cinque deuce.

COGDIE. Oh! Blood! And death! And fire! (*Rises and walks about in a passion.*)

VALERE. Nine. (*Throws*).

BOX-KEEPER. Nine's the main.

COGDIE. There, sir, I'll set you two hundred guineas upon that note.

VALERE. Note, sir! Whose note is it, pray?

COGDIE. Why, 'tis very good, sir; 'tis upon Sir F—s Ch—d.

VALERE. At it, egad. (*Throws*).

BOX-KEEPER. Nine. Cinque and quattor;[48] the box is due.

COGDIE. Um! (*Throws away the dice; breaks the box.*) Sir, I bar that throw.

VALERE. Sir, I did not see you—and I won it fairly.

COGDIE. The devil! I that understand play so well, to be bubbled of my
    money. Sir, I say this hat's white—who dares say the contrary?

VALERE. Not I indeed, sir.

COGDIE. I say 'tis black.

VALERE. Why, as you say; I think 'tis black.

COGDIE. I say, 'tis neither black nor white.

VALERE. Then it shall be green, blue, red, yellow, or what you please, sir.
    I have more manners than to quarrel now I'm on the winning side, ha,
    ha, ha.

FIRST GENTLEMAN. Prithee, don't quarrel with him; you'll get nothing
    by it. Valere will fight you know.

COGDIE. And so will I, sir. You're all a parcel of—[*Aside.*]—If ever I play
    upon the square again, I'll give 'em leave to make dice of my bones.

VALERE. Ha, ha, ha, hold; let me pay my debts. There sir (*to second
    gentleman*).

BOX-KEEPER. You owe a box, sir, an' please you.

VALERE. There— (*Gives a shilling.*)

BOX-KEEPER. You own me a teaster[49] for a backhand tip,[50] a little while
    ago, master.

VALERE. There, you dog. (*Gives him sixpence.*)

BOX-KEEPER. Thank you master—I'll thank any gentleman that will put
    that shilling in the box.

Enter Angelica in man's clothes.

ANGELICA. Aye, here he is.

VALERE. Come, seven.

BOX-KEEPER. Seven's the main.

FIRST GENTLEMAN. That—

---

48   Five and four.
49   Sixpence (slang).
50   Bribe (slang).

SECOND GENTLEMAN. That—

VALERE. 'Tis mine.

BOX-KEEPER. Eleven—

SECOND GENTLEMAN. I never saw such fortune.

FIRST GENTLEMAN. Here's the last of a hundred; if luck turn not, I'm broke.

ANGELICA. Save you, gentlemen! May one fling off a guinea or two with you— (*This while Cogdie sits disordered and plays by himself at another table.*)

VALERE. Aye, a hundred if you please. A pert young bubble this; flung six—

BOX-KEEPER. Six is the main.

ANGELICA. Fifty pieces, sir.

VALERE. Well said, stripling. Down with 'em: six or a dozen dice—deuce ace—ah split it— (*Throws down the box.*)

BOX-KEEPER. Deuce ace.

ANGELICA. Out, sir! Give me fifty guineas, sir.

VALERE. There 'tis, sir. (*Cogdie rises and comes to Angelica.*)

COGDIE. (*To Angelica.*) Sir, will you do me the favor to let me go two pieces with you; I am just stripped.

ANGELICA. With all my heart, sir. Come gentlemen. (*Throws.*) Set boldly—

BOX-KEEPER. Five's the main.

VALERE. A hundred guineas.

ANGELICA. Along. (*Throws.*) 'Tis mine. (*Sweeps the money.*)

BOX-KEEPER. Five, trae, deuce.

ANGELICA. (*To Cogdie.*) There's your two pieces, sir.

COGDIE. I go the four, sir. If you please?

ANGELICA. By and by, sir. You shall.

FIRST GENTLEMAN. I'm broke. But, I'll be here again instantly. (*Exit.*)

SECOND GENTLEMAN. I'll throw off this stake; if luck turn not I must home for recruits too.

ANGELICA. Come on then, sir—six. (*Throws.*)

BOX-KEEPER. Six is the main.

VALERE. In my conscience, I believe this young dog will strip us all. There, sir.

ANGELICA. And there, sir. (*Sweeps the money.*)

BOX-KEEPER. A dozen.

SECOND GENTLEMAN. I hope you'll stay till my return?

ANGELICA. If these gentlemen can hold me play.

BOX-KEEPER. I hope, gentlemen, you won't stay late for fear of the pressmasters;[51] here was two gangs last night before twelve o'clock. (*All the sharpers sneak off, and leave Angelica and Valere together.*)

ANGELICA. Pshaw, hang the press-masters! Come, sir, five—

BOX-KEEPER. Five's the main.

VALERE. That upon five.

ANGELICA. Nick—

BOX-KEEPER. Five, quattor ace; you owe a box, sir.

VALERE. Confusion! Did ever man see the like? That watch at twenty guineas. (*Sets a gold watch.*)

ANGELICA. Done, sir; nine. (*Throws*).

BOX-KEEPER. Nine's the main.

ANGELICA. 'Tis mine. (*Throws*).

BOX-KEEPER. Nine, six, and three; a main above a box.

VALERE. Furies and hell—that ring at ten guineas.

ANGELICA. Ha, ha, ha, with all my heart, sir; six again. (*Throws.*)

BOX-KEEPER. Six is the main.

ANGELICA. Nick, again, ha, ha, ha.

BOX-KEEPER. Six, cinque ace, two mains above a box.

VALERE. The devil—I'll set you a hundred guineas upon honor, sir.

ANGELICA. I beg your pardon, sir; I never play upon honor with strangers. If you have nothing else to set your humble servant—

VALERE. Death, shall he carry off my money thus. Hold, sir! Friends will be here presently; I'll borrow some of them.

ANGELICA. That's balking my hand—I can't stay, sir. Have you nothing else?

VALERE. Yes, one thing, but that's dearer to me than life. (*Takes out the picture.*)

ANGELICA. What can that be, pray?

VALERE. 'Tis a picture, the original of which is nearest to my soul. (*Kisses it.*)

ANGELICA. Pish, a trifle!—Oh my heart (*aside*).—Yet you shan't say I'm ungenerous. Whate'er you value it at, I'll answer it.

VALERE. Value it at? It is not to be valued.

ANGELICA. Then you'll not set it, sir; your servant.

VALERE. Stay, sir! Luck may turn—I'll set the diamonds at 200 guineas.

ANGELICA. [*Aside.*] Oh villain!—Well, sir, seven—

BOX-KEEPER. Seven's the main. (*Angelica throws at the picture.*)

---

51   Authorized military recruiters, notorious for their heavy-handed methods.

BOX-KEEPER. Four or seven.

VALERE. I bar the first throw.

BOX-KEEPER. Bar. (*Angelica throws two or three times and then wins it.*)

ANGELICA. 'Tis mine, sir.

BOX-KEEPER. Four, trae, ace; you owe me three boxes, sir.

VALERE. Eternal furies! Lost!—He shall restore it, or I'll cut his throat
   (*aside*). —Well, sir, take the diamonds, but I must have the picture—

ANGELICA. The picture, sir?

VALERE. Aye, the picture, sir.

ANGELICA. I won it, sir, and I shan't restore it, I assure you.

VALERE. But you shall restore it, sir, e're you and I part.

ANGELICA. (*Aside.*) If I should draw a duel upon my hands here, I'm in a
   fine condition.—Nay, sir, if you are angry, goodbye!

VALERE. Nay, nay, nay! (*Runs between him and the door.*) You shan't carry
   off the picture, by Hercules. Lookee, sir, either take my bond, or fight
   me for it— (*Draws.*)

ANGELICA. (*Trembling.*) Sir!—What shall I do? I must be obliged to discover myself (*aside*).

Enter first and second gentlemen

FIRST GENTLEMAN. Hold, Valere.

SECOND GENTLEMAN. What's the meaning of this? (*Lays hold of Valere.*)

ANGELICA. Ha! A lucky escape! (*Runs off.*)

VALERE. Away! Stand off, or I shall cut my passage through you, traitor!
   Dog! Oh, I could tear my flesh, cut off these hands that laid the jewel
   down—and stab my heart for having once consented— (*Walks about
   raving.*)

FIRST GENTLEMAN. What can be the cause of this passion?

SECOND GENTLEMAN. Ho, he has lost his money—prithee, don't let that
   trouble thee. I'll lend thee more. Come, let's throw for the box.

VALERE. Throw for the devil. No, henceforth a gamester is my foe. Nor
   should the Indies bribe me even to touch a die; nor after this moment
   will I e'er set foot in such a house again.

FIRST GENTLEMAN. The man is mad.

EMAN. Prithee, let's go seek out better company. (*Exit.*)
behold what a monster this darling sin has made me, and
f for my long race of folly—
t, but oh it comes too late,
tice now that she should hate;

He that flies virtue still to follow vice,
'Tis fit, like me, he lose his paradise.

ACT V

Scene: Valere's lodgings.

Valere solus.

VALERE. What shall I do? There's no going near Angelica; the action
 I have done carries such a face that she can ne'er forgive me. (*Enter
 Hector.*)

HECTOR. Another 'scape, sir; another 'scape. Your father was just at the
 gaming house door upon the hunt for you, but thanks to my wit, I
 found a way to send him packing. He's gone to Angelica's with a lawyer. Follow him! Follow him, sir. If he gets there before you, the old
 gentleman will believe me no more, for I told him you stayed for him
 there. Ha, he minds me not! Sir! Sir! Don't you hear me?

VALERE. No. I'll neither hear, nor see, nor eat, nor drink, nor ever rest
 again.

HECTOR. Ah, the devil. I shall be as slender as a hazel switch in a little
 time, then, for I suppose I must keep you company in that thin diet.
 Ah! What I dreaded is come to pass. What, then, is all the money lost?

VALERE. Money! My life, my soul is lost.

HECTOR. Hey day, what's the matter now?

VALERE. The picture.

HECTOR. (*With a frightful look.*) The picture, sir? Mercy on us! Shake
 your pockets. Shake your pockets, sir. (*Runs to Valere and shakes his coat
 pocket.*)

VALERE. Hold off; I tell thee I've lost it at play.

HECTOR. Why, then you have played fair. Why, what will you do now, sir?

VALERE. Cut your throat, sirrah, and then my own. (*Clapping hold of
 Hector.*)

HECTOR. 'Twas none of my fault, sir. (*Half weeping.*)

VALERE. Oh! No, it was my own, for had I ta'en thy council, this curse
 had been prevented.

HECTOR. Aye, sir, but a gamester's life was the most genteel of any: their
 fob was a fund, and their hands philosophers' stones. Aye, sir.

VALERE. No more. Go, fetch me a book— (*Sits down.*)

HECTOR. What book, sir?

VALERE. The first that comes to your hand, no matter which. (*Exit Hector; returns with a book.*)

HECTOR. Here's Seneca, sir.

VALERE. Well, read. Was ever man so unfortunate? (*Walking about in a thinking posture.*)

HECTOR. Who? I read Seneca, sir?

VALERE. Why not?

HECTOR. I seldom read anything, sir, but almanacs.

VALERE. Oh, read! Read at a venture! To lose upon seven, when the chance was four! Confusion! (*Stamps.*)

HECTOR. (*Reads.*) Be not taken with the glittering dreams of riches; their possession brings trouble. Tranquility is a certain equality of mind, which no condition of fortune can either exalt or depress. If his fortune be good, he tempers it; if bad, he masters it.

VALERE. The devil was in me, that I could not leave off when I was a winner.

HECTOR. "What is the end of ambition and avarice? We are but stewards of what we falsely call our own. All those things which we pursue with so much hazard, for which we break faith and friendship, what are they but the mere depositor of fortune and not ours, but already inclining towards a new master." Now, I will be hanged if Seneca himself was not given to gaming.—Sir, don't you think this looks like a moral reflection after a loss? In my conscience, I'm half in the mind that he played away a mistress's picture too.

VALERE. Ha! Name it not, for if thou dost, I'll shake thee into atoms. (*Shaking him.*)

HECTOR. Ah, sir, I've done; I've done. But, sir, this Seneca was a wondrous man—was he ever in London, sir?

VALERE. No, he lived at Rome.—Not one in ten, oh wretched luck.

HECTOR. That's a long way off. I thought indeed 'twas something made his morals so little minded. Come, sir, courage.

VALERE. Yes, I'll to the camp; there in the service of my country, expiate my follies.

HECTOR. To the camp, sir? What do you mean? Odsbud, sir, go to Angelica this minute and marry her out of hand; she does not know you have lost the picture, and when once she's secure, if she asks for it, stop her mouth with kisses, sir.

VALERE. Well, I will go, if but to take my leave of her. For I much fear she'll read guilt in my face—

This I resolve whatever fates in store,

To touch the cursed infectious dice no more.

HECTOR. Aye, stick you but there, and I warrant we prosper.

Scene: The Lady Wealthy's house.

Enter Lady Wealthy; Mrs. Betty to her.

BETTY. Madam, Mr. Lovewell to wait on your ladyship.

LADY WEALTHY. [*Aside.*] How shall I see him! Shame and confusion rises
in my face, yet it is not in my temper to own myself in the wrong. If he
upbraids me, this is his last visit. Bring him up. (*Enter Mr. Lovewell.*)
—I suppose you come triumphant, but know I give account of my
actions to no man. Am free, and will so remain.

LOVEWELL. 'Tis my hard fortune still to be mistaken; my love's too blind
to think you do amiss. I have since been with Valere, sworn to him the
letter was a plot of mine, the hand and bill all counterfeits, to satisfy
my jealous scruple if there were affairs between ye; he believed it, and
your honor's free from all ill tongues—and the wretch doomed to be
hated still. Am come to take my everlasting leave.

LADY WEALTHY. (*Aside.*) This generosity shocks me.—Farewell, you have
cleared me to your rival, but to yourself can say she was ungrateful
and despised me. Love without esteem is a forced plant and wants
its root; therefore, my ill conduct parts us, and thank your generous
carriage for this confession. Great spirits hardly yield themselves to
blame.

LOVEWELL. Nor are you. I have not watched so many years your temper,
each turn and sally of your mind, but I can judge it right. Honor is
centered in your soul, nor would you wrong it in an essential part. All
your little affectations are but the effects your glass produces, which
tells ye, beauty like yours, may take ten thousand liberties.

LADY WEALTHY. You have chose a cunning way to move my heart, when
I was armed for accusations to extenuate my faults. And if I could
persuade myself to trust a man, I think it would be you.

LOVEWELL. Oh, cherish that kind opinion, and if ever you do repent it,
proclaim me to the world—a villain.

LADY WEALTHY. This I resolve in favor of your noble usage, to banish
from my house that senseless train of fop admirers, which I always
laughed at, and only kept to feed my vanity.

LOVEWELL. On my knees I thank you, but do not, do not, dash my
transports by delay. Your year of widowship is just expired. Reward
my constant love and make me happy; a husband will fright the fool

pretenders from approaching, and these fond arms secure you ever mine.

LADY WEALTHY. Bless me, is the man mad? Here would be a strange leap, indeed, from mortal odds into matrimony. No, no, a little longer time must try you first.

LOVEWELL. If time be now required, you may defer my joys till age has strewed my head with hoary hairs, for from my very infancy I have adored you. 'Tis but a month ago when my auspicious stars inclined you to a fit of mercy. I flew, got a license, came with eager hopes, and you denied to see me; the same authority will do now. Nor will I leave you, till your hand is mine.

Enter Betty.

LADY WEALTHY. Betty, come to my aid. Here's an audacious man will marry me, in spite of my teeth, this very instant.

BETTY. Oh madam, the luckiest moment in the world. I have just been looking in *Erra Pater*,[52] and there's the happiest conjunction—and the chaplain sauntering about the gardens ready for employment.

LOVEWELL. Nay, look not back; your eyes consent, and I'll have no denial.

LADY WEALTHY. Well, this is the maddest thing.

LOVEWELL. The happiest thing. Thus—
The wandring fair, are by long courtships kind,
And constant love does luckiest minutes find. (*Exeunt.*)

Enter Angelica.

ANGELICA. Lovewell and my sister happy pair. I am only cursed in a loose reprobate, whom no chance, no obligations can fix. I must resolve to blot him from my soul. But how hard 'tis to efface the first impression. Valere, if I can part with thee, mankind will be upon the square; thy uncle may succeed, old or young, for I shall never look with living eyes again. Let me think—to lose my picture! Oh, unpardonable fault—

Enter Dorante and Mrs. Favorite, at a distance.

---

52   William Lilly's almanac, well-known seventeenth-century books of Christian astrology.

FAVORITE. Now, sir, is your time; she is horridly out of humor. I know
'tis with Valere, for nothing else makes her so.

DORANTE. Madam, I hope you will pardon my intrusion, when 'tis to
warn you of approaching danger; I can prove to you my nephew has
broke all his oaths and played with the veriest rakes the town affords
in a public gaming house.

ANGELICA. Malice, malice, all.

DORANTE. As this is true or false, may I your love enjoy.

ANGELICA. Suppose it true. Am I confined to make my choice in your
family, or indeed choose at all? Perhaps I'll never marry.

DORANTE. Oh say not so. Let not so much beauty lose the end of its
creation. You should bless the world with your increase.

ANGELICA. Methinks you are too much in the wane to think of increase;
however, I am yet resolved on nothing, and desire to be freed from
importunity. (*Enter Valere and Hector.*) —'Tis well you are come; your
uncle has been using all his rhetoric to supplant you.

HECTOR. (*Aside.*) The day's our own; she's in a pure humor.

VALERE. No clandestine dealings, uncle, I beseech you. Give me fair play,
and let the lady choose—

ANGELICA. (*Aside.*) With what assurance he approaches.

DORANTE. However her choice may go, I know who deserves her most.
I'm no gamester, sir! Her peaceful hours of rest shall ne'er be broken
by me.

HECTOR. (*Aside.*) That I dare swear.

VALERE. No reflections, sir, on former follies; you in your youth doubtless had your share, 'though now you are past 'em, and only rail at
what you can't enjoy. But I, in my full strength and vigor, give 'em over,
resolving never to indulge the tempting vice again.

DORANTE. This you have often sworn, and as often broke your vows.

VALERE. I have, but 'tis in the power of fate to make me do't again, and
what's past, this lady has forgiven.

ANGELICA. To end your disputes, Mr. Dorante, I'll now own to you that
my heart has been long since given to Valere—and this morning I
renewed my vows.

VALERE. Oh, transport! Now, uncle, I hope you are satisfied.

DORANTE. No, sir, I am not satisfied; nor can I believe what she says real,
without condemning her judgment.

ANGELICA. [*Aside.*] A strange positive old man this.—Valere, pray clear
his understanding; show him the present I made you today, then let
him judge who I design my heart for.

VALERE. (*Aside.*) Ha! What shall I say?

HECTOR. (*Aside.*) Oh! I'm thunderstruck!

VALERE. Oh, spare his age, madam; I forgive him. He is my uncle and I would not triumph: 'twould make him mad should I produce the picture.

ANGELICA. No, no, fear not. 'Tis rather charity, for since he refuses to believe my words, 'tis but reason he should have ocular demonstration.

VALERE. He that doubts what's uttered by that tongue, is unworthy of your farther care; therefore, pardon me, madam, a thing so sacred as your image shall never convince him.

HECTOR. (*Aside.*) Well hinted, i' faith.

ANGELICA. But when I desire it, methinks you should not refuse; obedience becomes a lover.

HECTOR. (*Aside.*) Lost again.

VALERE. You ever shall command me. (*Feeling in first one pocket, then in t'other.*) Ha! Where did I put it?

HECTOR. (*Lifting up his eyes.*) Humph.

ANGELICA. (*Aside.*) I am amazed at his impudence.

VALERE. Bless me, sure I did not leave it in the bed.—Which way shall I come off (*aside*)?—Hector—

HECTOR. (*Looking very simply.*) Sir?

VALERE. Did you not see a picture nowhere today?

HECTOR. A picture, sir! (*In a kind of fright.*)

VALERE. Aye, a picture! What makes you look so, sirrah? Ha! I suspect your rogueship has done something with it.

HECTOR. Oh dear, sir! (*Trembling.*)

VALERE. Where is it? Speak, rascal, or I'll cut your ears off. (*Draws.*)

HECTOR. Oh, sir, forgive me, and I'll tell you the whole truth. (*Falls on his knees*).

ANGELICA. (*Aside.*) What means the fellow?

VALERE. What will you tell me, sirrah?

HECTOR. Why, sir, fearing that your pocket might be picked, or your lodgings robbed, and you might lose the picture (and that, I thought, would break your heart)—knowing how much you did esteem the piece, I took it, sir, to a famous painter of my acquaintance to have it copied—sir, that's all.

ANGELICA. (*Aside.*) A well invented tale.

VALERE. Fly, sirrah, and fetch it. (*Slaps him on the back*).

HECTOR. Yes, sir. (*Going.*)

ANGELICA. Oh you may spare your pains, sir! The picture is already here. (*Pulls it out*). Now, sir, do you blush.

VALERE. (*Aside.*) I am amazed to think how she came by it.

HECTOR. (*Aside.*) Ruined past redemption. Oh, oh, oh, that such a complete lie should turn to no account.

ANGELICA. Ungrateful man!

DORANTE. How, how's this?

ANGELICA. Is this the price you set upon my favors? The sight of this should mind you of your duty—if I remember those were your words—but I presume you meant it should remind you of a last stake. How have I been deceived. Is it possible thou couldst be so base to expose my picture at a common board, amongst a crew of revelers?

VALERE. Madam.

ANGELICA. Be dumb, and make no impudent excuses.

DORANTE. Dol, dol , dery, dol, dery, dol. (*Sings*).

VALERE. No, madam, I shall not study to excuse myself. Only this, I am not guilty of all your charge, for there was none in presence when I lost it, but the youth that won it—who had not lived to have brought it you, had not an unlucky chance prevented me.

ANGELICA. Then to conceal your treachery, you would have committed murder? Excellent moralist! But, sir, the privacy of the act you boast of, does not in the least extenuate your crime. I told you whilst you kept that picture, my heart was yours, but you grew weary of the trifle, and restored it back, and now I have liberty to give to whom I please.

DORANTE. I hope you are satisfied now, nephew, ha, ha, ha.

VALERE. I am with everything this lady is pleased to inflict; I know she can use me no worse than I deserve. I own the foulness of my guilt and will not hope for pardon.

Enter Sir Thomas Valere with a lawyer.

HECTOR. Nay, then, we are friendless, indeed.—Sir, sir, shall I see what Seneca says upon this head? (*Aside to Valere.*)

VALERE. Away, and plague me not.—Ha, my father!

SIR THOMAS. I'm blessed beyond expression. Blessed! Madam, I wish you joy. My son, I have brought Mr. Demur, the lawyer. I'll reserve but five hundred a year for myself. The rest is thine, boy—full two thousand pound per annum.

ANGELICA. Sir Thomas, your words carry a meaning in 'em, which I'm a stranger to.

SIR THOMAS. Meaning, madam! I hope my son and you understand one another's meaning—and I understand it too, madam. Come, Mr.

Demur, where are the writings of my estate? He shall make thee a
swinging jointure,[53] my girl.

ANGELICA. You must pardon me, Sir Thomas; my mind's altered.

SIR THOMAS. How? Did you not promise?

ANGELICA. I suppose I did. When a man breaks all his oaths to me, I
know no reason I should keep my word with him.

HECTOR. (*Aside.*) Ah, Hector, Hector, what will become of thee?

SIR THOMAS. Why, I understood these quarrels were made up, and as
a token of your being reconciled, you made him a present of your
picture.

ANGELICA. True—and that's the thing that parts us.

SIR THOMAS. What do you mean?

DORANTE. He gamed it away, brother. Now do you understand her?

SIR THOMAS. Malice and marriage, brother, ill becomes your years. She
does not mean it so.

ANGELICA. Indeed, but I do!

SIR THOMAS. Say you so, madam? Then I'll do you justice immediately.
(*Draws.*) Sirrah, I'll save the hangman a labor—I will, you bastard.

VALERE. Do kill me, sir. You shall find I will not vent one groan, for
my soul has ta'en its flight already. My base ingratitude has deeper
stabbed my heart, than now your sword can do.

SIR THOMAS. Say you so, sirrah? Then I hope you'll live to want nothing,
for I'll take care you shall have nothing to support your extravagance.
Mr. Demur, I desire you to make my will this minute—and put the
ungracious rogue down a shilling. Sirrah, I charge you never to come
in sight of me, or my habitation more; nor, do you hear, dare to own
me for your father. Go, troop,[54] sirrah. I shall hear of your going up
Holbourn Hill[55] in a little time.

HECTOR. (*Aside.*) So, there's all my wages lost.

ANGELICA. (*Aside.*) Ha! This usage shocks me.

VALERE. Sir, I promise to obey you to a tittle—and this undutiful child
shall ne'er offend you with his presence more. You but enjoin, but I
before had chose, for England now would be the worst of fates.

ANGELICA. (*Aside.*) My heart beats as if the strings were breaking.

VALERE. Madam, there is but one request that I will make—then I will
take my leave forever, and if you grant it not, I shall be so much more
unhappy. My being disinherited weighs not a hair compared with

---

53   Unrestricted settlement.
54   Be off!
55   The way to the gallows.

what I've lost in losing you, whom my soul prefers before all wealth, friends, or family. Then, where should I ask pardon but where I most have injured? Thus on my knees, I beg you not to hate my memory, nor suffer the follies which I have now cashiered forever from my breast (but, oh, too late) to drive my name as distant as my body from you. Sometimes, vouchsafe to think on lost Valere.

ANGELICA. There is nothing so indifferent but we think of it sometimes.

SIR THOMAS. Sirrah, be gone I say. (*Pushes him.*)

VALERE. I have done. Now madam, eternally adieu.

ANGELICA. [*Aside.*] Shall I see him ruined? No, that would be barbarous beyond example.—Valere, come back. Should I forgive you all, would my generosity oblige you to a sober life? Can you upon honor (for you shall swear no more) forsake that vice that brought you to this low ebb of fortune?

VALERE. Ha! Oh, let me fold thee in my repenting arms, and whisper to thy soul that I am entirely changed. (*Embraces her.*) Yes, my love, I swear the course of life that I've run hitherto is grown more hateful to me than toads or adders, and I would as soon keep those animals in my bosom, whose sting I know would kill me as once indulge in my former follies.

ANGELICA. Then I am happy. Know I was the youth that won the picture, and you parted with it to myself.

HECTOR. (*Aside.*) I shall die with joy, that's certain.

VALERE. Then I did not break my oath entirely; you were excepted, madam.

SIR THOMAS. How lucky a turn is this! Madam, your example is too good not to be followed. Valere, I forgive thee, and confirm my first design. Bless you both. Now, brother, I hope you'll believe you can't get my boy's mistress from him. Ha, ha, ha.

DORANTE. Nor he shall never get a penny of my estate, brother; remember that. (*Exit.*)

SIR THOMAS. He wants it not. Ha! Who have we here? My Lady Wealthy, and her old lover.

Enter Lovewell and Lady Wealthy.

LOVEWELL. Wish me joy, friends; wish me joy.

SIR THOMAS. With all my heart, for in my conscience thou deserv'st her.

ANGELICA. I wish you joy, sister; here let all quarrels cease. (*Salutes her.*)

LADY WEALTHY. I overheard your reconciliation—and I wish you the same.

LOVEWELL. Oh, my friend! (*To Valere.*) Sure never man was blest like me.

VALERE. Yes, I can boast a happiness beyond thee. I that merited her endless scorn, am, by her sweet, forgiving temper, raised to lasting joy.

Enter the Marquis of Hazard.

MARQUIS. I understand you are married, madam, and come to wish you joy. I do it with a *bon cour la dioble in en port.*[56]

LADY WEALTHY. Oh Monsieur Marquis, I'm infinitely obliged to you e'er since your knight errantry with Valere in defense of my honor.

MARQUIS. A deuce of that unlucky story. No words on't now, madam, I beseech you.

VALERE. How's that?

MARQUIS. [*Aside.*] By the honor of France I shall be discovered.

Enter Betty.

BETTY. Madam, Mrs. Security has brought a pair of very fine diamond earrings to show you; they was lost in pawn, she says, and therefore she can afford them an extraordinary pennyworth.

LADY WEALTHY. Bring her in— (*Enter Mrs. Security.*) Well, Mrs. Security, are they very fine ones?

MRS. SECURITY. As fine a pair as ever your ladyship saw in all your life, madam. (*Gives her the earrings.*) Bless me, what do I see? (*To the Marquis.*) My cousin, Robin Skipp, I'm glad to see thee with all my heart.

LADY WEALTHY. Do you know what you say, Mrs. Security? That is a French nobleman.

MRS. SECURITY. A nobleman! What, do you think I don't know my brother's son?

MARQUIS. [*Aside.*] A pox of such kindred. Now all will out—

MRS. SECURITY. Why, how long hast thou been in England, Robert? I hear thou wert a footman to the Prince of Conti. Thy old master, Sir William, asks mightily how thou do'st.

OMNES. Ha, ha, ha, ha.

VALERE. How's this? The Marquis of Hazard a footman? Ha, ha, ha.

HECTOR. Brother, give me thy hand. Hold! Now I think on't, keep your distance friend, for *valet de chambre* is above a footman. (*Struts.*)

---

56   He probably means to say "I do it in good heart" and then, under his breath, "the devil at the gate."

LADY WEALTHY. My footmen, sir, will show you into the buttery: a horn
of small beer may quench your thirst of honor. Ha, ha.

VALERE. This morning he boasted of his royal blood at my lodgings, but
his cowardice confirmed him what he is.

LADY WEALTHY. He told me he was at your lodgings, and presented you
with a tweak by the nose.

VALERE. How! Scoundrel, beneath my sword, and therefore take this.
(*Kicks him.*)

MARQUIS. Very fine, very fine breeding, gentlemen, truly. Well, this is my
maxim still—
    Who once by policy a title gains,
    Merits above the fool that's born to means. (*Exit.*)

MRS. SECURITY. 'Tis dirtily done of you, Mr. Valere, so it is, to kick a
man for nothing. His father, though I say it, was as honest a man as
ever broke bread, and I could find in my heart to, to—

LADY WEALTHY. No more of your noise. Wait without there. (*Exit Mrs.
Security.*)

SIR THOMAS. Come, come a pies[57] of this nonsense. Let's have a dance.

A Country Dance.

VALERE. Now virtue's pleasing prospect's in my view,
    With double care, I'll all her paths pursue;
    And proud to think I owe this change to you. (*To Angelica.*)
    Virtue that gives more solid peace of mind
    Than men in all their vicious pleasures find,
    Then each with me the libertine reclaim,
    And shun what sinks his fortune and his fame.

FINIS.

EPILOGUE.

Spoke by Mr. Verbruggen.

As one condemned, and ready to become
For his offences past, a pendulum;[58]

---

57   An exclamatory expression
58   I.e., to be hanged.

Does, ere he dies, bespeak the learned throng,
Then, like the swan, expires in a song.
So, I (though doubtful long which knot to choose,
Whether the hangman's, or the marriage noose)
Condemned good people, as you see, for life
To play that tedious, jangling game, a wife,
Have but one word of good advice to say,
Before the doleful cart draws quite away.

You roaring boys,[59] who know the midnight cares
Of rattling tatts,[60] ye sons of hopes and fears,
Who labor hard to bring your ruin on,
And diligently toil to be undone;
You're fortune's sporting footballs at the best.
Few are his joys, and small the gamester's rest:
Suppose, then, fortune only rules the dice,
And on the square you play; yet who that's wise,
Would to the credit of a faithless main
Trust his good dad's hard-gotten hoarded gain?
But then such vultures round a table wait,
And hovering watch the bubble's sickly state;
The young fond gambler covetous of more,
Like Aesop's dog,[61] loses his certain store.

Then the sponge squeezed by all, grows dry—and now
Completely wretched, turns a sharper too;
These fools for want of bubbles too, play fair,
And lose to one another on the square;
So whores the wealth from numerous culls they glean,
Still spend on bullies, and grow poor again.

This itch for play has likewise fatal been,
And more than Cupid, drawn the ladies in,
A thousand guineas for basset prevails,
A bait, when cash runs low, that seldom fails;
And when the fair one can't the debt defray,

---

59   Young gentlemen known for riotous behavior.
60   False or loaded dice.
61   Proverbial for greed. In Aesop's fable, a dog with a piece of meat in his mouth sees
his reflection in a stream. As he opens his mouth to seize the other piece of meat he sees,
he loses the one he has into the water.

In sterling coin, does sterling bounty pay.
In vain we labor to divert your care,
Nor song, nor dance can bribe your presence here.
You fly this place like an infectious air;
To yonder happy quarter of the town
You crowd, and your own fav'rite stage disown.
We're like old mistresses; you love the vice,
And bate[62] us only 'cause we once did please.
Nor can we find how else 'tis we deserve,
Like Tantalus,[63] 'midst plenty, thus to starve.

NOTE ON THE TEXT

The Gamester: A Comedy was first performed in late January, 1705, at Lincoln's Inn Fields. It was published anonymously in the same year. The British Library first edition, a quarto, is my copy text here. It bears the imprint "London: Printed for *William Turner*, at the Angel at *Lincolns-Inn, Back Gate*, and *William Davis* at the Black-Bull in Cornhill." I call this text Q1. A self-proclaimed second edition, printed for James Knapton and William Turner, appeared in 1708; this quarto text seems to be a reissue of Q1 with reset preliminary materials. I call this Q2A. Also in 1708, another "second edition" was issued in a different typeset. It bears the same imprint as Q2A but has slight variations; I call it Q2B. A "third edition" appeared in 1714 in duodecimo, printed as well for James Knapton, here called D3. The first "fourth edition," from James Knapton is a duodecimo, dated 1734, here D4. In 1736 W. Feales issued at least two more duodecimo "fourth" editions, with slight variations—here D5A and D5B. Another "fourth edition" from James Knapton appears in 1760—here D6. There are at least two duodecimo "fifth editions," one from James Knapton in 1756 (here D7) and one from T. Lowndes in 1767 (here D8). All the editions from 1734 onwards declare the author as "Mrs. Centlivre."

TEXTUAL VARIATIONS

Prologue and dramatic personae do not appear in Q1. The texts for these preliminary materials I have taken from Q2A. The dedication appears only in Q1, Q2A&B, and D3.

---

62 Abide.
63 In Greek mythology, a king who was condemned in the afterlife to stand in water that receded when he stooped to drink, and below branches of fruit that were always just beyond his reach.

Dedication

QI, Q2A&B: than your Lordship's

D3: than your Lordship

QI, Q2A&B: Whereas I, in complaisance … have reclaimed him

D3: Whereas, in complaisance … I have reclaimed him

QI, Q2A&B: men of rank and quality as indifferent

D3: men of rank and quality were as indifferent

Dramatis Personae

Q2A&B, D3: Mr. Lee

ALL OTHER COPIES: Mr. Francis Lee

I.I

(p. 109)

QI, Q2A&B, D3: *arm'd chair*

ALL OTHER COPIES: *elbow-chair*

QI, Q2A&B, D3: enjoy the four and twenty hours

ALL OTHER COPIES: enjoy thee four and twenty hours

(p. 110)

QI, Q2A&B, D3: dare to ask him

ALL OTHER COPIES: dare ask him

(p. 111)

QI, Q2A&B: empty as a Capuchin

ALL OTHER COPIES: empty as a Capuchin's

QI, Q2A&B: sweet Mr. Hector, adieu.

ALL OTHER COPIES: sweet Mr. Hector, adieu. (*Exit.*)

(p. 112)

QI, Q2A&B, D5A, D6, D8: have power to forget

D3, D4, D5B, D7: have not power to forget

(p. 113)

QI, Q2A&B, D3, D4: She's the only woman

ALL OTHER COPIES: She is the only woman

QI, Q2A: Lovel

ALL OTHER COPIES: Lovewell

D7, D8: No, he's too much

ALL OTHER COPIES: No, he is too much

QI, Q2A&B, D3: as the Whigs against plays

ALL OTHER COPIES: as the Fanatics against plays

QI, Q2A&B, D3: What, are you up?

ALL OTHER COPIES: What, what, are you up?

(p. 114)

QI, Q2A&B: I'll forgive your faults

ALL OTHER COPIES: I'll forgive your fault

(p. 115)

QI, Q2A&B, D3: look'ee, Valere

ALL OTHER COPIES: look ye, Valere

QI, Q2A&B, D3, D4: Now, sir, here's your true dice

ALL OTHER COPIES: Now, sir, here is your true dice

(p. 116)

D7, D8: hearing of his continued extravagance

ALL OTHER COPIES: hearing his continued extravagance

(p. 118)

QI, Q2A&B, D3: just sealing of a bond

ALL OTHER COPIES: just sealing a bond

D8: You have your ring again, Mr. Valere

ALL OTHER COPIES: You had your ring again, Mr. Valere

II.1

(p. 120)

Q1, Q2A&B, D3: make our judgments err

ALL OTHER COPIES: make our judgment err

(p. 121)

Q1, Q2A&B: *Exit Favorite*

ALL OTHER COPIES: *Exeunt Angelica and Favorite*

(p. 122)

Q1, Q2A&B, D3: *Sung to the widow*

ALL OTHER COPIES: *Marq. sings to the widow.*

Q1, Q2A&B, D3: *Sung to the gamester, when he has won money.*

ALL OTHER COPIES: *Sings to the gamester, when he has money.*

Q1, Q2A&B, D3: till her hand be out

ALL OTHER COPIES: till her hand is out

Q1, Q2A&B, D3: 'Tis the only way

ALL OTHER COPIES: It is the only way

(p. 123)

Q1, Q2A&B, D3: Forgive the score

ALL OTHER COPIES: Forgive her the score

Q1, Q2&B: She's jealous already

ALL OTHER COPIES: (*Aside.*) She's jealous already

Q1, Q2A&B: my weed

ALL OTHER COPIES: my weeds

(p. 124)

D6, D7, D8: send in their messages

ALL OTHER COPIES: send in their message

(p. 126)

D5A, D6, D8: but I can guess the design

ALL OTHER COPIES: but I can guess

their design

(p. 127)

D8: and show I have no such power

ALL OTHER COPIES: and shows I have no such power

Q1, Q2A&B: love for play

ALL OTHER COPIES: play for love

ALL COPIES BUT Q2B: when I do (*kissing it*),

Q2B: when I do (*kisses it*),

(p. 128)

Q1, Q2A&B: *Holds the picture up to the nose*

ALL OTHER COPIES: *Holds the picture up to his nose*

II.2

(p. 128)

Q1, Q2A&B, D3: *Hector, with several papers*

ALL OTHER COPIES: *Hector, with papers*

(p. 129)

Q1, Q2A&B: noblemen that pays no body

ALL OTHER COPIES: noblemen that pay no body

(p. 130)

Q1, Q2A&B, D3: I, I, I, I, I—

ALL OTHER COPIES: o Lud, o Lud, o Lud—

Q1, Q2A&B: patient, I say

ALL OTHER COPIES: patience, I say

III.1

(p. 131)

Q1, Q2A&B, D3, D4: if thou know'st

D6, D7, D8: if thou knew'st

(p. 135)

Q1, Q2A&B: least Fortune wheel

ALL OTHER COPIES: lest Fortune

wheel
QI, Q2A&B, D3, D4, D5B, D7: your heart still runs counter
D5A: your heart runs counter
D8: your heart run counter
QI, Q2A&B: produce more luster
ALL OTHER COPIES: produces more luster
(p. 136)
QI: Allom Courage
Q2A&B, D3, D4, D5B, D7: Alloon Courage
D5A, D6, D8: Allons Courage
(p. 137)
ALL COPIES EXCEPT Q2B: vie with quality
Q2B: lie with quality
(p. 138)
QI, Q2A&B, D3: Marquis. Let me go; let me go. Valere. Aye, aye, prithee, let him go. He's not so dangerous as thou imagin'st, Hector—ha, ha, ha.
D4, D5B: [Marquis' speech omitted and Valere's attributed to Marquis.]
D5A, D6, D7, D8: [Marquis' speech omitted; Valere's the same as QI etc.]
QI, Q2A&B: country are fitter
ALL OTHER COPIES: country is fitter

III.2
(p. 138)
QI, Q2A&B, D3: *Scene changes: a table; pen, ink, and paper set out.*
ALL OTHER COPIES: *Scene changes: a table, with pen, ink, paper on it.*
(p. 141)
QI, Q2A&B, D3: that never was

guilty
ALL OTHER COPIES: that never were guilty
QI, Q2A&B: till he's here
ALL OTHER COPIES: till I'm there

IV.1
(p. 142)
ALL COPIES EXCEPT Q2B: seven or eleven
Q2B: seven or a eleven
ALL COPIES EXCEPT Q2B: golden shower
Q2B: golden shown
(p. 143)
QI, Q2A&B: I heard all this
ALL OTHER COPIES: I heard this

IV.2
(p. 145)
QI, Q2A&B: Over whom were this conquest?
ALL OTHER COPIES: Over whom was this conquest?
(p. 146)
QI, Q2A&B: though I have valor
ALL OTHER COPIES: though I love valor

IV.3
(p. 146)
QI, Q2A&B, D3: master and lady's
ALL OTHER COPIES: master's and lady's
QI, Q2A&B: I think an age
ALL OTHER COPIES: I think it an age

IV.4
(p. 147)
QI, Q2A&B, D3: *box-keeper and*

attendance
ALL OTHER COPIES: *box-keeper and attendants*
(p. 148)
QI, Q2A&B: I'll warrant the luck
ALL OTHER COPIES: I warrant thee luck

V.2
(p. 155)
ALL COPIES EXCEPT Q2B: generosity shocks me
Q2B: generosity shooks me
(p. 156)
ALL COPIES EXCEPT Q2B: time be now required
Q2B: time be now requited
QI, Q2A&B, D3: with living eyes
ALL OTHER COPIES: with loving eyes
(p. 158)
QI, Q2A&B: a picture nowhere today?
ALL OTHER COPIES: a picture anywhere today?
(p. 159)
QI, Q2A&B: use me worse
ALL OTHER COPIES: use me no worse
(p. 163)
QI, Q2A&B: in my heart to, to—
ALL OTHER COPIES: in my heart to—
QI, Q2A&B: a pize of this nonsense
ALL OTHER COPIES: enough of this nonsense

EPILOGUE
Q2A&B: Spoke by Mr. Verbruggen.
D5B, D6, D7, D8: Spoke by Mrs. Santlow

QI, D3, D4, D5A: [No epilogue]
(p. 164)
D8: that tedious, juggling game
ALL OTHER COPIES: that tedious, jangling game

THE
REHEARSAL:
O R,
BAYS in PETTICOATS.

A
COMEDY
In Two ACTS.

As it is performed at the

Theatre Royal in *Drury-Lane*.

Written by Mrs. C L I V E.

The MUSIC compofed by Dr. B O Y C E.

L O N D O N:
Printed for R. DODSLEY in Pall-mall. 1753.
Price One Shillin3.

ADVERTISEMENT

This little piece was written above three years since, and acted for my benefit.³—The last scene was an addition the year after. Whatever faults are in it, I hope, will be pardoned, when I inform the public, I had at first no design of printing it; and do it now at the request of my friends, who (as it met with so much indulgence from the audience) thought it might give some pleasure in the reading.—The songs were written by a gentleman.⁴

I take this opportunity to assure the public, I am, with great gratitude and respect,
Their most Obliged,
Humble Servant,
C. Clive

PERSONS

MEN

Witling	Mr. Woodward
Sir Albany Odelove	Mr. Shuter
Tom	Mr. Mozeen
Prompter	Mr. Cross⁵

WOMEN

Mrs. Hazard	Mrs. Clive
Miss Giggle	Miss Minors
Miss Crotchet	Miss Hippisley
Miss Sidle	Mrs. Simson
Miss Dawdle	Mrs. Toogood
Gatty	Mrs. Bennet

---

3   The play was first performed at a benefit night for Clive on 15 March 1750. (The mainpiece was *Hamlet*.) The play remained popular throughout 1750, and was revived in March, 1753 with a revised second act (the basis of the present text).

4   The pastoral in Act II, *Corydon and Miranda*, seems to have been performed independently of Clive's play—certainly the extant score, with music by William Boyce, contains some material not in the play, and vice versa. However, the identity of the librettist remains unknown.

5   Richard Cross (d. 1760), who was the prompter at Drury Lane from 1740 until his death, began his career as an actor, both at the Haymarket and at Drury Lane.

PASTORAL CHARACTERS

Corydon	Mr. Beard
Miranda	Miss Thomas
Marcella	Mrs. Clive

ACT I: A DRESSING-ROOM
IN MRS. HAZARD'S HOUSE.

Gatty preparing the toilet. Enter Tom with tea things.

GATTY. Well, I believe we are at present the most melancholy family in town, that used to be the merriest. Since these devils, the Muses, (as my Lady calls 'em) have got into the house, they have turned her head, and she distracts every body about her. She really was once a sweet-tempered woman; but now I can't speak, or stir, but she flies at me, and says I have flurried her out of one of the finest thoughts!—Hang her! I wish her farce may be hissed off the stage.

TOM. That's but a foolish kind of wish; for if she's so sweet-tempered now, what do you think she'll be then?

GATTY. I don't care what she'll be; for I'm determined not to stay with her. I am sure she uses me like her dog.

TOM. Does she?—Then you are an ungrateful hussy to complain: for she is fonder of that, than ever she was of her husband.—I fancy this farce of hers is horrid stuff: for I observe, all her visitors she reads it to (which is indeed every body that comes to the house) whisper as they come down stairs, and laugh ready to kill themselves.

GATTY. Yes, but that's at her assurance. Why, do you know 'tis none of her own? a gentleman only lent it her to read; he has been ill a great while at Bath; so she has taken the advantage of that, made some little alterations, had it set to music, and has introduced it to the stage as a performance of her own.

TOM. I hear Mr. Surly, that every body thought she was going to be married to, is so enraged at her, that he'll never speak to her, or see her again. One of his footmen told me of it yesterday, as a great secret, so I promised him never to mention it. (*Rings.*) —Don't you hear her bell ring?

GATTY. Hear her! yes, yes, I hear her; but I should have a fine time on't, if I was to go to her, as often as she takes it in her head to ring. (*Rings again.*) Ay, ay, ring away.

TOM. Ay, ay, ring away—I'gad here she comes. I wish you well off. (*Exit.*)

Enter Mrs. Hazard.

MRS. HAZARD. Why, what is the meaning I must ring for an hour, and none of ye will come near me, ye animals?—

GATTY. I was coming as fast as I could.

MRS. HAZARD. As fast as you could! why, you move like a snail that has been trod upon, you creeping creature.—Let me die, but she has provoked me into a fine simile. Come, get the things to dress me instantaneously. (Tom *with tea and coffee. She repeats recitative,* Oh, Corydon, *&c.*) You, Tom, I'm at home to no human being this morning but Mr. Witling. I've promised to carry him to the rehearsal with me. (*Repeats recitative,* Gatty *waiting with her cap.*)

GATTY. Madam, will you please to have your Cap on?

MRS. HAZARD. No! you idiot; how durst you interrupt me, when you saw me so engaged? As I am a Critic, this creature will distract me!—Give me my bottle of salts.—She has ruined one of the finest conclusions.—O Cor—Lord! I can't sing a note.—What are you doing?

GATTY. Lord, Madam, I can't find them!

MRS. HAZARD. Here's a provoking devil! sees 'em in my hand, and would not tell me of it! Get out of my sight. (*Repeats recitative.*) Why, where are you going? am I to dress myself?

GATTY. Madam, Mr. Witling.

Enter Witling.

WITLING. My dear Widow! you're hard at it, I see. Come, give me some tea. What is it, your prologue, or epilogue, pray?

MRS. HAZARD. O Lord! dear Witling!—Don't be ridiculous; for I'm in a horrid humour.

WITLING. Yes; and a horrid dress, too, I think. Why, 'tis almost ten.— What, is this your rehearsal habiliment?

MRS. HAZARD. Why, that creature that you see standing there, won't give me any thing to put on.

WITLING. Well, do you know I have had such a quarrel with Frank Surly upon your account? We met last night at Lady Betty Brag's rout;[6]—

---

6   A large fashionable assembly, usually attended by great crowds.

there was a vast deal of company,—and they were all talking of your new piece.

MRS. HAZARD. So, I suppose I was finely worried.

WITLING. You shall hear: as soon as ever it was mentioned, we all burst out a-aughing.

MRS. HAZARD. You did!—and pray what did you laugh at?

WITLING. Hey!—why—oh—, at Frank Surly; he looked so like a—ha, ha, ha, i'gad I can't find such a simile that can give you an idea of such a face. Oh, thinks I, my dear, you're in a fine humour to make us some diversion. So, says I, Frank, I hear the match is quite concluded between Mrs. Hazard and you; and that she has fixed the first night of her comedy for your wedding-night.—Sir, says he (with a very grave face), you may say what you please of Mrs. Hazard; for as she's going to expose herself, she must expect that every fool will be as impertinent as she is ridiculous:—but I would advise you not to mention my name any more in that manner, for, if you do, I shall take it extremely ill. Lord! says Miss Giggle, Mr. Surly, how can you be so cross? expose herself?—I'll swear, I believe Mrs. Hazard can write a very pretty play, for she has a great deal of wit and humour.—Wit and humour! Says he, why, there are not ten women in the creation that have sense enough to write a consistent *N.B.*—Marry her! I would sooner marry a woman that had been detected in ten amours, than one who, in defiance to all advice, and without the pretence that most people write for (for every body knows she's a woman of fortune), will convince the whole world she's an idiot.

MRS. HAZARD. A bear! a brute! Let me hear no more of him.

WITLING. Yes, but I must tell you a very good thing that I said to him.

MRS. HAZARD. No, that you can't I'm sure, Witling; for you never said a good thing in your life.

WITLING. Nay, why should you be so ill-natured to me? I'm sure I took your part. Why, says I, Frank, how can you be such a fool to quarrel with her? I wish she liked me half so well, as I'm sure she does you; she should write, and be hanged if she would, for any thing I cared; for let them do what they will with her performance, they can't damn her eight hundred a year.

MRS. HAZARD. You said so, did you?

WITLING. I said so!—No; Lord, Child!—How could you think I could say such a thing. No, no, to be sure it was said by somebody in the company. But upon honour I don't know who.

MRS. HAZARD (*Aside*). What a wretch is this?—But he is to carry a party for me the first night; so I must not quarrel with him.

WITLING. Well, but my dear Hazard, when does you farce come out?

MRS. HAZARD. Why some time next week; this is to be the last rehearsal: and the managers have promised they shall all be dressed, that we may see exactly what effect it will have.

WITLING. Well, but don't your heart ache, when you think of the first night? hey—

MRS. HAZARD. Not in the least; the Town never hiss any thing that is introduced to them, by a person of consequence and breeding. Because they are sure they'll have nothing low.

WITLING. Aye, but they mayn't be so sure they'll have nothing foolish.

MRS. HAZARD. Ha!—Why perhaps they mayn't find out one so soon as t'other. Ha, ha, ha, well, let me die if that is not a very good thing.— But 'tis well for me, Witling, the Town don't hear me; not that I mean quite what I say neither, for to do them justice, they're generally in the right in their censure; tho' sometimes indeed they will out of human- ity forgive an author stupidity, and overlook his being a fool; pro- vided he will do them the favour not to be a beast; for which reason, Witling, I have taken great care to be delicate; I may be dull, but I am delicate; so that I am not at all afraid of the Town: I wish I could say the same of performers: Lord, what a pity 'tis the great tragedy actors can't sing! I'm about a new thing, which I shall call a burletto,[7] which I take from some incidents in Don Quixote,[8] that I shall believe will be as high humour, as was ever brought upon the stage. But then I shall want actors; oh! if that dear Garrick could but sing, what a Don Quixote he'd make!

WITLING. Don't you think Barry[9] would be a better! he's so tall, you know, and so finely made for't. If I was to advise, I would carry that to Covent-Garden.

MRS. HAZARD. Covent-Garden! Lord, I would not think of it, it stands in such a bad air.

---

7   More properly, "burletta," a short, operatic piece, of which Pergolesi's *La serva padrona* is probably the best-known example. Burlettas were quite new to England in the 1750s; Mrs. Hazard's English burletta would have been quite innovative, since, according to the *Grove Dictionary*, the first English burletta, Kane O'Hara's *Midas*, was not performed until 1760.

8   Cervantes' novel (Part One, 1605, Part Two, 1615) was well known to English read- ers in the eighteenth century, especially in Thomas Shelton's versions of Part One (1612) and Part Two (1620), Charles Jervas's 1742 translation, or Tobias Smollett's 1755 version. Thomas D'Urfey wrote a hugely popular stage version in 1695, with music by a number of composers, including Henry Purcell. The premise was lampooned in a number of novels, most notably Charlotte Lennox's *Female Quixote* (1750).

9   Spranger Barry (1717?-77), manager of Covent Garden at this time. Barry was gener- ally considered during the period as David Garrick's major rival.

WITLING. Bad air!

MRS. HAZARD. Aye; the actors can't play there above three days a week. They have more need of a physician, than a poet, at that house.

WITLING. But pray, Madam, you say you are to call your new thing a burletto; what is a burletto?

MRS. HAZARD. What is a burletto? why haven't you seen one at the Haymarket?[10]

WITLING. Yes, but I don't know what it is for all that.

MRS. HAZARD. Don't you? why then, let me die if I can tell you, but I believe it's a kind of poor relation to an opera.

WITLING. Pray how many characters have you in this thing?

MRS. HAZARD. Why I have but three; for as I was observing, there's so few of them that can sing: nay I have but two indeed that are rational, for I have made one of them mad.[11]

WITLING. And who is to act that, pray?

MRS. HAZARD. Why Mrs. Clive, to be sure; tho' I wish she don't spoil it; for she's so conceited, and insolent, that she won't let me teach it her. You must know when I told her I had a part for her in a performance of mine, in the prettiest manner I was able (for one must be civil to these sort of people when one wants them), says she, Indeed, Madam, I must see the whole piece, for I shall take no part in a new thing, without choosing that which I think I can act best. I have been a great sufferer already, by the manager's not doing justice to my genius; but I hope I shall next year convince the Town, what fine judgment they have: for I intend to play a capital tragedy part for my own benefit.

WITLING. And what did you say to her, pray?

MRS. HAZARD. Say to her! why do you think I would venture to expostulate with her?—No, I desired Mr. Garrick would take her in hand; so he ordered her the part of the madwoman directly.

WITLING. Well, I think the Town will be vastly obliged to you, for giving them such an entertainment, as I am told it is from every body that has heard it; tho' the ill-natured part of your acquaintance say 'tis none of your own.

MRS. HAZARD. Why whose do they say it is, pray?—Not yours, Witling; not quite so bad as that I hope. No, my motive for writing, was really compassion; the Town has been so overwhelmed with tragedies lately,

---

10   The Haymarket Opera House—also known as the Queen's Theatre, the King's Theatre, and Her Majesty's Opera House—featured Italian opera and musical theater. It was destroyed by fire in 1789.

11   "Mad songs" were a popular operatic convention. *Corydon and Miranda* contains a mad aria from Marcella, but the rehearsal is interrupted before Mrs. Hazard can sing it.

that they are in one entire fit of the vapours.[12]—They think they love 'em, but it's no such thing. I was there one night this season at a tragedy, and there was such an universal yawn in the house, that, if it had not been for a great quantity of drums and trumpets, that most judiciously every now and then came in to their relief, the whole audience would have fallen asleep.

Enter Tom.

TOM. Madam, there's a young Miss desires to speak to you upon particular business.

WITLING. Heark'e Tom, are you sure 'tis a young Miss?—If 'tis an old one, don't let her come up; for they are a sort of creatures I have a great aversion to.

MRS. HAZARD. Why, thou impertinent, stupid wretch! did not I bid you deny me to every body? Don't you know I am going out this instant?

TOM. Madam, 'tis not my fault; I was not below, and they let her in.

MRS. HAZARD. I don't believe there is a woman in the world has such a collection of devils in her house as I have.

Enter Miss [Crotchet].[13]

MISS. Mame,[14]—your servant.—Not to interrupt you.

MRS. HAZARD. Yes, Miss; but you have done that—What is your business pray?

MISS. Why, Mame—I was informed as how that there was a new play of yours, Mame, a-coming out upon the stage, with some singing in't.

MRS. HAZARD. Coming out upon the stage! (Lord! where could this creature come from!) Well, Miss.

MISS. So, Mame, I have a desire, (not that I have any occasion) but 'tis my fancy, Mame, to come and sing upon the stage.

MRS. HAZARD. And a very odd fancy I believe it is.—Well, Miss, you say, it is your fancy to sing upon the stage; but, pray are you qualified?

---

12   "A morbid condition supposed to be caused by the presence of such exhalations; depression of spirits, hypochondria, hysteria, or other nervous disorder" (OED).

13   "The "Miss" who enters here must be the "Miss Crotchet" referred to in the Dramatis Personae. "Crotchet," a term for a musical note, is a fitting name for this would-be singer.

14   Miss Crotchet's unsophisticated pronunciation of "Ma'am."

MISS. O yes, Mame; I have very good friends.[15]

MRS. HAZARD. This girl's a natural![16]—Why, Miss, that's a very great happiness; but I believe a good voice would be more material to your fancy;—I suppose you have a good voice.

MISS. No, Mame; I can't say I have much voice.

MRS. HAZARD. Ha, ha, she's delightful! I am glad they let her in. Well, Miss, to be sure then you are a mistress!

MISS. Mame—what do you mean?

MRS. HAZARD. Ha, ha; I say, I imagine you understand music perfectly well.

MISS. No, Mame, I never learnt in my life; but 'tis my fancy.

WITLING (*Aside*). Miss is a very pretty girl, I wish she'd take a fancy to me, I believe it would answer my purpose better than singing will hers.

MRS. HAZARD. Well; but, my dear, as you confess you have neither voice nor judgment, to be sure you have a particular fine ear!

MISS. Yes, Mame, I've a very good ear—that is when I sing by myself; but the music always puts me out.

MRS. HAZARD. Ha, ha. Well, Child, you have given an exceeding good account of yourself, and I believe will make a very extraordinary performer.

MISS. Thank you, Mame. Yes, I believe I shall do very well in time.

WITLING. Pray, Miss, won't you favour us with a song?

MISS. Yes, Sir; If you please, I'll sing "Powerful Guardians of all Nature":[17] I've brought it with me.

MRS. HAZARD. Pray let's hear it. (*Miss sings.*) Oh fie! Miss! That will never do; you speak your words as plain as a parish-girl;[18] the audience will never endure you in this kind of singing, if they understand what you say: you must give your words the Italian accent, Child.—Come, you shall hear me. (*Mrs. Hazard sings in the Italian manner.*) There, Miss, that's the taste of singing now.—But I must beg you would excuse me

---

15   Miss Crotchet misinterprets Mrs. Hazard's question, confusing "qualified" (i.e., able to sing) with "quality" (i.e., one of the upper classes).

16   Simpleton.

17   A popular song of mid-century. The words, as printed in *The Aviary*, a song collection *c.* 1750, are as follows:

> Powerful Guardians of all Nature,
> O preserve my beauteous Love!
> Keep from Insults that dear Creature,
> Her Virtue sure has Charms to move.
> Powerful Guardians of all Nature,
> O preserve my beauteous Love, &c.

18   An orphan child, one supported by the parish in which she lives. The OED records the first use of the word in 1705.

at present; I'm going to the play-house, and will certainly speak to
the managers about you; for I dare believe you'll make a prodigious[19]
figure upon the stage.

WITLING. That you will indeed, Miss.— (*Aside*) The strangest that ever
was seen there.

MISS. Sir, I thank you, Mame, I thank you. Mame, I'll wait on you
another time.

MRS. HAZARD. Miss, your servant. (*Exit* Miss.) —No; that you shall not
do, I promise you.

Enter Tom.

TOM. Madam, your chair has been waiting a great while; 'tis after ten,
above half an hour.

MRS. HAZARD. My stars! This driveling girl has ruined me. Here, Gatty,
get me my shade; I'll go as I am.

WITLING. Shall I set you down?

MRS. HAZARD. Oh! not for the world! an authoress to be seen in the
chariot of a fool, would be the greatest absurdity in Nature; we shall
meet at the house.

WITLING. Very well, Mame, and I shall be in the pit the first night;
remember that.—Come, give me your hand, however.

Exeunt.

ACT II. SCENE: THE PLAY-HOUSE.

Enter Mrs. Hazard, Mr. Witling, and Mr. Cross.

MRS. HAZARD. Mr. Cross, your servant. Has any body been to ask for me
this morning?

MR. CROSS. Not any body, Madam.

MRS. HAZARD. Well, that's very surprising! I expected half the Town
would have been trying to get in: but 'tis better as 'tis; for they would
only have interrupted the *Rehearsal*.[20] So, Mr. Cross, I'll be denied

---

19   OED defines this as "caus[ing] wonder or amazement," which is how Miss Crotchet
is expected to take it; however, the term can also mean either "appalling" or "freakish,"
which is clearly Mrs. Hazard's intention.

20   Mrs. Hazard treats the rehearsal as if it were the title of her play, or at least as a
proper name in its own right. It also appears to be a sly allusion to Buckingham's original
play.

to every body. Well, Witling, how do you like the play-house in a morning?

WITLING. Why, I think 'tis like a fine lady; it looks best by candlelight.

MRS. HAZARD. But pray, Mr. Cross, get every body ready; is the music[21] come?

MR. CROSS. Yes, Madam, the music has been here this half hour, and every body but Mrs. Clive; and, I dare say, she'll not be long, for she's very punctual; Mr. Beard and Miss Thomas are gone to dress.

MRS. HAZARD. Mr. Cross, you have had a great deal of trouble with this thing; I don't know how I must make you amends; but pray, when your benefit is,—you have a benefit, I suppose?—set me down all your side-boxes, and every first row in the front; I may want more, but I shall certainly fill those.

MR. CROSS. Thank'ye, Madam.

Enter a servant.

SERVANT. Mr. Cross, there's a person wants to speak to you. (*Exit* Mr. Cross).

MRS. HAZARD. Well, I swear these poor players have a very slavish life; I wonder how they are able to go through it!

Enter Mr. Cross.

MR. CROSS. Madam, Mrs. Clive has sent word, that she can't possibly wait on you this morning, as she's obliged to go to some ladies about her benefit. But you may depend on her being her perfect, and ready to perform it whenever you please.

MRS. HAZARD. Mr. Cross, what did you say? I can't believe what I have heard! Mrs. Clive send me word she can't come to my *rehearsal*, and is gone to ladies about her benefit! Sir, she shall have no benefit. Mr. Witling, did you ever hear of a parallel to this insolence? Give me my copy, sir; give me my copy. I'll make Mrs. Clive repent treating me in this manner. Very fine indeed! to have the assurance[22] to prefer her benefit to my *rehearsal*! Mr. Cross, you need not give yourself the trouble to set down any places for me at your benefit, for I'll never come to the play-house any more.

---

21 I.e., musicians.
22 "Confidence; want of modesty" (Samuel Johnson's *Dictionary*).

WITLING. Nay; but, my dear Hazard, don't put yourself into such a passion, can't you rehearse her part yourself? I dare say you'll do it better than she can.

MR. CROSS. Why, Madam, if you would be so good, as the music are here, and the other characters dressed, it would be very obliging: And if you please to put on Mrs. Clive's, her dresser is here to attend, as she expected her, and I believe it will fit you exactly, as you're much of her size.

MRS. HAZARD. O yes; to be sure it will fit me exactly, because I happen to be a head taller, and, I hope, something better made.

WITLING. Oh, my dear Hazard! put it on; put it on. Oh Lord! let me see you in a play-house dress.

MRS. HAZARD. Well, let me die, but I have a great mind;—for I had set my heart upon seeing the poor thing rehearsed in its proper dresses.— Well, Witling, shall I?—I think I will. Do you go into the Green Room and drink some chocolate, I'll slip on the things in a minute. No; hang it, I won't take the trouble; I'll rehearse as I am.

Enter Performers dressed.

Miss Thomas, your servant. Upon my word, I am extremely happy to have you in my performance; you'll do amazing well. Only I must beg you'd throw in as much spirit as you can, without overdoing it; for that same thing the players call *Spirit*, they sometimes turn into Rant and Noise. Oh, Mr. Beard! your most obedient. Sir, I shall be vastly obliged to you, I am sure; do you know that you sing better than any of 'em? But I hope you'd consider the part you are to act with Marcella, is to be done with great scorn: Therefore, as you have such a smiling, good-humoured face, I beg you'll endeavour to smother as many of your dimples as you can in that scene with her. Come, come, let us begin. We may omit the overture.[23]

Miranda, sola.

Recitative.
It must be so—my shepherd ne'er shall prove
A renegade from the faith of Love.
Nor shall Marcella tear him from my arms,
Even tho' her wealth be boundless as her charms.

---

23   Interestingly, the surviving score of *Corydon and Miranda* has no overture.

MRS. HAZARD. That's pretty well, Madam, but I think you sing it too
much; you should consider *Recitative* should be spoken as plain as
possible; or else you'll lose the expression—I'll show you what I
mean.—No, no, go on now with the symphony[24] for the song.

Air.
If Cupid once the mind possess,
All low affections cease;
No troubles then can give distress,
No tumult break the peace.
Oh had I thousand gifts in store,
Were I of worlds the queen,
For him I'd covet thousands more,
And call profusion mean.

2.
Then let my swain my love return,
And equal raptures feel;
Nor let his passions cool, or burn,
As Fortune winds her wheel.
If his fond heart I may believe
Immutably secure,
No sorrow then can make me grieve,
No loss can make me poor.

Recitative.
But see he comes—I'll wear a short disguise;
Be false my tongue!—be hypocrites my eyes!
Nor to the youth too wantonly impart
The secret history of a faithful heart.

Enter Corydon.

What! from Marcella come!—Insulting swain,
Come ye to wake, and triumph in my pain,
Warm from those lips whose cruel sentence gave
Thy friend Philander an untimely grave?

Recitative.

---

24   Short introductory instrumental passage.

Corydon.
Marcella! Name not the capricious fair,
One smile from thee is worth possession there.

Miranda.
Did not I hear her, in yon hawthorn bower,
With transport boast o'er Corydon her power?

Air.

Corydon.
In vain, my fair one, you complain,
And charge the guiltless boy in vain,
Who ne'er was found untrue;
The sweetest image thought can find,
Thou best Idea of my mind,
My soul is fill'd with you.

2.
Let but those eyes, benignly bright,
That look the language of delight,
The spacious globe review;
If they can find an equal fair,
Be jealous then—and I'll take care
You shall have reason, too.

Miranda.[25]
Well—wou'd you ease my breast, and peace restore,
Oh never see the vain Marcella more.

Duet.[26]
Air.

Miranda.
At length return, luxuriant Thought,
Return and settle where you ought,
Fix'd by experience dearly bought

---

25   This is sung as a recitative.
26   The music for this duet is not in the extant score, although the last verse is sung as
the closing Chorus.

For sweet and useful ends.
Oft did I dread her subtle care,
And oft was jealous, tho' secure,
What agonies did I endure?
But Love has made amends.

Corydon.
Joy were no joy, and pleasure vain,
Were there not intervals of pain;
The captive who has felt a chain
Is doubly blest when free.
I view with transports the abyss,
Which powers propitious made me miss,
And rush with aching thoughts of bliss
To safety, and to thee.

Both.
Joy were no joy, and pleasure vain,
Were there not intervals of pain;
The captive who has felt a chain
Is doubly blest when free.
'Tis clouds that make the sun more bright,
'Tis darkness that sets off the light,
'Tis sorrow gives to joy its height,
By Heaven's most kind decree.
(Witling *falls asleep.*)

Corydon.
Soft! she approaches—seek yon poplar glade,
And wait beneath the thick embowering shade.
Yourself shall be a witness to my truth.
(Miranda *retires.*)

Enter Marcella.
Oh Corydon,[27] *ah cruel charming youth,*
Look not so stern, I have no hopes to blast;
My love is come in sighs to breathe its last.

---

27   This is the recitative Mrs. Hazard was attempting to sing in Act I; see above, p. 175.

Air.
The silver rain, the pearly dew,
The gales that sweep along the mead,
The soften'd rocks have sorrow knew,
And marbles have found tears to shed;
The sighing trees, in every grove,
Have pity, if they have not Love.

2.
Shall things inanimate be kind,
And every soft sensation know;
The weeping rain, and sighing wind,
All, all, but thee, some mercy show.
Ah, pity—if you scorn t'approve;
Have pity, if thou hast not Love.[28]

A noise without. Enter Miss Giggle, Sir Albany Odelove, Miss Sidle, and Miss Dawdle.

MISS GIGGLE. My dear Creature, I immensely rejoice to find you; do you know we have been at your house, and could not meet with a creature that could give the least account of you? Your servants are all abroad, ha, ha, ha; they are certainly the worst servants in the world, ha, ha, ha. Well, but my dear, have you done? for we must have you with us. We are going to one of those breakfasting places, but we don't know which yet, for they are all so immensely superb, that I can't touch my breakfast at home, ha, ha, ha! Lord, dear Creature, what makes you look so miserable? your new thing isn't a tragedy, is it?

MRS. HAZARD. Giggle, I'm astonished at you: Pray who are all these people you have brought upon me?—

MISS GIGGLE. Who are they, my dear? I'll introduce you to them; they're immensely agreeable, all of them, ha, ha, ha.

MRS. HAZARD. Lookee, Miss Giggle, if they are ever so immense, they must not stay here, for I'm going to be immensely busy, and will not be interrupted.

MISS GIGGLE. My dear Creature, as to leaving you, 'tis not in the nature of things; I would not go without you for the world; Sir Albany Odelove, Mrs. Hazard, desires to be introduced to you. Madam, this

---

28   While this is all the sung text that appears in the copy-text, it continues in the extant score: see Note on the Text below, p. 192.

gentleman is immensely fond of the Muses, and therefore must be agreeable to you. Miss Sidle, Miss Dawdle (*introduces 'em*).

MRS. HAZARD (*Aside*). Mr. Cross—I want to speak to you; I shall run mad.

MISS GIGGLE. Lord, Witling, what's the matter with Mrs. Hazard? She looks as if she could kill me.

WITLING. The matter with her? ha, ha, ha! why, you have interrupted her rehearsal. Ah, I could indulge such a laugh! if you'll join with me, we shall have the finest scene in the world.—She has made me sick to death with her stuff, and I will be revenged. You must know one of the actresses has disappointed her, and she is going to sing her part herself; so the moment she begins, do you burst into a violent laugh; we shall all join with you, you may be sure; and then you'll see the consequence.—

MISS GIGGLE. See! nay, I believe I shall feel the consequence, for she'll certainly beat us immensely. Oh, I'll tell you what, let's set Odelove upon her, to enquire into the plot of her play—he'll plague her to death, for he's immensely foolish.

WITLING. Well—that's an admirable thought.—Mum.[29]—

MISS GIGGLE. Well, but my dear Mrs. Hazard, don't let us interrupt you, for we are all immensely fond of a rehearsal.

MISS DAWDLE. Yes, so we are indeed, Madam, immensely.

WITLING. So we are, immensely. (*Catches her hand.*)

MISS DAWDLE. Lord! don't paw one so, Mr. Witling.—

MISS GIGGLE. And so this is the play-house; I'll swear 'tis immensely pretty, and all the music; well, if there was but a scene of green trees, we might fancy ourselves at Ranelagh,[30] ha, ha, ha.

MRS. HAZARD. Why really, by the noise you make, and the nonsense you talk, I think you might. Lookee, Miss Giggle, I shall be very plain with you; if you think it is possible for you to be quiet for half an hour, I shall be glad of your company; if not, I must beg you'd depart.

SIR ALBANY. Why really what the lady says, is very pathetic and consequential to the foregoing part of Miss Giggle's behaviour; for when a person of parts (as we are to suppose this lady to be) is assassinated with incoherences, it is such an aggravation to our intellects, as does in fact require supernatural patience to acquiesce thereto.

ALL. Ha! ha! ha!

---

29   I.e., keep quiet (presumably because Mrs. Hazard is attempting to overhear their conversation).

30   Fashionable eighteenth-century resort by the Thames, in London. Also mentioned in *The Runaway*: see below, p. 227.

MISS GIGGLE. Very well, Sir Albany, I'll remember you for this—No, upon honour, now I will be very good, I won't interrupt you indeed, won't speak another word.—O la, Witling, do you know Miss Lucy Loveshuffle had such an immense ill run[31] last night, she bragged[32] every thing that came into her hand, and lost every thing she bragged—'till she really looked as ugly as a fiend.

WITLING. I fancy you won, then, Giggle: for I never saw you look so well.

MRS. HAZARD. Nay, as to that matter, let Giggle win or lose, it will be pretty much the same thing with her beauty; but come, Mr. Cross, pray let us go on. Let me see, I begin my Recit.

SIR ALBANY. *Corydon*—

WITLING. Giggle, I can tell you who's going to be married.

MISS SIDLE AND MISS DAWDLE. Oh Lord! who?—pray tell us?

WITLING. The celebrated Miss Shrimp to Lord Lovelittle, a man of very great fortune.

MISS DAWDLE. Really! well then, I think we none of us need to despair.

WITLING. Come, don't you be envious now; for she's a charming girl, and deserves her good fortune.

MISS GIGGLE. Charming!—nay then I shall never have done, I'm sure she's immensely little.

SIR ALBANY. Oh fie, Miss, that's nonsense; horrid nonsense! immensely little! Oh Lord!

WITLING. Why, to be sure she is rather small, that must be allowed; she is certainly the least woman that ever was seen for nothing.

SIR ALBANY. Madam, as I was not so auspicious as to be here at the beginning of this affair, will you give me leave to ask you a few questions?—

MR. CROSS. Madam, if you won't go on, the music and performers can't possibly stay any longer.

MRS. HAZARD. Why what can I do, Mr. Cross? you see how I'm terrified with 'em.

WITLING. She begins to be in a fury.—Look at her, Giggle.

SIR ALBANY. I say, Madam, will you give me leave, as you're going to entertain the Town (that is, I mean endeavour, or attempt to entertain them), for let me tell you, fair lady, 'tis not an easy thing to bring about. If men, who are properly graduated in learning, who have swallowed the tincture of a polite education, who, as I may say, are hand

---

31   Bad luck at cards

32   Called, as in poker. Lucy Loveshuffle is presumably playing the game of brag—an ancestor of poker—in which the object is to assemble the strongest hand and to "brag," or challenge the other players' hands.

and glove with the classics, if such geniuses as I'm describing, fail of success in dramatical occurrences, or performances ('tis the same sense in the Latin), what must a poor lady expect, who is as ignorant as the dirt?

MRS. HAZARD. Pray, Sir, how long have they let you out?

SIR ALBANY. Therefore, I hope you have had the advice of your male acquaintance, who will take some care of your diction, and see that you have observed that great beauty, neglected by most dramatic authors, of time and place.[33]

WITLING. Oh Sir Albany, I'll answer she has taken care of time and place; for it will begin about half an hour after eight, and be acted at Drury-Lane Theatre.—Ha, ha, ha, there's time and place for you.

MRS. HAZARD. And so, you're hand and glove with the classics, are you? Why thou elaborate idiot, how durst you venture to talk to any thing that's rational?—Consult my male acquaintance! I thank my stars, thou art not one of 'em. Where did you pick up this creature?—What's his name?—Can you spell your own name, you ugly brute?

MISS GIGGLE. Oh Lord! it will never come to her singing.

MISS SIDLE. Pray, Madam, will there be any dancing this morning?

MRS. HAZARD. No—Mr. Cross, who let these people in? I do assure you I shall complain to the managers;—I have been so plagued there's no bearing it—I could tear these—I'm unfit for any thing now.—So the rehearsal must be put off, 'till another morning.

WITLING. Aye do;—and let us go to—

MRS. HAZARD. Go to—

WITLING. To Ranelagh—I knew you would not name an ungenteel place.

SIR ALBANY. The lady has been somewhat underbred in her behaviour to me; but as I have a regard to the fair sex, I would have some of you advise her to cry; it will give relief to her passion.

MRS. HAZARD. Sir, will you go out of this place?

SIR ALBANY. I protest, Madam, I will, directly (*Exit*).

ALL. Ha, ha, ha!

WITLING. Well, but my dear Creature, you are not angry with me?—

---

33   Sir Albany's pedantic observation that Mrs. Hazard's play must follow the classical "unities" of time and place (though not, interestingly enough, of action—the one rule Aristotle specifically insists on) is designed to show off his classical education, but not his deeper understanding of dramatic structure: even neoclassical theorists acknowledged that Shakespeare's greatness partly derived from his disregard for classical rules, and most accepted that dramatic effectiveness was ultimately more important than slavish attention to the rules.

MRS. HAZARD. Indeed I am, Witling, and very angry too; I don't believe
I shall ever speak to you again. As for those things, that run about
littering the Town, and force themselves into all public places only
to show their insignificance, they are beneath my resentment.—Mr.
Cross, I'll settle with you, when I would have another rehearsal; tho'
I am not sure I ever will have another.—I believe I shall tear it to
pieces.—Pray let somebody see if my chairmen[34] are there.

WITLING. Shall I wait on you?

MRS. HAZARD. No. (*Exit*).

WITLING. Well, as Sir Paul says, Odsbud, she's a passionate woman;[35]
but her tearing it will only save the audience the trouble of doing it for
her. Come, ladies, will you go? I'll see you to your coach.

MR. CROSS. As the ladies have been disappointed of Mrs. Hazard's
rehearsal, if they please to stay, we are going to practice a new dance.

ALL. Oh, by all means.

A Dance

FINIS

NOTE ON THE TEXT

The text is based on the first edition, published by Dodsley in 1753. A
Dublin edition published the same year (ESTC T046678) is a reprint of
the Dodsley edition, with one substantive change (Witling asks Mrs.
Hazard if her worries about the first night makes her "head ach" in the
Dublin edition). The text has been modernized along the following lines:

- Spelling has been modernized throughout, although the majority
  of words in the original are spelled according to modern usage.
- The contracted form "-'d" has been expanded to "-ed" throughout,
  as have the contracted forms for modal verbs ("wou'd," "cou'd,"
  "shou'd"). Both contracted and expanded forms are used
  interchangeably in the original printing.
- Capitalization of nouns—a practice that was becoming old-
  fashioned by 1753—has been eliminated, except in a few cases:

---

34   Servants who carry a sedan-chair.
35   Witling is quoting Sir Paul Plyant in William Congreve's *The Double Dealer* (1694).

      "the Town," for example, refers to a distinctive entity, and the capital in the original serves to emphasize that usage.

- Italics for proper nouns have been replaced with roman type throughout.
- Stage directions have been left unexpanded, but since eighteenth-century plays indicated asides, speeches directed to particular characters, and actions to which characters respond *after* the text, I have moved them for the sake of clarity.

Punctuation, on the other hand, I have left largely unchanged. Because eighteenth-century punctuation often followed natural speech rhythms more closely than modern punctuation does, the punctuation of a play can serve as a guide for performers experimenting with ways of speaking a line.

As noted on p. 187 above, n. 28, the extant score contains additional sung text as follows:

RECITATIVE.

Corydon.
Away, away; nor ever see me more,
Unless thou can'st my murder'd friend restore.
Remember all thy fierceness, all thy pride,
When poor Philander lov'd, despair'd, and died.
That mercy he receiv'd, vain nymph, from you;
That mercy I return: adieu, adieu!
Exit *Corydon.*

Marcella.
He's gone, he's gone! the wild inhuman swain.
God of my joys and demon of my pain!
His cruelty has fix'd the fatal dart;
It tears, it rives my bleeding heart.

AIR.

Rise, Tempests, rise, cloud the skies!
Ye Surges, why are you at rest?
Are there no storms but in my breast?
Collect, ye Winds, each plague that's dire,
And let the world in pain expire!
Down, down, ye Towers of State!

Vain tools of the great
To atoms fall! Nor let the mighty ruin cease
'Till it has crush'd me into peace.
But O, take heed, take heed,
Let my dear charmer bleed.
Hear, O ye Winds, my cries!
Now listen to my sighs!
Ye gentle Zephyrs, fan his breast,
While pleasing dreams attend his rest.
Ye feather'd songsters, all prepare
With grateful notes, to soothe his ear.

No, no, let him die, let him die!
Rain vengeance from the sky!
In pangs of passion let him be,
In endless pangs—like me!

CHORUS.

Joy were no joy, and pleasure vain,
Were there not intervals of pain;
The captive who has felt a chain
Is doubly blest when free.
'Tis clouds that make the sun more bright,
'Tis darkness that sets off the light,
'Tis sorrow gives to joy its height,
By Heaven's most kind decree.

THE
RUNAWAY.
A
COMEDY.

Performed at the

THEATRE = ROYAL

IN

DRURY=LANE.

A New Edition.[1]

Isaac Taylor del. et sculp

LONDON:

Printed for I. DODSLEY, in Pall Mall; T. BECKET, and

T. CADELL in the Strand; T. LONGMAN in Paternoster

Row & CARNAN & NEWBERY in S.t Paul's Church Yard.

(Pr. 1.s 6.d)

To David Garrick, Esq;

Sir,

Amidst the regrets I feel for your quitting the stage,[2] it is peculiarly gratify-
ing that a play of *mine* closes your *dramatic* life. It is the highest pleasure to
me, that *that* play, from its success, reflects no dishonor on your judgment
as a manager.

Posterity will know, through a thousand channels, that Mr. Garrick was
the ornament of the eighteenth century, that he possessed the friendship
of those whose names will be the glory of English history, that the first
ranks in the kingdom courted his society. May my small voice be heard
amongst those who will inform it, that Mr. Garrick's *heart* was no less an
honor to him than his *talents*!

Unpatronized by any *name*, I presented myself to you, obscure and
unknown. You perceived *dawnings* in my comedy, which you *nourished* and
improved. With attention and solicitude, you *embellished* and presented it to
the world—*that* world, which has emulated your generosity, and received it
with an applause, which fills my heart with most lively gratitude. I perceive
how much of this applause I owe to my *sex*. *The Runaway* has a thousand
faults, which, if written by a man, would have incurred the severest lash
of criticism. But the gallantry of the English nation is equal to its wisdom.
They beheld a *woman* tracing with feeble steps the borders of the Parnassian
mount;[3] pitying her difficulties (for 'tis a thorny path) they gave their hands
for her support, and placed her *high* above her level.

All this, sir, and whatever may be its consequences, I owe to you. Had you
rejected me, when I presented my little *Runaway*, depressed by the refusal,
and all confidence in *myself* destroyed, I should never have presumed to
dip my pen again. It is now my task to convince you and the world, that a
generous allowance for a young writer's faults, is the best encouragement
to genius—'tis a kindly soil, in which weak groundlings are nourished and
from which the loftiest trees draw their strength, and their beauty.

I take my leave of you, sir, with the warmest wishes for your felicity, and
Mrs. Garrick's—to whose *taste* and solicitude for me, I am highly indebted.
May your recess from the stage be attended with all the blessings of retirement and ease—and may the world remember, in its most distant periods,
that 'tis to Mr. Garrick the English theater owes its emancipation from
grossness and buffoonery. That to Mr. Garrick's *judgment* it is indebted for

---

2   See Introduction above, p. 10.
3   I.e., with ambitions to be a poet. Parnassus was a mountain in central Greece, sacred
to Apollo and home of the muses.

being the first stage in Europe and to his *talents* for being the delight of the most enlightened and polished age.

I am, sir, your most devoted, and humble servant,
The Author.

PERSONS OF THE DRAMA

MEN

Mr. Hargrave	Mr. Yates
George Hargrave	Mr. Smith
Mr. Drummond	Mr. Bensley
Sir Charles Seymour	Mr. Brereton
Mr. Morley	Mr. Aickin
Justice	Mr. Parsons
Jarvis	Mr. Palmer
First Hunter	Mr. Bannister

WOMEN

Lady Dinah	Mrs. Hopkins
Bella	Miss Younge
Emily	Mrs. Siddons
Harriet	Miss Hopkins
Susan	Mrs. Wrighten

Gentlemen, hunters, servants, &c.

Scene: Mr. Hargrave's house in the country.

PROLOGUE

Written by the author.
Spoken by Mr. Brereton.

Oh, the sweet prospect![4] What a fine parterre;[5]
Soft buds, sweet flowers, bright tints, and scented air! (*Boxes.*)

---

4   View.
5   Ornamental flower bed in a garden; also a name for the ground floor of the auditorium.

A vale, where critic wit spontaneous grows! (*Pit.*)
A hill, which *noise* and *folly* never knows! (*Gallery.*)
Let cits point out green paddocks to their spouses;
To me no prospect like your crowded houses—
If, as just now, you wear those smiles enchanting,
But, when you frown, my heart you set a-panting!
Pray, then, for pity, do not frown tonight;
I'll bribe—but how? Oh, now I've hit it right.
Secrets are pleasant to each child of Eve;
I've one in store, which, for your smiles, I'll give.

    Oh list! A tale it is, not very common,
Our poet of tonight, in faith's a—woman!
A woman, too, untutored in the school,
Nor Aristotle knows, nor scarce a rule
By which fine writers fabricate their plays,
From sage Menanders,[6] to these modern days;
How she could venture here I am astonished!
But, 'twas in vain the madcap I admonished;
Told her of squeaking cat-calls, hisses, groans,
Off-offs, and ruthless critics' damning moans.
I'm undismayed, she cried; critics are men,
And smile on folly from a woman's pen.
Then, 'tis the ladies' cause; there I'm secure.
Let him who hisses no soft nymph endure;
May he who frowns, be frowned on by his goddess,
From pearls, and brussel's-point[7] to maids in bodice.

    Now, for a hint of her intended feast:
'Tis rural, playful—harmless 'tis at least;
Not over-stocked with repartee or wit,
Though, here and there, *perchance* there is a hit.
For, she ne'er played with bright Apollo's[8] fire,
No muse invoked, or heard th'Aönian[9] lyre;
Her comic muse—a little blue-eyed maid,
With cheeks where innocence and health's displayed,
Her 'Pol[10]—in petticoats—a romping boy,

---

6   Athenian playwright *c.* 341-290 BCE; most celebrated writer of New Comedy.
7   Delicate and expensive lace made in Brussels.
8   Phoebus Apollo, Greek god of poetry and associated with the sun.
9   Part of ancient Boeotia, sacred to the muses.
10   Apollo; in the 1813 version of the prologue, the line reads "In lieu of Phoebus—but a romping boy."

Whose taste is trap-ball,[11] and a kite his joy;
Her nursery, the study, where she thought,
Framed fable, incident, surprise, and plot.
From the surrounding hints, she caught her plan
Lengthening the chain from infancy to man:
Tom plagues poor Fan; she sobs, but loves him still;
Kate aims her wit at both, with roguish skill.
Our painter marked those lines, which nature drew;
Her fancy glowed, and colored them—for you.
A mother's pencil gave the light and shades;
A mother's eye through each soft scene pervades.
Her children rose before her flattered view;
Hope stretched the canvas, whilst her wishes drew!
    We'll now present you drapery and features,
And warmly hope you'll like the pretty creatures;
Then Tom shall have his kite, and Fan new dollies,
Till time matures them for *important* follies!

ACT I

Scene: A garden

Bella and Harriet. Enter George.

GEORGE. Oh, for the luxury of nightgown and slippers! No jaded hack of
    Parnassus can be more tired than I am—the roads so dusty, and the
    sun so hot. 'Twould be less intolerable riding post[12] in Africa.
BELLA. What a wild imagination! But in the name of Fortune, why are
    you alone? What have you done with all the college youths? This is the
    first vacation you ever came home unaccompanied, and I assure you
    we are quite disappointed.
GEORGE. Oh, most unconscionable woman! Never to be satisfied with
    conquest—there's poor Lumley shot through by your wicked eyes.
BELLA. A notable victory indeed! However, his name serves to make
    a figure in the lists of one's conquests, and so you may give him just
    hope enough to feed his sighs—but not to encourage his presumption.

---

11   Old game involving a ball, trap (pivoted wooden instrument) and bat.
12   With speed, haste.

GEORGE. Paragon of generosity! And what portion of comfort will your ladyship bestow on Egerton and Filmer, who still hug the chains of the resistless Arabella?

BELLA. Upon my word, your catalog grows interesting—'tis worthwhile now to enquire for your vouchers. Proofs, George, proofs.

GEORGE. Why, the first writes sonnets in your praise, and the last toasts you till he can't see.

BELLA. Oh, excellent! The Dulcinea[13] of one—and Circe[14] of the other—ha! ha!—to transform him into a beast. I hope you have better love-tokens for the blushing Harriet. How does—

HARRIET. Fie, Bella—you use me ill.

GEORGE. Why, sister, you plead guilty, before the charge is exhibited. But tell me, my sweet Harriet, who is this favored mortal, of whom you mean to enquire?

HARRIET. Indeed, brother, I have no enquiries to make, but I imagine my cousin can inform you whom she meant.

BELLA. Oh, doubtless—but you look so offended, Harriet, that I dare not venture the enquiry. Ask for Sir Charles Seymour yourself.

GEORGE. (*Aside.*) Seymour! Ho, ho! Very fine truly!—If Seymour be the man, my sister, set your heart at rest: he is on the point of marriage, *if I am not mistaken*, with a fine blooming girl, not more than eighteen. Soft dove-like eyes, pouting lips, teeth that were, doubtless, made of oriental pearl, a neck—I want a simile now—ivory, wax, alabaster! No, they won't do.

HARRIET. (*With an air of pique.*) One would imagine, brother, you were drawing the picture of your own mistress, instead of Sir Charles's, your colors are so warm.

GEORGE. A fine woman, Harriet, gives warmth to all around her. She is that universal spirit, about which philosophers talk: the true point of attraction that governs nature, and controls the universe of man.

BELLA. Hey day, George! Did the charms of Lady Dinah inspire this rhapsody?

GEORGE. Charms! What, of that antiquated, sententious, delicate lady, who blessed us with her long speeches at dinner?

BELLA. You must learn to be more respectful in your epithets, sir; for that sententious, delicate lady designs you the honor of becoming your mother.

---

13   The name Don Quixote gives to the mistress of his imagination.
14   Enchantress from the island of Aeaea, who turned Odysseus's men into swine.

GEORGE. My mother! Heaven forfend[15]—you jest, surely.

BELLA. You shall judge. We met her in our late visit to Bath. She renewed her acquaintance with your father, with whom, in Mrs. Hargrave's lifetime, she had been intimate. He invited her to return with us, and she has been here this month; they are frequently closeted together. She has *forty thousand pounds*, and is sister to an Irish peer.

GEORGE. She might have been grandmother to the peer, by the days she has numbered—but her excessive propriety and decorum overcome me. How can they agree with my father's vociferation, October,[16] and hounds?

BELLA. Oh, I assure you, wondrously well: she kisses Jowler, takes Ringwood on her lap, and has, more than once, sipped out of your father's tankard—delicacies, cousin, are easily made to give way, when we have certain ends to answer.

GEORGE. Very true, and beware of that period, when delicacies *must* give way—tremble at the hour, Bella, when you'll rise from the labors of your toilette with no end in view, but the conquest of some Quixote gallant in his grand climacteric,[17] on whom you'll squander more encouraging glances, than all the sighs and ardor of two and twenty can extort from you now.

BELLA. *Memento mori!*[18] Quite a college compliment: you ought rather to have supposed that my power will increase, and that, like Ninon,[19] I might give myself the airs of eighteen at eighty—but here's John coming to summon us to coffee. Harriet!

GEORGE. Come, Harriet—why that pensive air? Give me your hand.

HARRIET. Excuse me—I'll only step and look at my birds, and follow you instantly. (*Exeunt George and Bella playfully.*) —"Set your heart at rest, my sister." Oh, brother! You have robbed that heart of rest forever. Cruel intelligence! Something has long sat heavy in my bosom—and now the weight is irremovable. Perfidious Seymour! Yet, of what can I accuse him? He never professed to love me. Oh yes, his ardent looks, his sighs, his confusion, his respectful attentions, have a thousand times professed the strongest passion. Surely, a man cannot, in honor, be exculpated, who by such methods defrauds a woman of her heart; even though the *word* "love" should never pass his lips. Yet I ought not

---

15   Forbid.
16   A strong ale traditionally brewed in October.
17   "A year of life, often reckoned as the 63rd, supposed to be especially critical" (OED).
18   A reminder of mortality; literally "Remember to die" (Latin).
19   Anne "Ninon" de l'Enclos (1620-1705), French author and courtesan celebrated for her wit and beauty.

to have trusted these seeming proofs. No! I must only blame my credulity. Oh partial Nature! Why have you given us hearts so replete with tenderness, and minds so weak, so yielding? [*Exit.*]

Scene: A garden parlor.

Enter George and Bella at the garden door; Bella seating herself at a tea table.

BELLA. Hang this Lady Dinah—one's forced to be so dressed, and so formal! In the country we should be all shepherds and shepherd-esses: meadows, ditches, rooks, and court manners, are the strangest combination!

GEORGE. Hist—she's in the hall, I see. I'll go and 'squire her in.

Exit George, and returns with Lady Dinah.

LADY DINAH. To you, sir, who have been so long conversant with the fine manners of the Ancients, the frivolous custom of tea drinking must appear ridiculous.

GEORGE. No custom can be ridiculous, madam, that gives us the society of the ladies. The young men of those days deserve your ladyship's pity, for having never tasted these elegant hours.

LADY DINAH. (*Aside.*) He is just what his father described.

Enter Mr. Hargrave [and a servant].

MR. HARGRAVE. No! Barbary Bess is spavined.[20] Let her be taken care of; I'll have Longshanks, and see that he's saddled by five. [*Exit servant.*] —So we sha'n't have you in the hunt tomorrow, George: you must have more time to shake off the lazy rust of Cambridge, I suppose. What sort of hours d'ye keep at college?

GEORGE. Oh, sir, we are frequently up before the sun, there.

MR. HARGRAVE. Hah! Then 'tis when you ha'n't been in bed all night, I believe. And how do you stand in other matters? Have the musty old dons tired you with their Greek, and their geometry, and their learned experiments to show what air, and fire, and water are made of? Ha! ha! ha!

BELLA. Oh, no, sir—he never studied them closely enough to be tired. His philosophy and mine keep pretty equal pace, I believe.

---

20   Lame.

GEORGE. As usual, my lively cousin. If you had said my philosophy and your coquetry, I should have thought you had meant to compliment me. However, sir, I am not tired of my studies—though Bella has not exactly hit the reason.

LADY DINAH. (*To Mr. Hargrave.*) The muses, sir, sufficiently recompense the most painful assiduities by which we obtain their favor. Their *true* lovers are never satiated with the pleasures they bestow. Those, indeed, who court them, like the toasts of the season, *because* it is the fashion, are neither warmed by their beauties, nor penetrated with their charms. But these are faithless knights; your son, I dare say, has enlisted himself among their sincerest votaries.

GEORGE. You do me great honor, madam—I have no doubt but you are perfectly acquainted with the muses. They shed their favors on a few only—but those who share them must, like you, be irresistible.—I'll catch her ladyship's style (*aside*).

MR. HARGRAVE. (*Aside.*) Humph—I am glad he likes her.

LADY DINAH. You men are so full of flattery! In Athens, in Lacedemon,[21] that vice was for ages unknown—it was then the Athenians were the happiest, and the Lacedemonians the—

BELLA. Oh mercy!—I have burnt my fingers in the most terrible manner. (*Enter Harriet from the garden.*) —I wish the misfortune had happened to her ladyship's tongue (*aside*).

HARRIET. Dear Bella, I am quite concerned.

BELLA. Pho!—I only meant to break in upon her harangue, there's no bearing so much wisdom [*aside*].

Enter servant.

SERVANT. Mr. Drummond!

Enter Mr. Drummond.

MR. DRUMMOND. *Benedicite!*[22] Ah! My dear godson! Why, this is an unexpected pleasure—I did not know you were arrived.

GEORGE. I have had that happiness only a few hours, sir, and I was on the point of paying my devoirs[23] to you at The Park.

---

21   Sparta.
22   Bless us! (Latin).
23   Dutiful respects.

MR. DRUMMOND. Ungracious rogue! A few hours, and not been with
me yet! However—stay where you are, stay where you are, George:
you cannot come under my roof with safety now, I assure you. Such a
pair of eyes, such a bloom, such a shape! Ah girls, girls!

HARRIET. Dear Mr. Drummond, of what, or whom, are you talking? You
make me quite jealous.

MR. DRUMMOND. Oh! You are all outdone, eclipsed—you have no
chance with my *Incognita*.24 Then she has the prettiest foot and moves
a grace!

BELLA. Teasing creature!

MR. DRUMMOND. Pretty Bella! Well, it shall be satisfied. Mr. Hargrave,
I wait on you, sir, to request an apartment for a young lady of beauty,
and honor, who hath put herself under my protection. But as I really
think my house a dangerous situation for her, considering that I am
single, young, and handsome (*stroking his face*), I cannot in conscience
expose her to it. You, being a grave, orderly man, and having a couple
of decent, well-behaved young women for a daughter and niece, I
think she will be more agreeably protected here—and this is my
business.

MR. HARGRAVE. A young lady who hath put herself under your protection! Who is she?

MR. DRUMMOND. Her name she wishes to conceal.

MR. HARGRAVE. That's very odd. Where did you meet with her?

MR. DRUMMOND. At the house of a widow tenant of mine, a few miles
from hence, where she had taken refuge from a marriage to which an
uncle would have forced her. She had no companion but the good old
lady, whom I found employed in assisting her to weep, instead of con-
soling her. In short, there were *reasons* to think her situation highly
dangerous, and I prevailed on her to leave it.

MR. HARGRAVE. And so your credulity is again taken in, and the air of a
weeping beauty is the trap that caught you? Ha, ha! ha! Will you never
be sick of impositions?

MR. DRUMMOND. I don't remember that I was ever imposed on.

MR. HARGRAVE. No! Don't I know how many people you have plagued
yourself about, who had not a grain of merit to deserve it?

MR. DRUMMOND. I want *merit* Mr. Hargrave; yet all the blessings of
health and fortune have not been withheld from me.

MR. HARGRAVE. Aye, aye—there's no getting you to hear reason on this
subject.

---

24   My "Unknown" or disguised woman.

MR. DRUMMOND. 'Tis too late to reason now. The young lady is at my house. I have promised to bring her here, and we must endeavor to raise the poor girl's spirits. She would have spoiled the prettiest face in England—beg pardon, ladies—*one* of the prettiest faces, with weeping at the old widow's.

BELLA. An old widow, a pretty girl, a lover, a tyrannical uncle—'tis a charming group for the amusement of a village circle.—I long to see this beauty.

LADY DINAH. Her beauty, according to Mr. Drummond, may be conspicuous enough—but her pretensions to *birth* and *honor* seem to be a more doubtful matter.

GEORGE. Pardon me, madam, why should we doubt of either? A lady in such a situation has a right to protection; (*to his father*) and I hope, sir, you will not withhold yours.

MR. HARGRAVE. Oh, no, to be sure, George. S'bud! Refuse protection to a fine girl! 'Twould be, with you, a crying sin, I warrant—but Mr. Drummond, I should suppose—

MR. DRUMMOND. Come, be satisfied! The weaknesses with which you reproach me, might have induced me to have snatched her from an alarming situation without much examination. But, in compliment to your delicacy, I have made proper enquiries. She was placed under the care of Mrs. Carlton by a person of credit. She has dispatched a messenger to her uncle, who, I presume, will be here tomorrow.

HARRIET. Pray, sir, permit us to wait on the lady, and conduct her here; I am strongly interested for her.

MR. HARGRAVE. 'Tis an odd affair—what say you to it, my lady?

LADY DINAH. As your family seem desirous to receive her, sir, I am sorry to perceive an impropriety in the request—but I should apprehend that any appearance of encouragement to young ladies in *disobedience*—particularly when accompanied with the glaring indecorum of an elopement—

MR. HARGRAVE. Aye, very true! S'bud, Mr. Drummond, how can you encourage such—

MR. DRUMMOND. Madam, I do not mean to encourage, but to restore the young lady to her family. She seems terrified at the peculiar severity of her uncle's temper; so we'll put ourselves in form, receive him in full assembly, and divide his anger amongst us. Your ladyship, I'm sure, must be happy to render the recovery of the *first false step* as easy as possible.

MR. HARGRAVE. Why aye, my lady—there can be no harm in that, you know.

LADY DINAH. Very well, sir—if you think so, I can have no farther objection.

MR. HARGRAVE. Well then, Harriet, you may go—I think.

BELLA. And I with you, cousin.

MR. DRUMMOND. Come then, my pretty doves—I'll escort you. George, steel your heart, steel your heart, you rogue. (*Exeunt [Mr. Drummond, Bella and Harriet].*)

GEORGE. It is steeled, sir.

MR. HARGRAVE. *You* need not go, George—I want to speak to you.

LADY DINAH. (*Aside.*) Bless me! What does he intend to say now? He's going to open the affair to his son. Well, these are the most awkward moments in a woman's life, but one must go through it.—I have letters to write, which I'll take this leisure to do, if you'll pardon my absence, gentlemen.

MR. HARGRAVE. (*Both bowing.*) To be sure, madam. (*Exit Lady Dinah.*)— Well, George, how do you like that lady?

GEORGE. *Extravagantly*, sir—I never saw a lady so learned.

MR. HARGRAVE. Oh, she's clever—she's an earl's sister too, and a forty thousand pounder, boy.

GEORGE. That's a fine fortune.

MR. HARGRAVE. Aye, very fine, very fine—and then her interest! Suppose I could prevail with her, eh, George. If one could keep her in the family, I say—would not that be a stroke?

GEORGE. An alliance with so noble a family, sir, is certainly a desirable circumstance.

Enter servant.

SERVANT. The gentlemen are in the smoking parlor, sir.

MR. HARGRAVE. Very well—are the pipes and October in readiness?

SERVANT. Yes, sir. (*Exit.*)

MR. HARGRAVE. Well then, we'll talk over the affair tomorrow. What—I suppose your stomach is too squeamish for tobacco and strong beer? You'll find the Justice, and some more of your old friends there.

GEORGE. Pardon me, sir, I have made too free with the bottle at dinner, and have felt the effects in my head ever since—I believe a turn in the garden is a better recipe than the fumes of tobacco.

MR. HARGRAVE. Well, well, we won't dispute the matter with you now, boy—but you know I don't like milksops.

GEORGE. (*Smiling.*) Nor I, sir. (*Bows and exit.*)

MR. HARGRAVE. Aye, aye, George is a brave boy—Old England is disgraced by a set of whipsters who affect to despise the jolly manners of their ancestors, while they only serve to show us, how greatly manners may be *altered* without being *mended*— (*Enter Justice.*) S'bud, I don't know that we are a bit wiser, happier, or greater, than we were in good old Bess's days[25]—when our men of rank were robust, and our women of fashion buxom.

JUSTICE. Aye, aye, a plague on all the innovations that tend to produce a race of *pretty fellows* instead of *Englishmen*—and puny girls, for the mothers of heroes. Give me a rosy buxom lass, with eyes that sparkle like the glasses we toast her in. Adod, I'd drink her health till the world danced round like a top. But, what a plague, 'squire, d'ye stay here for? Come into t'other room, and if you have a mind to make wise speeches there, we can drink in the meantime, and *then* what you say will have a proper effect.

MR. HARGRAVE. Well, well, I'll go, but I want to consult you—I have been thinking whether this Greenwood estate—

JUSTICE. Tush! You know very well, I can neither consider or advise, till I have had my brace; I am as dark, till the liquor sends its spirits into my brains, as a lantern without its candle—so, if you've any knotty point to propose, keep it till I'm enlightened.

MR. HARGRAVE. Well, come along. (*Going.*)

Enter Clerk.

CLERK. The people from the Crown, sir, and the Rose, and the Antelope, are here again about their licenses.

JUSTICE. (*To Mr. Hargrave.*) There, this is what I got by coming for you—I charged the butler not to let this dog in. (*To the Clerk.*) Why, how can I help it? Bid 'em come again tomorrow; 'tis of no consequence.

CLERK. And here's a pauper to be passed—a lame man with four children.

HARGRAVE. Well, turn him over to the cook, and let him wait till we are at leisure.

CLERK. And a constable has brought up a man, for breaking into farmer Thompson's barn last night.

---

25   The time of Queen Elizabeth I.

JUSTICE. (*Seeming irresolute.*) Has he? Well, tell *him* to wait too—we are going to be busy now, and can't be disturbed. But bid him take care he doesn't let the prisoner escape, as he did that dog Farlow, d'ye hear?

CLERK. Yes, sir—but—Justice Manly is now in the smoking room. I've spoken to him about the licenses, and we may'nt have another bench this—

JUSTICE. Will you please to march, sir? (*Exit Clerk.*)

MR. HARGRAVE. Well done, old boy. Burn himself[26] could not have dispatched business with more expedition. (*Going.*)

Enter servant.

SERVANT. The miller is here, sir, with a man that he cotched[27] with a hare that he had taken in the springe[28]—but the poor fellow, please your Honor, has a large family.

Hargrave and the Justice return.

MR. HARGRAVE. What! A hare. Come along, Justice. (*Exit another way.*)

A burst of laughter from the smoking room—the Justice looks wistfully back, and then follows Mr. Hargrave.

Scene: The garden.

Enter George reading.

GEORGE. Here's a special fellow of a philosopher now—would persuade that pleasure has no existence, when bounteous nature teems with her. She courts my senses in a thousand varied modes. She possesses herself of my understanding in the shape of reason—and she seizes my heart in the form of woman, dear, beauteous, all-subduing woman. And there is one—memory, be faithful to her charms! Show me the beauteous form, the animated face, the mind that beamed in her eyes, the blushing smile that repaid my admiration, and raised an altar in my heart, on which every other passion is sacrificed—on which every hope, desire, and wish, is sanctified by her.

---

26   Richard Burn (1709-85), legal writer and Church of England clergyman; his two-volume *The Justice of the Peace and Parish Officer* (1755) became a classic of its time.

27   Caught.

28   Snare for small game.

Enter Bella.

BELLA. Oh, monstrous! George Hargrave moralizing in the garden, whilst the finest girl in England is in the parlor! What is become of your gallantry?

GEORGE. Gone, sweet cousin, gone.

BELLA. Indeed! Who has robbed you of it?

GEORGE. A woman.

BELLA. Come then, and regain it from a woman, and such a woman—

GEORGE. Is she so beautiful?

BELLA. Beautiful! Look at me; I myself am not so handsome.

GEORGE. Ha! ha! ha! That, I confess, is an infallible criterion. But I'll bet this whole volume of wisdom against one of your billet-doux, that she's not within fifty degrees of her who witched away my heart.

BELLA. Witched it, indeed, if in six weeks it has not made one excursion. I never knew you so constant before. However, I prophesy *her* charm is broke; the divinity who will reign—perhaps for another six weeks—is coming down the steps with Harriet. But, that her rays may not dazzle your mortal sight, shelter yourself behind the clump, and examine her. (*George goes and returns.*) Well, how d'ye like her?

GEORGE. Like her! The air is all ambrosia—every happy constellation is in conjunction; each bounteous star has lent its influence; and Venus guided the event.

BELLA. Heyday! What event? Sure this cannot be your masquerade lady!

GEORGE. It is, it is. She is the sweet thief. She is my wood nymph. Oh, I am transported!

BELLA. And I—amazed! How can it—

GEORGE. No matter how, whether by chance or witchcraft. Now could I apostrophize—pshaw—away, and at her feet—these transports— (*Going.*)

Enter Mr. Drummond.

MR. DRUMMOND. So, so, so—and, pray, what's the cause of these transports?

GEORGE. You are the cause—'tis to you, my dear Mr. Drummond, I am indebted for the happiness which dawns on me.

MR. DRUMMOND. Then, God grant, my dear boy, the dawn may not deceive thee—I wish it to brighten into the fairest day. But how have I been instrumental to all this?

GEORGE. That lady I have seen before at a masquerade. She possessed herself of my heart at once, but I despaired of ever beholding her again. Pray present me— (*Going.*)

MR. DRUMMOND. Hold, George, hold—perhaps you'd better never be presented; for, though you may have put her in possession of your heart, 'tis by no means an evidence, that she has had the same complaisance for you. Suppose, for instance, such a trifle as *hers* being engaged.

BELLA. Oh unconscionable! To fancy the galloping imagination of a man in love, capable of so *reasonable* a supposition! But, pray have so much decency, George, to postpone your *entrée* till you are more composed. I'll go, and prepare her for the reception of a strange creature that you may appear to advantage. (*Exit.*)

GEORGE. Advantage! Oh, I will hope every advantage from so fortunate a chance. Her heart cannot—shall not—be engaged; and she shall be mine. Pardon, my dear sir, these effusions of my joy.

MR. DRUMMOND. I do pardon them—'tis an odd circumstance. Are you acquainted with the lady's name?

GEORGE. No one knew her. She seemed like an angel descended to astonish her beholders, and vanish the moment she had fixed their hearts. Unluckily Mrs. Fitzherbert stopped me, and a jealous coxcomb in her train seized that moment, to hurry her out of the room.

MR. DRUMMOND. That misfortune, perhaps, I can repair—but you seem so extravagantly disposed to raptures, that I hardly dare tell you I know something of her family.

GEORGE. I am rejoiced, for I am convinced you know nothing that will not justify my passion.

MR. DRUMMOND. This eagerness to *believe* might have been so fatal, that I tremble for you. But you are fortunate: she is the daughter of a deceased Major Morley, a man to whose friendship and elegance of manners I was indebted for happy and rational hours, amidst the bustle of a camp.

GEORGE. Fortunate indeed! For then my passion must have *your* sanction. But I thought you had not known—

MR. DRUMMOND. I knew her father's picture on her arm,[29] but her delicacy is so alarmed at the idea of exposing the name of her family

---

29   Miniature portrait; Cowley's friend, Richard Cosway, became the most celebrated miniaturist of the eighteenth century.

in such a situation, that she would not consent to be introduced here, but on condition of its being concealed.

GEORGE. Charming delicacy! I will keep her secret. My only consolation was, that such a woman could not be long concealed, and it would have been the business of my life till I had discovered her.

But[30] your goodness has brought about the event—your goodness to which I owe more than—

MR. DRUMMOND. Nay, stop your acknowledgments, and don't arrogate to your own merits the affection I have for you; for, transcendent as without doubt they are, you owe great part of it to circumstances, in which they have very little concern.

GEORGE. I am contented to hold your esteem by any tie.—But, dear sir, the lady—

MR. DRUMMOND. Impatient rogue! Well, come, I'll introduce you, and may the moment be auspicious! (*Exit.*)

GEORGE. May it! Oh Love, sweet tyrant! I yield my heart to thee a willing slave—to Love I devote my future life. Never more shall I experience the aching void of indifference, or know one moment unoccupied by thee. (*Exit.*)

ACT II

Scene: A court before the house.

Enter a hunt. A flourish of horns.

[ALL.] Hollo! Hollo! Ye hoicks, Hargrave, ille, ille, hoa.

FIRST HUNTER. Zounds, 'tis almost seven (*looking at his watch*); the scent will be cold. Let's rouse the lazy rogue with a song.

SECOND HUNTER. Aye, a good thought. Come begin.

Song.

Arouse, and break the bands of sleep;
Blush, idler, blush, such hours to keep.

---

30   Gray text in the play is omitted at the theater.

Somnus![31] What bliss canst thou bestow,
Equal to that which hunters know,
Whether the mountains they attain,
Or swiftly dart across the plain?
Somnus! What joys canst thou bestow,
Equal to those which hunters know?
Hark through the wood, how our music resounds!
The horns re-echoed, more sweet by the hounds.
Deep-throated and clear,
Our spirits they cheer;
They give us such glee,
No danger we see,
But follow with pleasure:
'Tis joy beyond measure
To be the first in at the death—at the death,
To be, &c.

Enter George from the house.

FIRST GENTLEMAN. Hah, my young Hercules! But how now, in this
  dress! Don't you hunt with us?
GEORGE. Oh, I have only changed liveries: I used to wear that of
  Adonis[32] but now I serve his mistress, Venus.[33]
SECOND GENTLEMAN. And a most hazardous service you have chosen.
  I would rather subject myself to the fate of Acteon,[34] than to the
  caprice and insolence of the handsomest coquette[35] in England.
GEORGE. Acteon's fate would be less than you'd deserve, if, knowing my
  goddess, you should dare profane her with such epithets.
SECOND GENTLEMAN. May I never start puss, if I believe your goddess to
  be more than a very woman; that is, a being whose soul is vanity, taste
  voluptuousness, form deceitful, and manners unnatural.
GEORGE. Heyday! Turned satirist on the sex at eight and twenty! What
  jilting Blowsalind[36] has worked this miracle?

---

31   Sleep!
32   Beautiful young hunter in Greek mythology.
33   Adonis's lover, the goddess of love (Roman equivalent of Aphrodite).
34   After incurring the wrath of Artemis, Greek goddess of the hunt, Acteon was turned
into a stag and torn apart by his own hounds.
35   Flirt.
36   Poetical character who jilted her lover, Strephon. He is also mentioned in *The
Emperor of the Moon*: see above, p. 97.

SECOND GENTLEMAN. Faith, I take my copies from higher schools. Amongst the Blowsalinds there is still nature and honesty, but examine our drawing rooms, operas, and water-drinking places—you'll find the first turned fairly out of doors, and the last exchanged for affectation and hypocrisy. So henceforward (*smacking his whip*) I abandon all ladies, but those of the woods, and chase only the harmless game, to which my sagacious hounds conduct me. (*Exit*).

GEORGE. Ha! ha! And in a short time be fit society for your hounds only. Good morning, sir.

Enter Mr. Hargrave and the Justice.

MR. HARGRAVE. So, George, come; you'd better mount. I'll give you a lecture upon air, and the advantages of a good constitution, on our downs, worth all you could hear in a musty college these fifty years.

GEORGE. I beg, sir, to be excused this morning; tomorrow I'll resume my usual post, and lead where you only will venture to follow me.

MR. HARGRAVE. Well, we shall put you to the test. (*Exit.*)

JUSTICE. (*To George.*) Yes, yes, you're a keen sportsman. I saw the game you are in pursuit of, scudding away to the garden. Beat the bushes, and I'll warrant you'll start her, and run her down too.

THIRD GENTLEMAN. Egad! I started a fine young puss a few days ago. She seemed shy, and made her doublings. But I stuck to the scent, and should infallibly have got her, if that poaching rogue, Drummond, had not laid a springe in her way.

JUSTICE. Why, she's the very puss I mean; he housed her here. (*Exit.*)

THIRD GENTLEMAN. Oh, ho! Then I suppose he only pointed the game for you. Sweet sir, your humble—. After college commons, a coarser dish than pheasant, I think, might have gone down.

GEORGE. Your whip, sir—your bit wants lashing. To talk thus of Mr. Drummond, whom you *do* know, is not more insolent than your profanation of a lady whom you do *not* know.

THIRD GENTLEMAN. Oh! Cry you mercy. Plague take me if I quarrel for any wench in England. You are heartily welcome for her, sir; only I hope another time you'll be honest, and hunt without a stalking horse. (*Exit.*)

GEORGE. Barbarian! How critically did Mr. Drummond relieve the lovely girl. This brute had discovered her, and she would have suffered every

indignity that ignorance, supported by the pride of fortune, could
have inflicted. In the garden—that's fortunate beyond my expectations—'midst groves and fountains, the very scene where a lover
should tell his tale. And the sweet consciousness, which beamed in her
eyes last night, flatters me that she will not *hate* me for my tale. I'll go,
in all the confidence of hope. (*Exit.*)

Scene: The garden.

Enter Emily.

EMILY. What an heavenly morning! Surely 'tis in *England* that summer
keeps her court, for she's nowhere else so lovely. And what a sweet
garden this is! But tell me, my heart, is it the brightness of the morning, the verdure of the garden, the melody of the birds, that gives thee
these enchanting sensations? Ah, no! It is that thou hast found thy
lord. It is, that I have again seen the man, who, since I first beheld
him, has been the only image in my mind. How different from the
empty, the presuming Baldwin. Yet, I owe *him* this obligation: if his
hateful perseverance had not forced me from London, I might never
have seen, but once, the man, who, *that once*, possessed himself of my
tenderest wishes. Ha! (*Starting.*)

Enter George.

GEORGE. Abroad so early, madam! The fine ladies in London are yet in
their first sleep.
EMILY. It would have been impossible to have resisted the cheerful call
of the hunters, if the morning had been less enticing.
GEORGE. Oh, do not imagine yourself obliged to the hunters, madam; it
was my good genius[37]—I thank her—that inspired them, and did me
the favor to lead me here.

EMILY. If she usually influences you to no better purpose, her claims to
your gratitude are but weak.
GEORGE. Till lately I thought so, and supposed myself influenced by
the worst genius that ever fell to the lot of a poor mortal. But she has
entirely retrieved herself in my opinion, and by two or three capital

---

37   Personal protective god or attendant spirit.

strokes has made me forget her unlucky pranks, and believe her one of the best disposed sylphs[38] in all the regions of Fancy.

EMILY. (*Smiling.*) You recommend this aerial attendant very strongly. Have you any intention to part from her?

GEORGE. I would willingly exchange her—if your genius would be so obliging to take a fancy to me. I'll accept her with all my heart—and give you mine.

EMILY. You would lose by the exchange.

GEORGE. Impossible! For my quondam[39] friend would say a thousand things for me, that I could not for myself—so I should gain your good opinion, and that would be *well gained*, whatever I might lose to attain it.

EMILY. Your genius is, at least, a gallant one, I perceive, but I was on the point of leaving the garden, sir.

—The ladies, I imagine, are risen by this time.

GEORGE. Indeed they are not, but if they should—these are precious moments, which I must not lose. May I presume to use them in telling you how happy I am, in the event which placed you in my father's house? But you have, perhaps, forgot the presumptuous Tancred,[40] who gave such disturbance to the gentleman honored by protecting you, at the masquerade?

EMILY. No, sir, I remember—and if I don't mistake, you were nearly engaged in a *fracas* with that gentleman. I was happy, when I observed you stopped by a mask, and seized that moment to leave the room.

GEORGE. A moment, madam, that I have never ceased to regret till now. But *that* which I at present possess, is a felicity so unexpected, and unhoped for—

EMILY. You forget, sir, these gallantries are out of place here. Under a mask, a shepherd may sigh, or an eastern prince amuse himself in saying the most extravagant things, but they know there are delicacies to be observed in real life, quite incompatible with the freedoms of a masquerade.

---

38   Spirits supposed to inhabit the air. See also Charmante's explanation in *The Emperor of the Moon* above, p. 47.

39   Former.

40   In James Thomson's tragedy *Tancred and Sigismunda* (1745), Tancred is the passionate lover of Sigismunda, who despaired when she was tricked into marrying someone else.

GEORGE. Whilst you are thus severe on mere gallantries, I will venture to hope that a most tender and respectful passion will be treated more favorably.

EMILY. Sir!

GEORGE. I comprehend, madam, what your delicacy must feel, and will therefore only add, that from the first moment I beheld you, my heart has known no other object. *You* have been the mistress of its wishes, and you *are* the mistress of its fate.

EMILY. (*Hesitatingly.*) Indeed, sir, this declaration, at a time when I must appear in so strange a light to your family, hurts me greatly. I can scarcely believe you mean it a compliment. But, surely, my situation here ought—

GEORGE. I acknowledge, madam, the confession I have dared to make, is premature; it is ill-timed. Nothing can excuse it but the peculiarity of our situation. When I reflect that in a few minutes your uncle may arrive, that he may snatch you from us, and that such an opportunity never may be mine again—

Enter Mr. Drummond.

MR. DRUMMOND. So, so, my young ones; have I found you? 'Tis a most delicious morning. But is it usual with you, madam, to take the air so early?

EMILY. Yes, sir! In the country, at least, I seldom murder such hours in sleep.

MR. DRUMMOND. Aye, 'tis to that practice you are indebted to the roses in your cheeks. What, I suppose, you brought the lady into the garden, George, to read her a lecture on vegetation, to explain the nature and cause of heat, or, perhaps, more abstracted subjects have engaged—

GEORGE. Stop, dear sir! I assure you I am not abstracted enough to enter on these subjects with such an object before me. I found the lady here, and had scarcely paid her my morning compliments when you appeared.

MR. DRUMMOND. For which you do not thank me, I presume—but come, madam, you are *my* ward till I have the pleasure of presenting you to your uncle, and I come to conduct you to breakfast. George, you may follow, but take care you keep your distance. (*Exeunt Mr. Drummond and Emily.*)

GEORGE. Distance! As well you might persuade the shadow to forsake its sun, or erring mortals give up hopes of mercy. With what sweet confidence she gives her hand to Mr. Drummond! If these are the privileges of age, I'll be young no longer. (*Exit.*)

Scene: Lady Dinah's dressing room.

Lady Dinah dressing; Susan attending.

LADY DINAH. Both in the garden—and in deep conversation!

SUSAN. It appeared so, my lady, as I saw them from the window; he looked eagerly in her face, and she blushed, and seemed confused.

LADY DINAH. Confused indeed! Yes, so the impertinent affected to appear last night, though it was evident she had neither eyes nor thoughts but for Mr. Hargrave's son, who paid her those attentions, which, from the present habits of life, are paid to *every* woman—though I think Mr. George Hargrave should be superior to these modern gallantries.

SUSAN. I dares to say she is some impostor. Husbands, in good truth, are not so plenty that a woman need run away to escape one.

LADY DINAH. I have no doubt of her being a low person, and as to her prettiness, 'tis of the kind one sees in wooden dolls: cherry-color cheeks and eyes that from the total absence of expression might be taken for glass.

SUSAN. I wonder Mr. Hargrave did not stand by his own opinion and let her stay where she was. But whatever Mr. Drummond says is law here.

LADY DINAH. Because Mr. Hargrave imagines he'll make his son his heir. But if he does, he'll only share with the paupers of the neighboring villages; for these Mr. Drummond seems to consider his family, and I am mistaken if he doesn't find it a pretty expensive one.

SUSAN. Oh, ma'am, he believes every melancholy tale that's told him as proof of his piety.—Here's the bow, my lady.—But as he fancies her prettiness was in danger, he had better have kept her in his own house and stood guard himself.

LADY DINAH. Aye, that employment or any other that would keep him at home might be useful. Want of rest (*looking in the glass*) absolutely transforms me. The detestable horns and their noisy accompaniment waked me from the most delightful dream. How do I look today, Susan?

SUSAN. Oh, charmingly, my lady.

LADY DINAH. 'Tis a most provoking circumstance, the color of my hair should be so soon changed, but Mrs. Gibson's liquid[41] entirely hides that accident, I believe.

---

41   Mrs. Gibson's "Innocent Liquid" was hair water or dye.

SUSAN. Entirely, my lady, and then her bloom; it is impossible to distinguish from nature.

LADY DINAH. You need not speak so loud. In compliance with the custom of modern times, a woman is forced to keep the use of these sort of things as secretly as she would an illegitimate birth. It was not so among the Ancients. The Roman ladies made a point of excelling in arts of this kind; and the empress Poppea[42] was not ashamed to carry in her train five hundred asses, in whose milk she bathed every morning for the benefit of her complexion.

SUSAN. Five hundred asses in one lady's train! Thank heaven we have no such engrossing now-a-days. *Our* toasts have all their full share.

LADY DINAH. Indeed! Mrs. Susan, (*half smiling*) this wench has ideas. Pray, what do you think of the young collegian?

SUSAN. Oh, my lady, he is the sweetest, smartest man—I think he is exactly like the picture of your ladyship's brother that died when he was eighteen.

LADY DINAH. People used to say *that* brother and myself bore a strong resemblance.

SUSAN. I dare say you did, my lady, for there's something in the turn of young Mr. Hargrave's face, vastly like your ladyship's. (*Laughing behind her.*)

LADY DINAH. Well, Susan, I believe I may trust you. I think you can be faithful.

SUSAN. Most surely, my lady. I would rather die than betray your ladyship.

LADY DINAH. Well, then—I protest I hardly know how to acknowledge it, but—

SUSAN. But what, my lady? Your ladyship alarms me.

LADY DINAH. I too am alarmed. But I know your faith— (*Sighs.*) There will soon be a most intimate and never to be dissolved connection between me—and—young Mr. Hargrave.

SUSAN. Young Mr. Hargrave, madam!

LADY DINAH. Yes, young Mr. Hargrave, madam. What dost stretch thy eyes so widely at, wench? Mr. George Hargrave, I say, is to be my husband. I am to be his wife. Is it past comprehension?

SUSAN. I most humbly beg your ladyship's pardon. It was my surprise: the whole house concludes your ladyship is to marry old Mr. Hargrave. But to be sure, the son is a much more suitable match for your ladyship.

---

42   Poppea Sabina (d. 65 CE), treacherous second wife of the emperor Nero.

LADY DINAH. Old Mr. Hargrave indeed! The whole house is very impertinent in its conclusions. Go and bring the Bergamot[43] hither. (*Exit Susan.*) I marry Old Mr. Hargrave! Monstrous absurdity! And by so preposterous an union to become the mother of that fine fellow, his son! 'Twould be insupportable. No, mistress Susan, 'tis young Mr. Hargrave I am to marry. (*Enter Susan with the Bergamot.*) Here, scent that handkerchief, while I write to my agent to prepare matters for the writings. (*Exit.*)

Susan alone, scenting the handkerchief.

SUSAN. To prepare matters for the writings! A very fine business indeed; and what you'll sorely repent of, my good lady, take my word for it. All those scented waters, nor any other waters, will be able to keep up your spirits this time twelvemonth. A "*never to be dissolved connection,*" between fifty and twenty-one. Ha! ha! ha! I shall burst with the ridiculous secret; I must find Jarvis, and give it vent—"never to be dissolved connection!" Ha! ha! ha!

Scene: An apartment.

Enter George, Harriet, and Bella.

BELLA. What transformations this Love can make! You look as grave, George, and speak as sententiously, as an Old Bailey[44] fortune teller.
GEORGE. And is it only to preserve your spirits, Bella, that you keep your heart so cold?
BELLA. The recipe is certainly not a bad one, if we may judge from the effects of the opposite element on *your* spirits, But, I advise you, whatever you do, not to assume an appearance of gravity—'tis the most dangerous character in the world.
GEORGE. How so?
BELLA. Oh, the advantages you would lose by it are inconceivable. Whilst you can sustain that of a giddy, thoughtless, undesigning, *great boy*, all the impertinent and foolish things you commit will be excused, laughed at—nay, if accompanied by a certain manner, they will be

---

43   Fragrant oil from the rind of fruit of the tree Citrus Bergamia.
44   London's central criminal court; Bella alludes facetiously to a judge pronouncing sentence.

applauded. But do the same things with a grave reflecting face, and an important air, and you'll be condemned, *nem. con.*[45]

Enter servant.

SERVANT. Sir Charles Seymour is driving up the avenue, sir. (*Exit.*)

GEORGE. Is he? I am rejoiced—

HARRIET. Sir Charles Seymour, brother? I thought you told us yesterday that he was on the point of marriage.

GEORGE. Well, my dear Harriet, and what then? Is his being on the point of marriage any reason why he should not be here? He is even now hastening to pay his devoirs to the lady. I left him yesterday at a friend's house on the road, and he promised to call on us in his way today. But I hear him— (*Exit.*)

BELLA. Harriet, you look quite pale. I had no conception that Sir Charles was of *serious* consequence to you.

HARRIET. My dear Bella, I am ashamed of myself. I'll go with you to your dressing room; I must not see him while I look so ridiculously. I dread my brother's raillery.

BELLA. Come then, hold by me. Deuce take it; what business have women with hearts? If I could influence the House,[46] handsome men should be shut out of society, till they grew harmless by becoming husbands! (*Exeunt.*)

Enter George and Sir Charles.

GEORGE. Ha! The birds are flown.

SIR CHARLES. Let us pursue 'em then.

GEORGE. Pho! They are not worth pursuing. Bella's a coquette and Harriet's in love.

SIR CHARLES. Harriet in love!

GEORGE. Aye, she's in for't, depend on't. But that's nothing. *I* have intelligence for the man. My Incognita's found; she's now in the house. My beauteous wood nymph!

SIR CHARLES. Miss Hargrave's heart another's!

GEORGE. Miss Hargrave's heart another's—why, my sister's heart is certainly engaged. But how's all this?

---

45   *Nemine contradicente*: with no one speaking against (Latin); unanimously.
46   I.e., Parliament.

SIR CHARLES. Oh, George! I love, I love your sister to distraction—dote on her.

GEORGE. A pretty time, for the mountain to give up its burthen truly! Why did you not tell me this before? If your heart had been as open to me, as mine has ever been to you, I might have served you. But now—

SIR CHARLES. Oh, reproach me not, but pity me. I love your sister—long have loved her.

GEORGE. And not entrust your love to *me*! You distrusted me, Charles, and you'll be *properly* punished.

SIR CHARLES. Severely am I punished—fool, fool, that I was, thus to have built a superstructure of happiness for all my life to come, that in one moment dissolves into air! I cannot see your sister; I must leave you.

GEORGE. Indeed, you shall not leave me, Seymour. On what grounds did you build your hopes, that you seem so greatly disappointed? Had my sister accepted your addresses?

SIR CHARLES. No, I never presumed to make her any. My fortune was so small, that I had no hopes of obtaining your father's consent, and therefore made it a point on honor not to endeavor to gain her affection.

GEORGE. (*Aside.*) Yes, yes, you took great care.

SIR CHARLES. But my uncle's death having removed every cause of fear on that head, I flattered myself I had nothing else to apprehend.

GEORGE. Courage, my friend, and your difficulties may vanish. 'Tis your humble distant lovers who have sung through every age of their scornful Phillises.[47] You never knew a bold fellow, who could love women without mistaking 'em for angels, whine about their cruelty.

SIR CHARLES. Do you not tell me your sister's heart is engaged? Then what have I to struggle for? It was her heart I wished to possess. Could Miss Hargrave be indelicate enough, which I am sure she could not, to bestow her hand on me without it, I would reject it.

GEORGE. Bravo! Nobly resolved! Keep it up by all means. Come now, I'll introduce you to one of the finest girls you ever saw in your life—but remember you are not to suffer your heart to be interested there, for that's my quarry, and death to the man who attempts to rob me of my prize!

---

47   Phyllis was the spurned lover of Demophon, the Athenian king, whose story is best known through Ovid and Callimachus.

SIR CHARLES. Oh, you are very secure, I assure you. My heart is ada-
mant from this moment. (*Exeunt.*)

Scene: The garden.

Enter Hargrave and a servant.

MR. HARGRAVE. Run and tell my son I want to speak to him here directly.
(*Exit servant.*) Her forty thousand pounds will just enable me to buy
the Greenwood Estate, and to my certain knowledge, that young
Rakehelly won't be able to keep it to his back much longer. We shall
then have more land than any family in the country, and a borough
of our own into the bargain. Humph! But suppose George should
not have a mind to marry her now? Why then—why then—as to his
mind, when two parties differ, the weaker must give way: the match is
for the advancement of your fortune, says I, and if it can't satisfy your
mind, you must teach it what I have always taught you—obedience.
(*Enter George.*) Oh, George, I sent for you into the garden, that we
might have no interruptions; for, as I was saying, there's an affair of
consequence I want to talk to you about.

GEORGE. I am all attention, sir.

MR. HARGRAVE. I don't design that you shall return to college any more.
I have other views, which I hope will not be disagreeable to you. You—
you like Lady Dinah, you say?

GEORGE. (*Hesitatingly.*) She is a lady of great erudition, without doubt.

MR. HARGRAVE. I don't know what your notions may be of her age; I
could wish her a few years younger, but—

GEORGE. Pardon me, sir, I think there can be no objection to her age,
and the preference her ladyship gives to our family is certainly a high
compliment.

MR. HARGRAVE. Ho, ho, then you are acquainted already with what I
was going to communicate to you; I am surprised at that.

GEORGE. Matrimonial negotiations, sir, are seldom long concealed; 'tis
a subject on which everybody is fond of talking—the young, in hopes
that their turn will come, and those who are older—

MR. HARGRAVE. By way of giving a fillip to their memories, I suppose
you mean, George, eh? Well, I am glad you are so merry; I was a little
uneasy about what you might think of this affair, though I never
mentioned it in my life. But perhaps Lady Dinah may have hinted it to
her woman, and then I should not wonder if the whole parish knew it.

However, you have no objection, and that's enough, though if you had,
   I must have my way, George.

GEORGE. Without doubt, sir.

MR. HARGRAVE. Have you spoken to Lady Dinah on the subject?

GEORGE. Spoke! N—o, sir; I could not think of addressing Lady Dinah
   on so delicate an affair without your permission.

MR. HARGRAVE. Well then, my dear boy, I would have you speak to her
   now, and, I think, the sooner the better.

GEORGE. To be sure, sir; I shall obey you—

MR. HARGRAVE. Well, you have set my heart at rest. I am as happy as
   a prince. I never fixed my mind on anything in my life, so much as I
   have done on this marriage, and it would have galled me sorely if you
   had been against it. But you are a good boy, George, a very good boy,
   and I'll go in and prepare Lady Dinah for your visit. (*Exit.*)

GEORGE. Why, my dear father, you are quite elated on the prospect of
   your nuptials, but why must *I* make speeches to Lady Dinah? I am
   totally ignorant of the mode that elderly gentlemen adopt on such
   occasions.

Enter Bella.

BELLA. What, have you been opening your heart to your father, George?

GEORGE. No, faith, he has been opening his to me. He has been making
   me the confidante of his passion for Lady Dinah.

BELLA. No! Ha!, ha, ha—is it possible? What style does he talk in? Is it
   flames and darts, or esteem and sentiment?

GEORGE. I don't imagine my good father thinks of either. Her fortune,
   I presume, is his object, and I shall not venture to hint an objection;
   for contradiction, you know, only lends him fresh ardor. Where is
   Seymour and Harriet?

BELLA. Your sister is in the drawing room, and Sir Charles I just now
   saw in the orange-walk, with his arms folded thus, and his eyes fixed
   on a shrub, in the most *penseroso*[48] style you can conceive. Why, he has
   no appearance of a happy youth on the verge of bridegroomism.

GEORGE. Ha, ha, ha, ha!

BELLA. Why do you laugh?

GEORGE. At the embarrassment I have thrown the simpletons into—ha,
   ha, ha!

---

48   Melancholic.

BELLA. What simpletons? What embarrassment?

GEORGE. That you cannot guess, my sweet cousin, with all your penetration.

BELLA. I shall expire, if you won't let me know it. Now do—pray, George—come, be pleased to tell it me (*curtsying*).

GEORGE. No, no, you look so pretty while you are coaxing, that I must, must see you in that humor a little longer.

BELLA. That's unkind. Come, tell me this secret, though I'll be hanged if I don't guess it.

GEORGE. Nay, then I must tell you, for if you should find it out, I shall lose the pleasure of obliging you. Seymour and my sister dote on one another, and I have made each believe that the other has different engagements.

BELLA. Oh, I am rejoiced to hear it.

GEORGE. Rejoiced! I assure you, I am highly offended.

BELLA. At what? Sir Charles is your friend, and every way an eligible match for your sister.

GEORGE. Very true; I am happy in their attachment, and therefore offended. Sir Charles has been as chary of his secret, as if I had not deserved his confidence.

BELLA. I believe he had never addressed your sister.

GEORGE. Aye, so he pretends, he never made love to her—ridiculous subterfuge! He stole into her heart by the help of those silent tender observances, which are the surest battery when there's time to play 'em off.[49] If any man had *thus* obtained my sister's heart, left her a prey to disappointment, and then said *he meant nothing*, my sword should have taught him, that his conduct was not less dishonorable, than if he had knelt at her feet, and sworn a million oaths.

BELLA. Why, this might be useful. But, mercy upon us! If every girl had such a snapdragon of a brother, no beau and very few pretty fellows would venture to come near her. Pray, when did you form this mischievous design?

GEORGE. Oh, Sir Charles has been heaping up the measure of his offences some time; 'twould have diverted you to have seen the tricks he played to get Harriet's picture. At last he begged it, to get the drapery copied for his sister's, and I know 'tis at this moment in his bosom, though he has sworn an hundred times 'tis still at the painter's.

---

49   I.e., the most effective weaponry when there's time to fire them.

BELLA. Ha! I'll fly and tell her the news. If I don't mistake, she'd rather have her picture there than in the Gallery of Beauties at Hampton.[50] (*Going.*)

GEORGE. S'death! Stop! Why are not you angry? Shut out by parchment provisoes from all the flutters of courtship yourself, you had a right to participate in Harriet's.

BELLA. Very true; this might be sufficient for *me*. But what pleasure can *you* have in tormenting two hearts so attached to each other?

GEORGE. I do mean to plague 'em a little, and it will be the greatest favor we can do them, for they are such sentimental people, you know, that they'll blush, and hesitate, and torment each other six months before they can come to an explanation. But, by alarming their jealousy, they'll betray themselves in as many hours.

BELLA. Oh, cry your mercy! So there's not one grain of mischief in all this, and you carry on the plan in downright charity. Well, really in that light there is some reason—

GEORGE. Aye, more reason than is necessary to induce you to join in it— even though there were mischief, so promise me your assistance with a good grace.

BELLA. Well, I do promise, for I really think—

GEORGE. Oh, I'll accept of very slight assurances.

BELLA. Apropos! Here's Harriet—I'm just as angry as you wish me. Leave us, and you shall have a good account of her.

Enter Harriet.

HARRIET. Brother! Mr. Drummond, I fancy, wonders at your absence. He's alone with the lady—

GEORGE. Then he possesses a privilege that half mankind would grudge him. (*Exit.*)

BELLA. Have you seen Sir Charles yet?

HARRIET. Indeed I have not. I confess I was so weak as to retire twice from the drawing room because I heard his voice, though I was conscious my absence must appear odd, and fearful the cause might be suspected.

BELLA. Ah! Pray be careful that you give *him* in particular no reason to guess at that. I advise you to treat him with the greatest coldness.

---

50   Picture collection at Hampton Court Palace, London, that included Peter Lely's Windsor Beauties (ladies of Charles II's court) and Godfrey Kneller's Hampton Court Beauties (ladies of William and Mary's court).

HARRIET. Most certainly I shall, whatever it costs me. It would be the most cruel mortification, if I thought he would ever suspect my weakness. I wonder, Bella, if the lady whom he is to marry is so handsome as George describes her.

BELLA. Of what consequence is that to you, child? Never think about it: if you suffer your mind to be softened with reflections of that sort, you'll never behave with a proper degree of scorn to him.

HARRIET. Oh, do not fear it. I assure you, I possess a vast deal of scorn for him.

BELLA. (*Aside.*) I'm sure you fib.—Well now, by way of example, he is coming this way, I see.

HARRIET. Is he? Come then, let us go.

BELLA. Yes, yes, you are quite a heroine, I perceive—surely you will not fly to prove your indifference? Stay and mortify him with an appearance of carelessness and good humor. For instance, when he appears, look at him with such an unmeaning eye, as one glances over an acquaintance shabbily dressed at Ranelagh,[51] and when he speaks to you, look another way; and then, suddenly recollecting yourself— "What were you saying, Sir Charles? I beg pardon, I really did not attend." Then, without minding his answer—"Bella, I was thinking of that sweet fellow who opened the ball with Lady Harriet. Did you ever see such eyes? And then the air with which he danced! Oh Lord! I never shall forget him."

HARRIET. You'll find me a bad scholar, I believe; however, I'll go through the interview, if you'll assist me.

BELLA. Fear me not.

Enter Sir Charles.

SIR CHARLES. Ladies, this is rather unexpected. I hope I don't intrude.

BELLA. Sir Charles Seymour can never be an unwelcome intruder.

SIR CHARLES. Miss Hargave, I have not had the happiness of paying my respects to you since I arrived—I hope you have enjoyed a perfect share of health and spirits, since I left Hargrave Place (*confusedly*).

HARRIET. I never have been better, sir, and my spirits are seldom so good as they are now (*affecting gaiety*).

---

51 Fashionable eighteenth-century resort by the Thames, in London. Also mentioned in *The Rehearsal*: see above, p. 188.

SIR CHARLES. Your looks indeed, madam, speak you in possession of that happiness I wish you (*sighing*). You, Miss Sydney, are always in spirits.

BELLA. In general, sir, I have not wisdom enough to be troubled with reflections to destroy my repose.

SIR CHARLES. Do you imagine it then a proof of wisdom to be unhappy?

BELLA. One might think so, for wise folks are always grave.

HARRIET. Then I'll never attempt to be wise; henceforward I'll be gaiety itself. I am determined to devote myself to pleasure and only live to laugh.

BELLA. Perhaps you may not always find subjects, cousin, unless you do as I do—laugh at your own absurdities.

HARRIET. Oh, fear not; we need not always look at home. The world abounds with subjects for mirth, and the men will be so obliging as to furnish a sufficient number, when every other resource fails.

SIR CHARLES. Miss Hargrave was not always so severe.

HARRIET. Fie, Sir Charles, do not mistake pleasantry for severity. But exuberant spirits frequently overflow in impertinence; therefore, I pardon your thinking that mine do.

SIR CHARLES. Impertinence! Surely, madam, you cannot suppose I meant to—

HARRIET. Nay, Bella, I appeal to you; did not Sir Charles intimate some such thing?

BELLA. Why—a—I don't know. To be sure there was a kind of distant intimation; though perhaps Sir Charles only means that you are awkward, ha! ha! But consider, sir, this character of Harriet's is but lately assumed, and new characters, like new stays,[52] never fit till they have been worn.

SIR CHARLES. Very well, ladies, I will not dispute your right to understand my expressions in what manner you please, but I hope you will allow me the same—and that, when lady's eyes speak disdain, I may, without offence, translate it into love.

HARRIET. 'Tis an error that men are apt to fall into, but the eyes talk in an idiom, warm from the heart, and so skillful an observer as Sir Charles will not mistake their language.

SIR CHARLES. Are they alike intelligible to all?

HARRIET. So plain, that nine times out of ten, at least, mistakes must be willful.

---

52   Stiff laced undergarment; panels of a corset.

SIR CHARLES. Then pray examine mine, madam, and by the report you make I shall judge of your proficiency in their dialect.

BELLA. Oh, I'll examine yours, Sir Charles; I am a better judge than Harriet. Let me see. Aye, 'tis so, in one I perceive love and jealousy; in the other, hope and a wedding. Now am I not a prophetess?

SIR CHARLES. Prove but one in the last article, and I ask no more of Fate. Now, will *you* read? Madam!

HARRIET. You are so entirely satisfied with Bella's translation, sir, that I will not run the risk of mortifying you with a different construction. Come, cousin, let us return to our company.

BELLA. (*Apart.*) Fie! That air of pique is enough to ruin all.

SIR CHARLES. Do you not think the garden agreeable, Miss Hargrave? I begin to think it charming.

HARRIET. Perfectly agreeable, sir, but the happy never fly society; I wonder to see you alone. Come, Bella.

BELLA. Bravo! (*Exeunt Bella and Harriet.*)

SIR CHARLES. Astonishing! What is become of that sweetness, that dove-like softness, which stole into my heart and deceived me into a dream of bliss? She flies from me, and talks of her company and returning to her society. Oh Harriet! Oh my Harriet! Thy society is prized by me beyond that of the whole world, and still to possess it, with the hope that once glowed in my bosom, would be a blessing for which I would sacrifice every other, that nature or fortune has bestowed. (*Exit.*)

ACT III

Scene: Lady Dinah's dressing room.

Lady Dinah and Mr. Hargrave sitting.

MR. HARGRAVE. I am surprised, madam, at your thinking in this manner; when I spoke to my son this morning, I assure you, he expressed a great deal of satisfaction about the affair. I wonder indeed he has not been here.

LADY DINAH. Now, I could almost blame you, Mr. Hargrave. Pardon me, but you have certainly been too precipitate. Your son has scarcely been at home four and twenty hours, and cannot possibly have received any impression or formed an idea of my character. He has been so much engaged, indeed, with other persons, that I have had no opportunity of conversing with him; and how, so circumstanced, can he have formed a judgment of his own heart?

MR. HARGRAVE. Good God! Madam, he has given the best proof in the world that he has formed a judgment, for he told me this morning that the prospect of the marriage made him very happy. I don't know what other proof a man can give that he knows his own heart—and let me tell you, madam, I have accustomed my children to pay a proper regard to my inclination.

LADY DINAH. I am apprehensive, sir, that Mr. George Hargrave's obedience may influence him more than I could wish, and, I assure you, I cannot think of uniting myself to any man, who does not prefer me for my own sake, without adverting to any other consideration.

MR. HARGRAVE. His obedience to me influence him more than you could wish! Why really I don't understand you, my lady.—Zounds! I thought she had been a sensible woman (*aside*).

LADY DINAH. Not understand me, Mr. Hargrave! I have too high an opinion of your good sense to suppose that I am unintelligible to you.

MR. HARGRAVE. My opinion, madam, is, that an obedient son is likely to make a kind husband. George is a fine young fellow as any in England, though I his father say it, and there's not a woman in the kingdom, who might not be proud to call him her husband. Too obedient—

LADY DINAH. (*Aside.*) Bless me! This man has no ideas.—You mistake me, Mr. Hargrave; I do not mean to lessen the merit of obedience in your son, but, I confess, I wish him to have a more delicate, more tender motive, for offering his hand to me.

MR. HARGRAVE. Look ye, madam, you have a great understanding to be sure, and I confess you talk above my reach, but I must nevertheless take the liberty to blame your ladyship. A person of your ladyship's experience, and—allow me to say—your date in the world, must know that there are occasions in which we should not be too nice.

LADY DINAH. Too nice! Mr. Hargrave— (*rising*).

MR. HARGRAVE. Aye, too nice, my lady. A boy and girl of sixteen have time before 'em; they may be whimsical, and be off and on, and play at shilly-shally as long as they have a mind. But, my lady, at a certain season we must leave off these tricks, or be content to go to the grave old bachelors and— (*shrugging his shoulders*).

LADY DINAH. I am utterly astonished, Mr. Hargrave. You surely mean to offend me: you insult me.

MR. HARGRAVE. No, by no means; I would not offend your ladyship for the world. I have the highest respect for you, and shall rejoice to call you my daughter. If you are not so, it will be your own fault, for

George, I am sure, is ready the moment you will give your consent. The writings shall be drawn when you think proper, and the marriage consummated without delay.

LADY DINAH. Well, sir, I really do not know what to say. When Mr. George Hargrave shall imagine it a proper period to talk to me in the subject—I—I—

MR. HARGRAVE. Well, well, madam, I allow this is a topic on which a lady does not choose to explain herself but to the principal. I waited on your ladyship only to inform you that I had talked to my son concerning the affair, and to incline you, when he waits on you, to give him a favorable hearing.

LADY DINAH. Mr. Hargrave, a person of your son's merit is *entitled* to a proper attention from any woman he addresses.

MR. HARGRAVE. There—now we are right again. I was fearful that you had not liked my boy, and that your difficulties arose from that quarter. But since you like George, 'tis all very well, very well.

LADY DINAH. Mr. Hargrave! I am surprised at your conceiving so unjust an idea. Mr. George Hargrave is, as you have said, a match for any woman, whatever be her rank.

MR. HARGRAVE. My dear Lady Dinah, I am quite happy to hear you say so. I am sure George loves *you*—odds bobs, I hear him on the stairs. I'll go and send him to you this moment, and he shall tell you so himself. You'll surely believe *him*. (*Exit*.)

LADY DINAH. Mr. Hargrave, Mr. Hargrave, bless me, what an impetuous obstinate old man. What can I do? I am in an exceedingly indelicate situation. He will tell his son that I am waiting here in expectation of a declaration of love from him. Sure never woman was in so awkward an embarras—I *wish* the son possessed a little of the father's impetuosity: this would not then have happened.

Enter George.

GEORGE. Your ladyship's most obedient servant.

LADY DINAH. S—i—r (*curtsying confusedly*).

GEORGE. My father permits me, madam, to make my acknowledgments to your ladyship, for the honor you design our family.

LADY DINAH. I must confess, sir, this interview is somewhat unexpected. It is indeed quite premature: I was not prepared for it, and I am really in great confusion.

GEORGE. I am sensible, madam, a visit of this kind to a lady of your delicacy must be a little distressing. But I entreat you to be composed.

I hope you have no reason to regret a resolution which myself, and the rest of the family, have so much cause to rejoice in—and I assure your ladyship, everything on my part, that can contribute to your felicity, you shall always command.

LADY DINAH. You are very *polite*, sir. We have had so little opportunity of conversing, Mr. Hargrave, that I am afraid you express rather your father's sentiments than your own. It is impossible, indeed, from so short a knowledge that you can have formed any sentiments of me yourself.

GEORGE. Pardon me, madam, my sentiments for you are full of respect, and I am convinced your qualities will excite the veneration of all who have the honor of being connected with you.—My father could hardly have done it better (*aside*).

LADY DINAH. (*Aside.*) Why, this young man has certainly been taught to make love by his tutor at college.

GEORGE. I am concerned this visit seems so embarrassing to your ladyship; I certainly should have deferred it, from an apprehension of its being disagreeable, but, in obedience to my father, I—

LADY DINAH. Then it is to your father, sir, that I am indebted for the favor of seeing you.

GEORGE. By no means, madam; it would certainly have been my *inclination* to have waited on your ladyship, but my father's wishes induced me to hasten it.

LADY DINAH. (*Aside.*) Really! A pretty extraordinary confession!

—I think it necessary to assure you, sir, that—that this affair has been brought thus forward by Mr. Hargrave, and the proposals he made, in which it was evident, *his whole heart* was concerned, were quite unexpected.

GEORGE. I have not the least doubt of it, madam, nor am I at all surprised at my father's earnestness on a subject so interesting.—What can she mean by apologizing to me (*aside*)?

LADY DINAH. It would certainly have been proper, sir, to have allowed you time to have formed a judgment yourself, on a point which concerns you so highly.

GEORGE. The time has been quite sufficient, madam. I highly approve the steps my father has taken, but if I did not, the respect I bear to his determination would certainly have prevented my opposing them.—I must end this extraordinary visit (*aside*). —Shall I have the honor of conducting your ladyship to the company?

LADY DINAH. N—o, sir, I have orders to give my woman; I'll rejoin the
ladies in a few minutes.

GEORGE. Then I'll wish your ladyship a good morning. (*Exit.*)

LADY DINAH. Amazement! Why, what a visit from a lover! Is this the
language in which men usually talk to women, with whom they are
on the point of marriage? Respect! Veneration! Obedience to my
father! And shall I have the honor of conducting your ladyship to the
company? A pretty lover-like request truly! But this coldness to me
proceeds from a cause I now understand. This morning, what fire
was there in his eyes! What animation in his countenance, whenever
he addressed himself to that creature Mr. Drummond brought here!
Would his request to her have been to conduct her to company? No,
no. But I must be cautious; I must be patient now. But you will find,
sir, when I possess the privileges of a wife, I shall not so easily give
them up. Your fiery glances, if not directed to me, shall at least, in my
presence, be addressed to no other. (*Exit.*)

Scene: Changes to an apartment.

Bella at her harpsichord.

Song.

Haste, haste, ye fiery steeds of day,
In ocean's bosom hide your beams!
Mild evening, in her pensive gray
More soft, and more alluring seems.
Yet why invoke the pensive eve,
Or, sighing, chide refulgent morn?
Their shifting moments can't relieve
The heart by pangs of absence torn.

[BELLA.] Hang music—it only makes me melancholy. Heigh-ho! These
lovers infect me too, I believe. Seducive Italy! What are your attrac-
tions? Oh, for Fortunatus's cap:53 I'd convince myself in a moment if
my doubts are justly founded. And suppose they should—what then?
Ah! They think I am made of ice, whilst the gaiety of my disposition
only serves to conceal a heart as tenderly susceptible as the most serious of my sex can possess— (*Enter Emily.*) Ah, my dear ma'am, I am

---

53   Magic wishing cap that would transport the wearer anywhere desired.

rejoiced to see you; I have been just long enough alone to be tired of myself and to be charmed at so agreeable a relief.

EMILY. Can that ever be the case with Miss Sydney? I thought you had possessed the happiest flow of spirits in the world.

BELLA. Pho! Your great spirits are mere jack-a-lanterns in the brain: they dance about, shine, and make vagaries, while those who possess happiness, *soberly* and quietly enjoy their treasure.

EMILY. Indeed! I hope *dullness* is not your criterion of happiness—if it is, there are few assemblies where you'll not find a great number to envy.

BELLA. Oh, no—dullness is the character of those who are too wise, not too happy.

Enter George.

GEORGE. Two ladies in council—on fashion or news?

BELLA. On a better subject: laughing at the slaves we have made, and forging chains for more.

GEORGE. That's not the business of fine women. Nature meant to save them the trouble of plotting—for traps and chains, she bestowed sparkling eyes and timid blushes, with a whole multitude of graces that hang about the form and wanton in the air. (*Looking at Emily.*)

BELLA. Well, after all, men are delightful creatures: flattery, cards, and scandal help one through the day tolerably well. I don't know how we should exist without 'em in the country.

GEORGE. And which of 'em would you relinquish in town?

BELLA. Not flattery, because it keeps one in spirits, and gives a glow to the complexion. Scandal you may take away, but pray leave us cards, to keep us awake, with the fashionable world, on Sunday evenings.

GEORGE. And, in lieu of scandal, you'll be content with conquest.

BELLA. Ridiculous! Conquest is not such an object with women, as the men imagine. For my part, I should conceive a net that would catch the hearts of the whole sex, a property of very little value.

GEORGE. But, you would think it a very pleasant one, my gentle cuz or at least (*archly*) you'd pick out one happy favorite before you gave the rest to despair.

BELLA. Positively no! I don't know one that I should not let fly away with the rest.

GEORGE. Now, how can you fib, with such an unblushing face? This debate, madam (*to Emily*), will let you into Bella's secret: she has, at this moment, an image in her heart that gives flat contradiction to her tongue.

BELLA. Indeed! You make your assertion with great effrontery. But now, to compliment your discernment, whose image do you think of?

GEORGE. Ha, Bella. Listen with your greediest ears to catch the transporting sound. Breathe not, ye softest zephyrs! Be silent, ye harmonious spheres while I articulate the name of—

BELLA. (*Stopping her ears.*) Oh, I won't hear it.

GEORGE. Belville!

BELLA. Oh, frightful! Don't attend to him. George's belief is always under the influence of his fancy.

EMILY. In this instance, if I may judge from your looks, he has not hinted at a fiction.

BELLA. Indeed you are mistaken; his guess might have been as good, if you had named Prester John.[54]

GEORGE. Hum—I wish it may be so, for I have heard a story about a certain lady on the continent, whom a certain gentleman—

BELLA. Thinks handsomer than Bella Sydney—mortifying—ha, ha, ha!

GEORGE. Nay more, to whom he devotes his hours.

BELLA. (*Petulantly.*) His heart.

GEORGE. On whom he dotes.

BELLA. Psha!

GEORGE. Grows melancholy.

BELLA. Nonsense!

GEORGE. Nay, fights for her.

BELLA. Ridiculous!

GEORGE. Lives only at her feet.

BELLA. You really are very insupportable, sir; do find some other subject to amuse yourself.

GEORGE. Ha, ha, ha! The gudgeon[55] has bit. See, madam, a coquette struggling with the consciousness of love. Are not these pouts and angry blushes proofs of Belville's happiness?

EMILY. I cannot perceive these proofs. Mr. Belville, perhaps, is not in so enviable a state.

BELLA. Oh, you are a good girl, and, I assure you, perfectly right. Lovers—thank our stars!—are too plenty, for an absent one to give us much pain. What, turn your arms on your associates, George!—I'll break the league, and discover all (*apart to George.*).

GEORGE. You dare not; you love mischief too well. It is as dear to you as the sighs of your lover.

---

54   Legendary ruler of a Christian kingdom in Asia.
55   Small freshwater fish used as bait; hence a gullible person.

BELLA. A-propos! Where's Sir Charles?

GEORGE. In the garden probably, sighing to the winds, and I wish you'd find him—and leave us (*apart*).

BELLA. Ha! Perhaps they'll waft his sighs to Harriet, and she must not hear 'em yet, and so, Sir Charles— (*Exit.*)

EMILY. Oh, pray make me one of your party. (*Going*).

GEORGE. Stay, madam, I entreat you. Believe me, they will not thank you; I'll tell you the story.

EMILY. I'll hear it from Miss Sydney.

GEORGE. Nay, if you are determined— (*Exeunt.*)

Scene: The garden.

Enter Harriet.

HARRIET. In vain I do endeavor to conceal it from myself. This spot has charms for me, that I can find in no other; here have I seen, perhaps for the last time, Sir Charles Seymour. My cousin's presence was unlucky. I should have heard him, but it would have been a crime in him to have talked to me of love—an insult that I must have resented. And yet 'tis the only subject on which I could wish to have heard him. Bless me! He's here again; he haunts this place. But he does not observe me, and I'll conceal myself, for I feel I could not now behave with proper reserve. (*Goes behind an arbor*).

Enter Sir Charles looking round.

SIR CHARLES. Ha, not here then! Sweet *resemblance* of her I love come from thy hiding place! (*Takes a picture from his bosom and kisses it.*) In her absence thou art the dearest object to my eyes. What a face is this!
"'Tis beauty truly blest, whose red and white
"Nature's own sweet and cunning hand laid on."

Enter George. Catches his hand with the picture.

GEORGE. Ho ho! So the picture's come home from the painter's, is it, sir, and the drapery quite to your mind?

SIR CHARLES. (*Confused and recovering.*) The artifice I used to obtain it, those who love can pardon.

GEORGE. And how many times a day dost thou break the Decalogue[56] in worshipping that image?

SIR CHARLES. Every hour that I live, I gaze on it till I think it looks, and speaks to me; it lies all night on my heart, and is the first object I address in the morning.

GEORGE. Oh, complete your character and turn monk; 'tis plain you're half a papist.

SIR CHARLES. Why condemn me to cells and penitence?

GEORGE. That you mayn't violate the laws of nature, by pretending to a character for which she never designed you. Your bonds, instead of silken fetters, appear to be hempen cords. Come, confess: have not you been examining on which of these trees you would be most gracefully pendent?

SIR CHARLES. That *gaieté de coeur*,[57] George, bears no mark of the tender passion; and, to be plain, I believe you know very little about it.

GEORGE. You are confoundedly mistaken. We are both lovers, but the difference between us lies thus: Cupid to me is a little familiar rogue, with an arch leer and cheeks dimpled with continual smiles. To you, an awful deity, decked out in his whole regalia of darts, flames, and quivers, and so forth. I play with him; you—

SIR CHARLES. Spare yourself the trouble of so long an explanation. All you would say is, that you love with hope; I with despair.

GEORGE. Very concise, and most pathetically expressed: melancholy suits your features, Charles. 'Twere pity your mistress should encourage you; it would deprive you of that *something* in your air which is so touching. Ha! ha! ha! Poor Seymour! Come, let us go in search of the girls; they are gone to the wood. Who knows but you may find a nymph there, who'll have the kindness to put hanging and drowning out of your head?

SIR CHARLES. Oh, would sweet Celia[58] meet me there,
With softened looks, and gentler air,
Transported, to the wood I'd fly,
The happiest swain beneath the sky;
Sighs and complaints I'd give the wind,
And Io's sing, were Celia kind.

---

56   The Ten Commandments as a body of law.
57   Lightness of heart.
58   Conventional name in pastoral literature.

As he repeats the verses, George, laughing, scans them on his fingers. Exit Sir Charles.

GEORGE. Cupid is deaf, as well as blind. (*Exit.*)

Enter Harriet.

HARRIET. Her picture is in his bosom, and kiss it with such rapture too! Well, I am glad I am convinced; I am perfectly at ease. He loves then without hope, and George was mistaken in supposing him so near marriage. But he loves notwithstanding; her picture lies all night on his heart, and her idea is never absent from his mind. Well, be it so, I am perfectly at ease, and shall no longer find a difficulty in assuming an indifference that is become real—Oh, Seymour! (*Exit.*)

Scene: The wood.

Enter Lady Dinah.

LADY DINAH. Insolent wretch! Nothing less than the conviction of my own senses could have induced me to believe so shocking an inde-corum: I saw her myself look at him with eyes that were downright gloating; I saw him snatch her hand, and press it to his lips, with an ardor that is inconceivable—and when the creature pretended to blush, and made a reluctant effort to withdraw it, *my* youth, so full of veneration and respect to me, refused to resign it, till the creature had given him a gracious smile of reconciliation.—Heavens! They are coming this way. Sure they do not perceive me. See there! Nay, if you will come here. (*Goes behind a shrub.*)

Enter Emily, followed by George.

EMILY. I entreat you, sir, not to persist in following me. You'll force me to appeal to Mr. Drummond for protection.
GEORGE. You need no protection, madam, that you will not find in my respect. But you are barbarous to deprive me of conversing with you—'tis a felicity, I have so lately tasted, that 'tis no wonder I am greedy of it.
EMILY. If you believe your attentions would not displease me in my proper character, I ought to be offended that you address them to a person, of whose name and family you are ignorant.

GEORGE. Can a name deprive you of that face, that air, or rob you of your mind? Of what then am I ignorant? 'Tis those I address with the most passionate vows of—

EMILY. I positively will not listen to you. However, if the acquaintance should place us on a footing, I'll then converse with you—if on my own terms.

LADY DINAH. (*Listening.*) —Aye, or on any terms.

EMILY. I have no dislike to the charming freedom of English manners; you shall be as gallant as you please. But I give you notice, the instant you become dangerous, I shall be grave.

GEORGE. How dangerous—

EMILY. Oh, the moment you grow of consequence enough to endanger my heart, I shall shut myself from you. But as long as you continue harmless, you may play.

GEORGE. This is not to be borne. I will not be harmless; I declare open war against your heart, not in play, but downright earnest.

EMILY. Nay, then, I must collect my forces to oppose you; my heart will stand a long siege, depend on it.

GEORGE. If you'll promise it shall yield at last, a ten years siege will be richly rewarded.

EMILY. Oh no! I make no promises—try your forces. If you should possess yourself of it in spite of me, I can only bewail its captivity.

GEORGE. Your permission to take the field is all I can present hope; and thus, on my knees, dear charming creature—

LADY DINAH. (*Listening.*) There's veneration and respect!

EMILY. Hold, sir, I will be so generous to tell you, that whenever you kneel I shall fly. (*Runs out.*)

GEORGE. And I'll pursue—till my Atalanta[59] confesses I have won the prize.

As George is following Emily, Lady Dinah comes out against him with an angry reproachful air, and passes him.

GEORGE. (*Aside.*) So—there's a look! What a blessed mother-in-law I shall have! (*Exit.*)

LADY DINAH. What! Not stay even to explain, to apologize, follow her before my face. Oh, monsters, furies! Yes, yes, she'll yield without the

---

59   A beautiful huntress in Greek mythology who issued a fatal challenge to her suitors. Hippomenes succeeded by dropping golden apples, one at a time, which Atalanta stopped to pick up.

trouble of a ten years siege; she can scarcely hold out for ten minutes. Oh, ye shall both suffer for this. I will go this instant. I will do something. (*Exit*)

Enter Susan.

SUSAN. Hah, my good lady, is it so? Ha, ha, ha! I must see if I can't make myself useful here. A lady, who like my mistress gives way to her most unbridled passions, is the only one worth being served by a girl of spirit and intrigue. I'll follow, and aid your ladyship with my counsel before you have time to cool (*going, returns*). So, 'tis needless, here she ebbs, like a stormy sea.

Enter Lady Dinah, not seeing Susan.

LADY DINAH. A moment's reflection has convinced me I should be wrong; he must not suspect that I influence his father against the minion. Nor will I allow her the satisfaction of thinking she gives to me the pangs of jealousy, but I will not lose him. Something must be done.

SUSAN. Oh, my lady, I was witness to the whole affair. Oh, a base man! I could have trampled him under my feet.

LADY DINAH. Base indeed! But 'tis on *her* my resentment chiefly falls. Oh, Susan, revenge!

SUSAN. I am sure my heart aches for you, my lady; there's nothing I would not do. Oh, she's an artful slut.

LADY DINAH. She's as dangerous as artful.

I must be rid of her, yet I do not know how. Oh France! For thy *Bastille*,[60] for thy *Lettres de Cachet*![61]

SUSAN. There are ways and means here, my lady. Miss told a fine tale to get into the house, and I fancy I can tell as fine a tale to get her out of it, and I should think it neither sin nor shame in the service of so good a lady.

LADY DINAH. If thou can'st contrive any method—I care not what—any plan to rid me of her, command my fortune.

---

60   Famous prison in Paris.
61   Letters signed by the French king and closed with the royal seal, containing an executive order, often to authorize someone's imprisonment without trial.

SUSAN. Oh, dear my lady, as to that, as to your fortune, my lady, that's out of the question. But I know your ladyship's generosity. I think I could send her packing, perhaps before night.

LADY DINAH. Can you! The instant she goes, I'll give you two hundred pounds.

SUSAN. (*Curtsying.*) She shall go, my lady, if I have invention, or Jarvis a tongue.

LADY DINAH. Jarvis! Are you mad? I would not have him suspect that I am concerned in the affair for the universe.

SUSAN. Oh, dear my lady, I vow I would not mention your name to him— no, not for another two hundred pounds. No, no, miss shall be got rid of, without giving Jarvis, or any one, the least reason to suspect that your ladyship is privy to the matter.

LADY DINAH. I am convinced she is an impostor, and I wonder Mr. Hargrave doesn't see it. But there will be more labor in rousing his stupid apprehension, than in explaining to an enthusiast the conceptions of a Bolingbroke.[62]

SUSAN. I am more afraid of Mr. Drummond than him.

LADY DINAH. Aye, he will support that girl's interest, in order to mortify me—

SUSAN. That doesn't signify, my lady. I have a card as good as any he holds to play against him; your ladyship must have seen that the old Justice has full as much weight with the 'squire as Mr. Drummond.

LADY DINAH. I observe that Mr. Hargrave is continually wavering between them: they influence his actions like two principal senses. Mr. Drummond is the friend of his understanding, the other of his humor. But what is the card you mean to play?

SUSAN. I mean to play one of his senses against the other, my lady, that's all; for I am mistaken if I can't govern the Justice, as much as his whole five put together.

LADY DINAH. That is indeed a card: my hopes catch life at it. Susan, say to him what you will, promise what you will. I suppose you have the way to the old fool's heart, and know by what road to reach it. At all events the girl must be got rid of; the method I leave to you. There's the dinner bell. I must walk a little to recover my composure, and then, I suppose, I may have the honor of sitting for the young lady's foil. (*Exit.*)

---

62   I.e., an enthusiast's religious fervor would preclude any understanding of deist reasoning. Henry St. John Bolingbroke (1678-1751) was a Tory politician, orator, and writer known for his deist beliefs.

SUSAN. I am sure she's can't have a better—ha, ha, ha! Two hundred pounds! Oh the charms of jealousy and revenge. I might have served one of your good sort of orderly old women, till I have been grey; these two hundred will quicken Mr. Jarvis a little. We shall see him more attentive, I fancy, than he has been, and then farewell to servitude. Hah, Jarvis!

Enter Jarvis, bowing affectedly.

JARVIS. "So looked the goddess of the Paphian isle,[63]
 "When Mars she saw, and conquered with that smile."
 My dear goddess, I kiss your fingers; I have been hunting for you in every walk in the garden.
SUSAN. (*Tenderly.*) Why—what did you want with me, Jarvis?
JARVIS. Why, faith, I have the same kind of necessity for you, that a beau has for a looking-glass: you admire me, and keep me in good humor with myself.
SUSAN. Oh, if you want to be put in temper, I've got an excellent cordial. Now for your parts—now to prove yourself the clever fellow you think you are.
JARVIS. That you think, my dear, you mean, but what extraordinary occasion has occurred now, for the exhibition of my parts?
SUSAN. Listen! We have discovered that the young 'squire thinks eighteen a prettier age than fifty, that he prefers natural roses to Warren's,[64] and that gravity and wisdom are no match for the fire of two hazel eyes, assisted by the reasoning of smiles and dimples.
JARVIS. And he's in the right on't. Didn't I tell you this morning they reckoned without their host?
SUSAN. Here has he been on his knees at the feet of the damsel, and her ladyship behind that bush, amusing herself with his transports—ha, ha, ha!
JARVIS. Ha, ha, ha! I warrant her, 'tis the only transports *she'll* ever see him in. George Hargrave marry our old lady! No, no! I have a very good opinion of that young fellow; he's exactly what I should be, if I was heir to his father's acres—just such a spirited, careless deportment, a certain prevailing assurance. Upon my soul, Susan, you and I ought to have moved in a higher sphere.

---

63   Cyprus. Its coastal city Paphos was reputed to be the birthplace of Aphrodite, goddess of love.
64   Warren's "Milk of Roses," a product of the mid-eighteenth century that cleared and preserved skin.

SUSAN. Come, come, you must consider this affair in another light; 'twould be a shame, that because this girl has a pretty face, and was found weeping by a compassionate old gentleman—it would be a shame, I say, for these reason, she should marry into a great family, and cheat the sister of a peer, of a husband. Read the story *this* way, act with spirit, and our lady will, *on the day of our marriage*, give us two hundred pounds.

JARVIS. Humph! On the day of our marriage. Cannot you, child, prevail on your lady to give me the two hundred without tacking that condition to it?

SUSAN. Pho, sauce-box! Well, but these two hundreds now—what will you do for 'em?

JARVIS. Do for 'em? Oh, anything! The most extravagant thing in the world: run off with the girl, blow up the house, turn Turk—or marry you.

SUSAN. Upon my word, sir.

JARVIS. Well, but the business, child, the business.

SUSAN. The business is, that we must contrive to open some door for this girl to walk out of the house.

JARVIS. But how? Upon what ground? When, and where?

SUSAN. Why, if we could contrive the business, I have no doubt of the spirit and fire of your execution. Do you remember the occupation which once gave employment to these talents of yours—I mean that of itinerant player?

JARVIS. Oh, yes! I remember the barns that I have made echo with the ravings of Orestes,[65] and the stables in which I have sighed forth the woes of Romeo.

SUSAN. Well, but have you any recollection of a pretty Juliet, a tall elegant girl? In short, do you not remember one of the strolling party[66] exceedingly like the strange guest now in the house?

JARVIS. Hum! Why, what devil sent thee to tempt me this morning? So I am to sell my honor, my honesty—

SUSAN. Pho, pho, honesty and honor are sentiments for people whose fortunes are made. Let us once be independent, and we'll be as honorable and honest as the best of 'em. So let's go in, and settle our plan.

JARVIS. Well, 'tis the fate of great men to be in the hands of women; and therefore, my sweet Abigail, I am yours. (*Leads her off.*)

---

65   Ancient Greek tragic hero, who features in Ambrose Philips's *The Distrest Mother* (1712).

66   Group of traveling actors.

ACT IV

Scene: An apartment.

Enter Harriet, followed by Bella.

BELLA. Nay, but hear him—hear him, Harriet.

HARRIET. Can this be you, Bella, who this morning seemed fearful that I should not treat him with sufficient scorn, now persuading me to allow a private interview to a man, who is professedly the lover of another?

BELLA. How apprehensive you *very* delicate ladies are! Why must you suppose he wants to talk to you about love, or on any topic, that his approaching marriage would make improper?

HARRIET. Why, what *can* he have to say to me?

BELLA. Admit him, and he'll tell you. Perhaps he wants to consult your taste about the trimmings of his wedding clothes, or to beg your choice in his ruffles, or—

HARRIET. Pho! This is downright ridicule.

BELLA. Well then, you won't admit him? (*Seeming to go.*) I shall tell him you don't choose to see him, though he is going to leave us directly—but I approve your caution, Harriet; you are perfectly right.

HARRIET. Going to leave us directly, Bella!

BELLA. Immediately, my dear. I heard him order his chaise, and mutter something about insupportable, but I think you'll be exceedingly imprudent in receiving his visit, and advise you by all means to refuse it.

HARRIET. Dear Bella!

BELLA. Well then you will see him—I shall acquaint him with the success of my embassy, but remember scorn, Harriet, *scorn.* (*Exit Bella.*)

HARRIET. Now, what am I to expect? My heart beats strangely—but remember, foolish girl, the picture of his mistress is in his bosom.

Enter Sir Charles.

SIR CHARLES. The request I ventured to make by Miss Sydney, madam, must appear strange to you; the engagements which I—

HARRIET. Renders it an extraordinary request indeed, sir.

SIR CHARLES. I feared you would think so, and conscious of those engagements, I should not have presumed to have made it, but as it's probably the last time I may ever see you, I seize it to tell you that—I adore you.

HARRIET. Sir Charles! I am astonished; in my father's house, at least, I should have been secure from such an insult.

SIR CHARLES. Forgive me, I entreat you. Nothing could have forced this declaration from me but my despair.

HARRIET. The engagement you talk of, sir, ought to have prevented *these* effects of your despair.

SIR CHARLES. I acknowledge it, and they have kept me silent ever since I arrived, but when I thought of leaving you in a few moments, I found the idea insupportable.

HARRIET. The picture you wear, Sir Charles, might console you surely.

SIR CHARLES. Hah! I thought you were ignorant, madam, of my possessing it.

HARRIET. Without doubt you did, Sir Charles, but no, sir, I am acquainted with your wearing that picture, and wonder how you could presume—but I deserve the insult for listening to you a moment. (*Going.*)

SIR CHARLES. Oh, stay, Miss Hargrave, I entreat you; I will give up the picture, since it so offends you, yet how can I part from it?

HARRIET. Oh, keep it, sir; keep it by all means. You mistake me entirely, sir; I have no right to claim such a sacrifice. (*Going.*)

SIR CHARLES. You have a right, madam—here it is (*kissing and offering it*) but do not rob me of it.

HARRIET. Rob you of it! In short, Sir Charles, you redouble your rudeness every moment—

SIR CHARLES. I did not think you would have so resented it, but I resign it to you, madam—nay you must take it.

HARRIET. *I* take it, sir! (*Glances her eye on it, then takes it with an air of doubt.*) My picture! Astonishing!

Enter George and Bella, both laughing.

SIR CHARLES. Your picture, madam!

GEORGE. Look at the simpletons—ha, ha, ha!

BELLA. What a fine attitude! Do it again, Sir Charles. Ha, ha, ha! Well, Harriet, how do you like Sir Charles's mistress? Is she as handsome as George represented her?

GEORGE. Hold, hold! 'Tis time now to have mercy. My dear Harriet, allow me to present to you my most valued friend, as the man whom

I should rejoice to see your husband. To you, my Seymour, I present a sister, whose heart has no engagement that I am acquainted with to supersede your claim.

SIR CHARLES. I am speechless with joy, and with amazement.

GEORGE. Forgive the embarrassment I have occasioned you. You have suffered something, but your felicity will be heightened from the comparison. My dear Harriet, Seymour has always loved you—the picture which so offended you is a proof, you cannot doubt.

SIR CHARLES. And that you were so offended, is supreme felicity. Stupid wretch, not to perceive my bliss!

HARRIET. (*To George and Bella.*) You have taken a liberty with me that I cannot pardon.

GEORGE. Nay, but you shall pardon it, and as a proof, give him back your picture this minute.

SIR CHARLES. Return it to me, madam, I entreat you (*kneeling*). I will receive it as the most precious gift.

BELLA. Come, give the poor thing its bauble.

HARRIET. Well, take it, sir, since you had no share in this brilliant contrivance.

SIR CHARLES. (*Taking picture.*) Eternal blessings on that hand!

HARRIET. You, George, are never so happy, as in exercising your wit, at my expense.

GEORGE. And you, Harriet, never so heartily forgave me in your life, and therefore—

SIR CHARLES. Hold, George, I cannot bear Miss Hargrave's suffering in this manner; I will take on myself the transporting office of defending her. This hour, madam, I shall forever remember with gratitude, and will endeavor to deserve it by a life devoted to your happiness.

BELLA. Come, Harriet—I must take you away, that Sir Charles may bring down his raptures to the standard of common mortals. At present, I see his in the clouds.

HARRIET. 'Tis merciful to relieve me. (*Exeunt Harriet and Bella.*)

SIR CHARLES. Charming Miss Sydney, I'll never quarrel with your omvivacity again. But why have I been made to suffer thus?

GEORGE. Because you did not tell me *why* you wanted my sister's picture. But I have taken a friendly vengeance: my plot has told you more of my sister's heart in a few hours than all your sighs and humility would have obtained in as many months.

SIR CHARLES. For which I thank you, and my present happiness receives a brighter glow from this illusion of misery. I'll fly and pour out my joy and gratitude, at the feet of my charming Harriet. (*Going. Enter Bella.*)

BELLA. Oh, stay, stay—we may want your assistance. Here's your father coming, George. Your repartee to Lady Dinah at dinner, spoiled her digestion, and she's been representing you. That's all.

GEORGE. I hope she represented her sneer too, which suffused with tears the loveliest eyes in the world. Could I do less than support her against the ill-humor of that antiquated pedant? By Jupiter, I'll draw her in colors to my father, that shall make him shrink from the fate he is preparing for himself.

Enter Hargrave.

MR. HARGRAVE. Why, George, how's this? D'ye know what you've done? You've affronted Lady Dinah.

GEORGE. I did not design to affront her, sir; I only meant to convince her that she should not insult the amiable young lady, whom Mr. Drummond placed under your protection.

MR. HARGRAVE. Don't tell me—amiable young lady! How do you know what she is? On the footing you are with Lady Dinah, let me tell you, if she had insulted an hundred young ladies, you ought not to have seen it—at least, not resented it.

GEORGE. Pardon me, sir; I did not conceive that Lady Dinah should have assumed in your house—at least till she becomes your wife—a right to—

MR. HARGRAVE. *What's* that you say, sir?

GEORGE. Indeed, sir, to confess the truth, I am astonished at your partiality for that lady. She is the last woman in the world, whom I could wish to see in the place of my amiable mother.

MR. HARGRAVE. Your mother!

GEORGE. I should think it a breach of my duty, to see you plunge yourself into so irretrievable a fate, without acquainting you with my sentiments. If you saw her in the light I do, sir, you would think on your wedding day with horror.

MR. HARGRAVE. Why—why—are you mad?

GEORGE. If you wished to keep your engagements a secret, sir, I am sorry I mentioned the affair, but—

BELLA. Oh, 'tis no secret, sir, I assure you: everybody talks of it. For my part, I shall be quite happy in paying my respects to my new aunt. I have put a coral string in my tambour[67] already, that I may finish it time enough for her first boy to wear at its christening.

---

67   Circular embroidery frame.

MR. HARGRAVE. Look ye, sir, I perceive that you have all that backwardness in obeying me that I expected, and, in order to conceal it, are attempting to throw the affair into ridicule. But I tell you it will not do; I know what I am about, and my commands shall not be disputed.

GEORGE. Commands, sir! I am quite at a loss—

MR. HARGRAVE. Well, then, to prevent further mistakes, I acquaint you that I design Lady Dinah for your *wife*, and not your mother—and, moreover, that the marriage shall take place in a very few days. (*Going.*) And—d'ye hear?—acquaint your pert cousin that the coral string will do for *your* first boy. (*Exit Hargrave.*)

A long pause, staring at each other.

BELLA. So, so, so! And is this the end of all the closetings?

SIR CHARLES. What the devil! It must be all a dream.

GEORGE. Wife!! Lady Dinah *my* wife!

BELLA. Ha, ha, ha! Dear George, forgive me, but I must laugh, or I can't exist—ha, ha, ha! Oh, my cousin Dinah!

GEORGE. Pray, Bella, spare your mirth, and tell me what I am to do, for I am incapable of thinking.

BELLA. Do! Why run to Lady Dinah. Fling yourself at her feet, tell her you have no idea of the bliss that was designed for you, and that you'll make her the tenderest, fondest husband in the world. Ha, ha, ha!

GEORGE. Oh, cousin, for once forget your sprightliness—I cannot bear it. Seymour, what am I to do?

SIR CHARLES. My dear George, I pity you from my soul, but I know not what advice to give you.

BELLA. Well, then seriously I think—ha, ha, ha! But 'tis impossible to be serious. I am astonished you are not more struck with your father's tender cares for you.

GEORGE. Have you no mercy, Bella?

BELLA. You have none upon yourself, or instead of standing here with that countenance *si triste*,[68] you would be with Mr. Drummond.

GEORGE. He is, indeed, my only resource. I'll fly to him on this instant, and if it fails me, I am the most miserable man on earth. (*Exit.*)

SIR CHARLES. What can induce Mr. Hargrave to sacrifice such a fellow as George, to a Lady Dinah? Preposterous!

BELLA. Her rank and fortune—and I dread the lengths to which his obstinacy may carry him. He has no more respect for the divinity of

---

68   So sad (French).

Love, than for that of the Egyptian Apis.[69] Let us find Harriet, and
tell her the strange story; she is not the only person, I fear, to whom it
will be painful.

SIR CHARLES. Is it possible that Lady Dinah, in the depth of her wisdom,
can imagine such an union proper?

BELLA. Be merciful. Love has forced heroes to forget their valor, and philosophers their systems. No wonder he should make a woman forget
her wrinkles. (*Exeunt*.)

Scene: the garden.

Enter Jarvis and Susan.

JARVIS. Egad, 'tis a service of danger.

SUSAN. Danger! Sure you've no qualms?

JARVIS. No, no, child, no qualms. The resolution with which I could go
through an affair of this sort, would in another hemisphere make my
fortune. But hang it, in these cold northern regions there's no room
for a man of genius to strike a bold stroke: the fostering plains of Asia,
for such talents as mine!

SUSAN. Now I think England's a very pretty soil.

JARVIS. Why, aye, if one could be sure of keeping clear of a dozen ill-bred
fellows, who decide on the conduct of a man of spirit at the Old Bailey,
then indeed we need not care; for an air of ton,[70] and a carriage, on
whatever *springs* it moves, introduces one to the best circles. But let
us consider our bottom; this girl was placed under the care of the old
gentlewoman, by a person of credit.

SUSAN. Pho, pho, what! She brought a recommendation. Don't we know
how easily a character is to be had—spotless as silver, or as bright as
gold! 'Tis a wonder she did not afford a name too; I warrant she had
sufficient reasons to conceal her own.

JARVIS. It does look like it, and there's a mystery in the affair. Now, mysteries, *as my lady says*, we have a right to explain as we please.

SUSAN. Aye, to be sure—and this is the explanation. She is an unpro-
tected, artful girl, who having caught a taste for the life of a fine
lady, thinks the shortest way to gratify her longing, is by gaining the
heart of some credulous fool, who'll make her his wife for the sake of
her—beauty.

---

69   A bull-deity.
70   Fashionable society.

JARVIS. True! That with this view she told her story to Mr. Drummond, who, innocent soul, not seeing her drift, introduced her here, where she attempts to succeed, by playing of her artillery on the gunpowder constitution of George Hargrave Esq., the younger.

SUSAN. Oh, delightful! Why if I continue with my lady, I shall be her mistress as long as she lives, and now I think on't, I believe that must be our plan. You and I can be married just the same, you know.

JARVIS. Oh, just the same, my dear, just the same; nothing shall prevent that—but my being able to coax you out of the two hundred (*aside*).

SUSAN. Hark! Here comes the Justice; slip away, and leave me to manage him. I know I can make him useful. You need not be jealous now.

JARVIS. Jealous! No, no; I have lived among the great too long, to be tormented with so vulgar a passion. (*Exit Jarvis*.)

Enter Justice.

JUSTICE. Hah, hah! Have I caught you, my little pixie? Come, no struggling—I will have a kiss, by jingo.

SUSAN. (*Resisting*.) Lud! You are the strangest gentleman.

JUSTICE. You are wondrous coy, methinks.

SUSAN. Coy, so I should. What have gentlewomen without fortunes to recommend 'em else?

JUSTICE. Aye, but that rosy, pouting mouth tells different tales, I warrant, to the fine gentlemen in London. I have been thinking you'd make a pretty little housekeeper; yes, you would, hussy, yes you would. Will you come and live with me?

SUSAN. Oh, dear sir, I should like it vastly, but I think you had better go to London with me. I assure you, my lady speaks very highly of your talents in the law, and she has great interest—so, as soon as she is Lady Dinah Hargrave. Your worship is acquainted with that affair, I suppose.

JUSTICE. Yes, yes; my friend has told me of it—but under strict injunctions of secrecy.

SUSAN. Secrecy! Aye, to be sure, but I dare say Mr. Drummond has been informed of it.

JUSTICE. Oh, I know nothing of *him*; he's queer and close. One can never get him in a bout; he's not staunch.[71]

---

71   I.e., because Mr. Drummond doesn't drink to excess, the Justice considers him untrustworthy.

SUSAN. I believe he is not staunch to our match, and if that is prevented, we shall leave the country directly.

JUSTICE. Why, what can prevent it, sweety?

SUSAN. Perhaps Mr. Drummond's advice, for *he* can manage Mr. Hargrave.

JUSTICE. Ah, but my advice will go as far as his, I believe; and do you think I'll part with you, you little wicked rogue you? (*Chucking her chin.*)

SUSAN. Then if you find the match is likely to go off, you must use all your interest to bring it to bear; and then we sha'n't part, you little wicked rogue you. (*Chucking his chin.*)

JUSTICE. That I will. I'll plead for the wedding as vigorously, as if I had an hundred guineas with a brief.

SUSAN. Well, but d'ye mind me? I don't like the stranger this same 'squire ushered here.

JUSTICE. Not like her! Why, she's a devilish fine girl. Adod, the warm sparkling of her eyes catches one's heart, as if it was made of tinder.

SUSAN. Upon my word—a devilish fine girl—the sparkling of her eyes!

JUSTICE. Oh, I don't mean—that is—Oh, I would rather have one kind look of thine, sweet Mrs. Sukey, for t'other I dare not squint at.

SUSAN. Hah! I believe you are a coquette, but however I have certain reasons to wish this beautiful angel out of this house. I have observed looks that I don't like, between her and young Hargrave, and—you comprehend me—whatever interrupts the marriage, we are gone.

JUSTICE. I understand you; you may depend upon me. Let me see! How shall we manage to get her out of Drummond's clutches?

SUSAN. That's your business; I say that it must be done, and you must do it.

JUSTICE. To be sure, Mrs. Susan, let me consider—

SUSAN. We must have no qualms, Mr. Justice.

JUSTICE. We will have none, but what your smiles, sweet Sukey, can disperse. I must venture a little; the tender passions make one do anything. *Omnia vincit amor,*[72] say no more.

SUSAN. She shall be sent packing.

JUSTICE. Have I not given you the word of a magistrate? But come now, give me one kiss, you little dear, cruel, soft, sweet, charming baggage.

SUSAN. Oh, fie! You won't ask for wages before you've done your work. (*Runs off.*)

---

72   "Love conquers all" (Virgil, *Eclogues* 10).

JUSTICE. (*Following.*) Stop! Don't run so fast; don't run so fast, hussy. (*Exit.*)

Scene: An apartment.

Enter Mr. Drummond and George.

MR. DRUMMOND. I wish I had known it before matters had been carried so far; on a subject of this nature no woman can be affronted with impunity.

GEORGE. I am careless of her resentment; I will never be her husband, nor husband to any woman but *her* to whom I have given my vows.

MR. DRUMMOND. Hah! Have you carried your affair so forward?

GEORGE. Yes, sir, I have made that enchanting girl the offer of my heart and hand, and though her delicacy forbids her, while our families remain unknown to each other, to give the assent my heart aspires to, yet she allows me to catch hopes, that I would not forfeit to become master of the universe.

MR. DRUMMOND. There's a little of the ardor of youth in this—the ardor of youth, George; however, I will not blame you, for twenty years ago, I might have been tempted to enter the lists with you, myself.

GEORGE. I should fear less to meet a Hector in the field; in such a cause the fury of Achilles[73] would inspire me, and I would bear off my lovely prize from amidst the embattled phalanx.[74]

MR. DRUMMOND. Bravo! I like to see a man romantic in his love, and in his friendships: the virtues of him who is not an enthusiast in those noble passions, will never have strength to rise into fortitude, patriotism, and philanthropy. But here comes your father: leave us.

GEORGE. May the subject inspire you with resistless eloquence! (*Exit.*)

Enter Mr. Hargrave.

MR. DRUMMOND. So, Mr. Hargrave.

MR. HARGRAVE. So, Mr. Drummond—what, I guess your business.

MR. DRUMMOND. I suppose you do, and I hope you are prepared to hear me with temper.

---

73   Greek hero who killed the Trojan prince Hector and dragged his body in the dust outside Troy.
74   Battle formation.

MR. HARGRAVE. You'll talk to no purpose for I am fixed, and therefore the temper will signify nothing.

MR. DRUMMOND. Strange infatuation! Why must George be sacrificed to your ambition? Surely, it may be gratified without tying *him* to your Lady Dinah.

MR. HARGRAVE. How?

MR. DRUMMOND. By marrying her yourself, which, till now, I supposed to have been your design—and that would have been sufficiently preposterous.

MR. HARGRAVE. What! Make me a second time the slave of hysterics, longings, and vapors! No, no, I've got my neck out of the noose—catch it there again if you can. What, her Ladyship is not youthful enough for George, I suppose?

MR. DRUMMOND. True, but a more forcible objection is the disproportion in their minds. It would not be less reasonable to expect a new element to be produced between earth and fire, than that felicity should be the result of such a marriage.

MR. HARGRAVE. Pshaw, pshaw! What, do you suppose the whole world has the same idle notions about love and constancy, and stuff, that you have? D'ye think, if George was to become a widower at five and twenty, *he'd* whine all his life for the loss of his deary?

MR. DRUMMOND. Not if his deary, as you call her, should be a Lady Dinah; and if you marry him with no other view than to procure him a happy widowhood, I admire the election you have made. But, if she should be like my lost love, my sainted Harriet, my—oh! Hargrave—

MR. HARGRAVE. Come, come, I am very sorry I have moved you so. I did not mean to affect you. Come, give me your hand; 'sbud if a man has anything to do with one of you fellows with your fine feelings, he must be as cautious as if he was carrying a candle in a gunpowder barrel.

MR. DRUMMOND. 'Tis over, my friend, but when I can hear my Harriet named, without giving my heart a fond regret for what I have lost, reproach me; for then, I shall deserve it.

MR. HARGRAVE. Well, well, it shall be your own way. But come, let me convince you that you are wrong in this business.

—'Sbud! I tell you it has been the study of my life to make George a great man. I brought Lady Dinah here with no other design, and now, when I thought the matter was brought to bear, when Lady Dinah had consented, and my son, as I supposed, eager for the wedding—why!—'tis all a flam.[75]

MR. DRUMMOND. My good friend, the motives from which you would sacrifice your son's happiness appear to me so weak.

MR. HARGRAVE. Weak! Why, I tell you, I have provided a wife for George, who will make him, perhaps, one of the first men in the kingdom.

MR. DRUMMOND. That is, she would make him a court dangler, an attendant on ministers' levees—one whose ambition is to be fostered with the chameleon food of smiles and nods, and who would receive a familiar squeeze with as much rapture as the plaudits of a nation. Oh, shame, to transform an independent English gentleman into such a being!

MR. HARGRAVE. Well, to cut the argument short, the bargain is struck, and George shall marry Lady Dinah, or never have an acre of my land; that's all.

MR. DRUMMOND. And he shall never possess a rood[76] of mine, if he does. (*Walking about.*)

MR. HARGRAVE. (*Aside.*) There, I thought 'twould come to this. What a shame it is for a man to be so obstinate! But hold! Faith, if so, I may lose more than I get by the bargain; he'll stick to his word.

Enter Justice.

JUSTICE. I am very much surprised, Mr. Drummond, sir, that I can't be left alone in the discharge of my magisterial duties, but must be continually thwarted by you.

MR. DRUMMOND. This interruption, Mr. Justice, is ill-timed, and rather out of rule. I could wish you had chosen another opportunity.

JUSTICE. No opportunity like the present; no time like the present, sir. You've cause, indeed, to be displeased with my not observing rules, when you are continually breaking the law.

MR. DRUMMOND. Ha, ha, ha! Let us hear: What hen-roost robbery have you to lay to my charge now?

JUSTICE. Aye, sir, you may think to turn it off with a joke, if you please, but for all that, I can prove you to be a bad member of society, for you counteract the wise designs of our legislators and obstruct the operations of justice. Yes, sir, you do.

---

75   Sham.
76   Quarter of an acre.

MR. HARGRAVE. Don't be so warm. What is this affair?

JUSTICE. Why, the poacher, whom we committed last night, Mr. Drummond has released, and given money to his family. How can we expect a due observation of our laws, when rascals find encouragement for breaking them? Shall Lords and Commons in their wisdom assemble in parliament to make laws about hares and partridges, only to be laughed at? Oh, 'tis abominable!

MR. HARGRAVE. Very true, and let me tell you, Mr. Drummond; it is very extraordinary that you will be continually—

MR. DRUMMOND. Peace, ye men of justice! I have all the regard to the laws of my country, which it is the duty and interest of every member of society to possess. If the man had been a poacher, he should not have been protected by me; the poor fellow found the hare in his garden, which she had considerably injured.

MR. HARGRAVE. Ho, ho—what, the rascal justifies himself! An unqualified man gives reasons for destroying a hare! Zounds, if a gang of ruffians should burn my house, would you expect me to hear their reasons?

JUSTICE. (*Aside.*) Ah, there it works: Susan's my own.—There can be no reasons; if he had found her in his house, in his bedchamber, in his bed and offered to touch her, I'd prosecute him for poaching.

MR. DRUMMOND. Oh, blush to avow *such* principles!

MR. HARGRAVE. Look'ee, Mr. Drummond, though you govern George with your whimsical notions, you sha'n't me. I foresee how it will be as soon as I'm gone: my fences will be cut down, my meadows turned into common, my cornfields laid open, my woods at the mercy of every man who carries an axe, and, oh—this is noble, this is great!

MR. DRUMMOND. Indeed, 'tis ridiculous.

MR. HARGRAVE. I'll take care that my property sha'n't fall a sacrifice to such whimsies: I'll tie it up, I warrant me, and so Justice, come along. (*Going.*)

MR. DRUMMOND. We were talking on a subject, Mr. Hargrave, of more importance, at present, than this; and, I'll beg you'll hear me farther.

MR. HARGRAVE. Enough has been said already, Mr. Drummond. Or, if not, I'll give you one answer for all: I shall never think myself obliged to study the humor of a man, who thinks in such opposition to me. I have a humor of my own, which I am determined to gratify, in seeing George a great man. He shall marry Lady Dinah in two days, and all

the fine reasoning in the world, you will see, has less strength than
my resolution. 'Sbud, if I can't have the willing obedience of a son, I'll
enjoy the prerogatives of a father. Come along, Justice. (*Exit.*)

JUSTICE. D'ye hear with what a fine *firm* tone he speaks. This was only a
political stroke, to restore the balance of power.

MR. DRUMMOND. Why don't you follow, sir? (*Exit Justice.*) "My son shall
be a great man!" To such a vanity as this, how many have been sacrificed! "He shall be great: the happiness of love, the felicities that flow
from a suitable union, his heart shall be a stranger to, but he shall convey *my name*, decked with titles to posterity, though, to purchase these
distinctions, he lives a wretch." This is the silent language of the heart,
which we hold up to ourselves as the voice of reason and prudence.
(*Enter Emily.*) Miss Morley! Why this pensive air?

EMILY. I am a little distressed, sir. The delicacy of the motive which
induced you to place me here, I am perfectly sensible of, yet—

MR. DRUMMOND. Yet, what, my dear child?

EMILY. Do not think me capricious, if I entreat you to take me back to
your own house, till my uncle arrives. I cannot think of remaining
here.

MR. DRUMMOND. (*Aside.*) Then 'tis as I hoped.—What can have dis-
gusted you? Come, be frank: consider me a friend, to whom you may
safely open your heart.

EMILY. Your goodness, sir, is excessive. Shall I confess? The lady who will
soon have most right here treats me unkindly.

MR. DRUMMOND. That you can't wonder at. Be assured, I will effectually
defend you from her insults. But do you not pity poor George, for the
fate his father designs him?

EMILY. Yes, I do pity him.

MR. DRUMMOND. If I dared, I would go still further—I would hope that,
as his happiness depends on you—

EMILY. Sir!

MR. DRUMMOND. Let me not alarm you. I am acquainted with his passion, and wish to know that 'tis not displeasing to you.

EMILY. So circumstanced, sir, what can I say? He is destined to be the
husband of another.

MR. DRUMMOND. It is enough. I bind myself to you from this moment,
and promise to effect your happiness, if within compass of my abilities or fortune. But, that I may know my task, favor me with the key to
your uncle's character.

EMILY. My uncle possesses a heart, sir, that would do him honor, if he
would be guided by it, but unhappily he has conceived an opinion that

his temper is too flexible—that he is too easily persuaded—and the consequence is, he'll never be persuaded at all.

MR. DRUMMOND. I am sorry to hear that: a man who is obstinate from *such* a mistake, must be in the most incurable stage of the disorder. However, we'll attack this man of might. His flexibility shall be besieged, and if it won't capitulate, we'll undermine it.

EMILY. Ah, sir! My uncle is in a state of mind ill prepared for yielding. He returned from Spain with eager pleasure to his native country, but the disgust he has conceived for the alteration of manners during his absence has given him an impatience that you will hardly be able to combat.

MR. DRUMMOND. Take courage. Let me now lead you back to your young companions. I am obliged to be absent a short time, but I'll watch over you, and, if possible, lead you to happiness. (*Exit Drummond leading Emily.*)

Enter Justice.

JUSTICE. (*Tipsy.*) Where the devil does my clerk stay with Burn! But I know I'm right—yes, yes, 'tis a clear case. By the statute *anno primo Caroli Secundum*,[77] obtaining goods on false pretences, felony, with benefit—hum—with benefit. Now obtaining entrance into houses, upon false pretences, must be worse; I have no doubt but it amounts to a burglary, and that I shall be authorized to commit. Ho, here they are! Where is my clerk and Burn? (*Exit.*)

Enter Mr. Hargrave and Lady Dinah.

MR. HARGRAVE. Aye, aye, here's a pretty business. Bringing this girl into my house now is the consequence of Mr. Drummond's fine feelings. He will never take my advice, but I'll show him who is best qualified to sift into an affair of this sort, and yet I *am* a little puzzled, a stroller—

LADY DINAH. It is, doubtless, a strange story, Mr. Hargrave, and I beg that you will yourself question my servant concerning it.

MR. HARGRAVE. Why, what can she mean—what can her design be?

LADY DINAH. To *you* I should imagine her design must be very obvious, though Mr. Drummond's penetration was so easily eluded. By assuming the airs and manners of a person of rank, she doubtless expects to

---

77   In the first year of the reign of Charles II; i.e., 1660.

impose on the credulity of some young heir, and to procure—a jaunt
to Scotland[78]—*that*, Mr. Hargrave, I take to be her design.

MR. HARGRAVE. Ho, ho, is it so? Now I understand your ladyship; if
your man can prove what he asserts, be assured, madam, she shall not
stay in my house another moment. I'll young heir the baggage!

LADY DINAH. But consider, dear Mr. Hargrave, before you take any steps
in this affair, that 'tis possible, we may have been deceived, for though
my servant avows having been on the most intimate terms with her,
he may be mistaken in her person, you know.

MR. HARGRAVE. Oh, madam, I shall inquire into that: she shall pick
up no young heirs here, I warrant her. I'll see into that immediately.
(*Going.*)

Enter Justice, leading in Jarvis by the button.

JUSTICE. Here's the young man—the witness. I have brought him up in
order to his examination. Here, do you stand there. In the first place,
(*settling his wig*) in the first place, how old are you?

MR. HARGRAVE. Fiddle de de. What signifies how old he is?

JUSTICE. Why, yes it does, for, if he is not of age—

MR. HARGRAVE. Pshaw, pshaw, I'll examine him myself. How long is
since you left the strollers you were engaged with?

JARVIS. It is about two years since I had the honor of being taken into
my lady's service, and at that time I left the company.

MR. HARGRAVE. And did you leave the young woman in the company at
that time?

JARVIS. I did, sir, and I have never seen her since till now.

MR. HARGRAVE. I am strangely puzzled—I don't know what to think—

JUSTICE. It is indeed a difficult case, a very difficult case; I remember
Burn in the chapter on vagrants—

MR. HARGRAVE. Prithee, be silent. At this time you are not likely to clear
up matters at all.

JUSTICE. A Justice be silent! A silent Justice! A pretty thing indeed—are
we not the mouth of the law?

MR. HARGRAVE. What does your ladyship advise?

LADY DINAH. I advise! I don't advise, Mr. Hargrave.

JUSTICE. Why then, let the parties be confronted—

MR. HARGRAVE. Aye, let the parties be confronted.

---

78   An elopement. As Scotland's marriage laws were much less strict than England's,
young English couples often eloped to Gretna Green on the Scottish border.

JARVIS. Aye, aye, let us be confronted. If I once speak to her, she'll be too much dashed to be able to deny the charge.

Enter Servant.

SERVANT. Did your honor call?

MR. HARGRAVE. Go and tell my daughter, that I desire she'll bring her visitant here—the young lady.

JARVIS. (*Aside.*) Two glasses of brandy, and tremble yet! I wish I had swallowed the third bumper.[79]

LADY DINAH. Now, Mr. Hargrave, it will be exceedingly improper, that I should be present at this interview, so I shall retire till the affair is settled. (*Going.*)

MR. HARGRAVE. 'Sbud, my lady, if you go, I'll go too, and the Justice may settle it as well as he can.

JUSTICE. Nay, if you are for that, I shall be gone in a crack; I won't be left in the lurch, not I.

LADY DINAH. Bless me! I am surprised: only consider what an imputation may be thrown on my character. (*Enter Harriet and Emily.*) So, now 'tis determined.

HARRIET. Robert informed us, sir, that you requested our attendance.

MR. HARGRAVE. Yes, Harriet, I did send Robert. 'Tis about an odd affair—I had rather—but I don't know—pray, madam (*to Emily*)—be so kind to tell us if you know anything of that person (*pointing to Jarvis*).

EMILY. No, sir, I believe not. I do not recollect. I may have seen him before.

JARVIS. Oh, Miss Jenny, you don't recollect—what you have forgotten your old companion, William Jarvis?

EMILY. I do not remember, indeed, that I was ever honored with such a companion, and the mistake you have made of my name, convinces me that I never was.

JARVIS. Pshaw, pshaw, this won't do *now*. You was always a good actress, but behind the scenes, you know, we used to come down from our stilts, and talk in our proper persons. Why, sure, you will not pretend to forget our adventures at Colchester, the affair of the Blue Domino at Warwick, nor the plot which you and Mrs. Varnish laid against the manager at Beconsfield.

---

79   Brim-full glass.

HARRIET. Dear sir, nothing is so evident, as that the man has mistaken this lady for another person. I hope you'll permit us to go without hearing any more of his impertinence.

MR. HARGRAVE. If he is mistaken, no excuses will be sufficient. I don't know what to say—'tis a perplexing business, but I wish you would be so kind to answer the man, madam.

EMILY. Astonishment has kept me silent till now, sir, and I must still be silent, for I have not yet been taught to make defenses.

Enter George behind Jarvis.

JARVIS. Dear madam, why surely you have not forgot how often you have been my Juliet, and I your Alexander.[80]

GEORGE. Hark you, sir, if you dare utter another word to that lady, I'll break every bone in your body. Leave the room, rascal, this instant.

MR. HARGRAVE. You are too hot, George—he shall stay, and since things have gone so far, I'll sift the story to the bottom. If the young gentlewoman is not what he represents her, she has nothing to fear. Speak boldly, where did you last see that lady?

JUSTICE. Aye, speak boldly—give her a few more circumstances. Perhaps some of them may hit. People on occasions of this sort have generally short memories.

GEORGE. Surely, sir, you cannot allow these horrid—

MR. HARGRAVE. I do allow, sir, and if you can't be silent, leave the room.

JUSTICE. Yes, sir, or else you'll be committed for contempt of court. Now, for your name, child, your name, and that of your family.

EMILY. The name of my family, demanded on such occasion, I think myself bound to conceal; my silence on that subject, hitherto arose from a point of delicacy. That motive is now greatly strengthened, and I refuse to discover a name, which my imprudent conduct has disgraced.

JUSTICE. Ho, ho, pray let the lady be treated with respect—a person of consequence—stands upon constitutional ground—a patriot, I'll assure you—she refuses to answer interrogatories.

GEORGE. Sir, I cannot be any longer a silent witness of these insults. Your presence, madam, supports that rascal, or he should feel the immediate effect of my resentment.

---

80   He seems to be conflating plays, imagining himself as the hero, Alexander the Great, and Emily as Shakespeare's famous heroine, Juliet.

LADY DINAH. *Your* resentment will be unnecessary, sir, if he is not supported by truth. I shall take care that he is properly punished. (*Enter servant.*)

SERVANT. A gentleman in a coach-and-six enquires for your honor. His name is Morley.

EMILY. Hah, 'tis my uncle. I no longer dread his presence. Now, sir, you will be satisfied concerning my family.

Exeunt Emily and Harriet.

MR. HARGRAVE. (*To Lady Dinah.*) Her uncle! Heavens, madam, what have we done! (*Exit Hargrave.*)

LADY DINAH. Done! Nothing.—Madness (*aside*).

JUSTICE. So, so—the niece of a man who keeps a coach and six! We are got into a wrong box here.

She can be no patriot; our patriots don't ride in coaches and six.

GEORGE. Stay, sir, we have not done with you yet. You must now exhibit another part in this scene. What says your oracle, Burn, to such a fellow as this, Justice?

JUSTICE. Aye, you rascal, 'tis now your turn. Thou art a vilifier, a cheat, an impostor—'tis downright conspiracy. The niece of a man who keeps a coach and six! Why, how dost think to escape? Thou'lt cut a noble figure in the pillory, Mr. "Alexander the Great."

JARVIS. Sir—your honors—I humbly crave pardon for my mistake. I could have sworn the lady had been my old acquaintance, the likeness is so strong. But I humbly ask pardon—my lady!

LADY DINAH. Expect no protection from me; I discharge you from my service from this moment. The dilemma into which you have deceived me excites my warmest resentment.

GEORGE. Since your ladyship gives him up, he has no other protection. Who's there? (*Enter servants.*) Secure this fellow till I have leisure to enquire into the bottom of the affair—*he* is only the agent, I am convinced.

JARVIS. (*Aside.*) Aye, sir, but I am dumb, or we shall lose the reward.—I beseech your honor; 'twas all a mistake.

GEORGE. Take him away. (*Exeunt servants with Jarvis.*)

LADY DINAH. (*Aside.*) Hah! Are you suspicious, sir! I hope Susan has not put me in this fellow's power. I must be sure of that. (*Exit.*)

JUSTICE. 'Tis a conspiracy, that's certain, and will, I believe, come under *Scan. Mag.*[81]

> For 'tis a most scandalous libel. But hold—'gad so—let me see. It can be no libel. 'Tis a false story. If it had been true, aye, then indeed—if it had been true. But I'll go home and consult Burn, and you shall know what he says.
> ——Egad, it won't be amiss to get out of this Morley's way (*aside*). (*Exit.*)

GEORGE. Surely she must have been privy to this scandalous plot. But 'tis no matter; my fate is at its crisis. Mr. Morley's arrival fixes it. At this moment my fortitude forsakes me and I tremble to meet the man, on whose caprice depends the value of my existence.

ACT V

Scene: An apartment.

Enter Mr. Morley and Emily.

MORLEY. A pretty freak indeed! A pretty freak, in return for the care and solicitude with which I have watched over you. I have broke with the doctor for his share in this romantic affair.

EMILY. I am much concerned, sir, that compassion to my situation should have led that worthy man to take any step that you can think unpardonable. But when he found he could not move my resolution, he thought it his duty to accommodate me with a retreat amongst persons of reputation.

MORLEY. Retreat! So, whilst I was condemning my sweet innocent niece for stubbornness, willfulness, and ingratitude, she was only gone to a *retreat* to sit under elms, listen to the cawing of rooks, and carve her melancholy story on the young bark. Oh Emily, Emily! You ought to be made repent of this retreat, as you call it, as long as you live.

EMILY. Indeed, sir, I do repent.

---

81   *Scandalum magnatum* (Latin): "the utterance or publication of a malicious report against any person holding a position of dignity" (OED).

MORLEY. What's that? Repent! My dear Emily, I am rejoiced to hear
you say so. I knew you was always a good girl, on the whole. Come,
it sha'n't be a misfortune to you. I'll make Baldwin swear, before the
ceremony, that he'll never reproach—

EMILY. Sir, I must not deceive you: my repentance does not concern Mr.
Baldwin. He is, pardon me, sir—my sentiments with regard to him,
are, if possible, strengthened.

MORLEY. Are they so, mistress? Then farewell to humorings. Since your
sentiments are so strong, your resolution cannot be weak. 'Twill
enable you to bear this dreaded fate with heroism.

EMILY. I am glad you can be so supportive with my unhappiness, sir.
Where you jest with misery, you always design to lessen it.

MORLEY. Aye, that won't do. The easiness of my temper, girl, has been
my great misfortune. I never made a mistake in trade in my life, never,
but have been *persuaded*, and listened to *advice*, till I have been half
ruined. But I'll be resolute now for your sake.

EMILY. Surely, sir—

MORLEY. Aye, aye! I understand that speaking face: there is not a line in
it, but calls me monster. However, madam, after your retreat, you can
never expect to be the wife of another, so snap Baldwin while you can.

EMILY. Oh, sir, allow me to live single; I have no wish for the married
state, since he to whom my heart is devoted must be the husband of
another.

MORLEY. No wish for the married state! Ha, ha, ha! Why, 'tis the ultimate wish of every woman's heart; you all want husbands, from your
doll to your spectacles.

EMILY. The person with whom one enters into so important an union
should be at least agreeable, or—

MORLEY. What an age this is! Why, hussy, in the days of your great grandmother, a girl on the point of marriage had never dared to look above
her lover's beard, and would have been a wife a week before she could
have told the color of her husband's eyes. But, now, a girl of eighteen
will stare her suitor confidently in the face, and, after five minutes
conversation, give an account of every feature and peculiarity, from
his brow to his buckle.
—But, pray, Madam, what is it in Baldwin now, that so particularly
hits your fancy?

EMILY. His person is ungraceful, his manner assuming, and his mind
effeminate.

MORLEY. Very true, and is not this the description of all young men of the age? But he has five thousand a year; that's not quite so common a circumstance. Come, take the pencil again; lay on coarser colors or you won't convince me the picture's a bad one—considering the times.

EMILY. (*Aside.*) Hah! How different is Mr. Hargrave! If I could urge his merit.—You have heard my objections so often, sir, that the repetition can have no weight. But, surely, I may urge my happiness.

MORLEY. By all means, it shall be considered; therefore, John, order my carriage up. We are going directly, though you don't deserve it. The very moment we reach Grosvenor Street, you shall be tied fast to Baldwin, who is now waiting there with the parson at his elbow, and we'll this moment step into the carriage, and away as briskly as if Cupid was our coachman. Come now, don't put on that melancholy air. 'Tis only to turn the tables: fancy that I hate Baldwin, that you are driving to Scotland, and I pursuing you. Why the horses will move so slowly, you'll be ready to swear they don't gallop above three rood an hour.

EMILY. I entreat you, dear sir, stay, at least, till tomorrow.—Oh, where is Mr. Drummond (*aside*)?

MORLEY. Not a moment.

EMILY. You have not yet seen Mr. Drummond, to whom I am so much obliged.

MORLEY. I have made enquiries, and have heard a very extraordinary character of Mr. Drummond. We can make him acknowledgments by letter, and you may send him gloves. I know your design. You hope he will be able to talk me out of my resolution and, perhaps, I may be a little afraid of it myself. And so, to avoid that danger, we'll go directly.

EMILY. 'Tis so late, sir, and the night is dark.—Yet why should I wish to stay here (*aside*)?

MORLEY. No more trifling. Conduct me to the family, that we may take leave. If you complain of this as an act of tyranny, be comforted, child; 'tis the last you'll experience from me. My authority will expire with the night, and tomorrow morning, I shall be my dear niece Baldwin's most humble servant. (*Exeunt.*)

Enter George and Sir Charles.

GEORGE. What, refuse me your assistance in such an hour? Talk to me of prudence in a moment when I must be mad, if I am human? Yes, be prudent, sir; be prudent. The man who can be discreet when his friend's happiness is at stake, may gain the approbation of his own heart, but mine renounces him. Where can Mr. Drummond be?

SIR CHARLES. I am at your command in everything; I ask you only to reflect.

GEORGE. Yes, I do reflect, that in a few hours she will be irrevocably another's, lost to me forever. Unfeeling brute! To sacrifice such a woman to a man whom she despises!

SIR CHARLES. What then is your resolution?

GEORGE. There is but one way. She hangs on the point of a precipice, from which, if I do not snatch her in an instant, nothing can retrieve her. We will follow the carriage on horseback; let your chaise attend us with our servants. I'll force her from this tyrant uncle, carry her instantly to Dover, and in a few hours, breathe out my soul at her feet, in sweet security in France.

SIR CHARLES. Considering your plan is an *impromptu*, I admire its consistency. But, my dear George, have you weighed all its consequences? Your father—

GEORGE. Will perhaps disinherit me. Be it so—I have six hundred a year independent of his will. And six hundred a year in France with Emily Morley: Kingdoms! Empires! Paradise!

SIR CHARLES. But are you certain she will partake it with you?

GEORGE. No! But supposing the worst, I shall, at least, have had the happiness to preserve her from a fate she dreads. For the rest, I will trust to time and my ardent passion.

SIR CHARLES. Pity the days of chivalry are over, or what applause might'st thou not expect, adventurous knight!

GEORGE. Come, we have not a moment to lose. Let us get our people ready to follow, the instant the carriage sets out.

SIR CHARLES. But, George, George, I'll not accompany you a step after the lady's in your protection, for if your father should surmise that I have any hand in the *enlevement*,[82] I can hope for no success when I ask him for my charming Harriet.

GEORGE. Agreed! Let me have your chaise, and leave me to my fortune. I will not endanger your happiness. This key will let you in at the garden door. You may give fifty reasons for your short absence. Now, Cupid, Venus, Jove, and Juno, leap into your chariots, and descend to our assistance. (*Exeunt Sir Charles and George.*)

Enter Lady Dinah.

---

82   Abduction (French).

LADY DINAH. She's gone, and my alarms are at an end. 'Tis plain I had never the least foundation for my fears. What passed in the garden was mere gallantry, and the effects of her art; he suffered her uncle to carry her off with an indifference that transports me. How weak I have been, to allow my credulity to be imposed on by their suggestions, and my temper ruffled at a time when 'twas of so much importance to me to have been serene!

Enter Susan.

SUSAN. Oh, my lady, she's gone—the delightful obstinacy of the old uncle. It is well Mr. Drummond was not here; I was afraid—

LADY DINAH. Your joy wears a very familiar aspect. I know she's gone.

SUSAN. I beg pardon, my lady; I thought I might congratulate your ladyship on her being carried off. I was terribly afraid—

LADY DINAH. Yes, you have had most extraordinary fears on the occasion. You ought to have known, that the man whom I had received as my lover, could never have felt anything like a serious passion for such a girl as that.

SUSAN (*Aside.*) So, so, so! How soon our spirits are got up!—I am sure, my lady, 'twas not I who occasioned the interview in the garden today that so enraged you and confirmed your fears. You was ready enough then to believe all that was said against her.

LADY DINAH. How dare you reproach me with the errors which you led me into? 'Twas your fears I was governed by, and not my own; and your ridiculous plot was as absurd as your fears.

SUSAN. As to the plot, my lady, I am sure 'twas a good one, and would have sent her packing if the uncle hadn't come. 'Twasn't our fault he came. We have had the same trouble, and—service is no inheritance, and I hope your ladyship will consider—

LADY DINAH. How dare you think of a reward for such conduct? If you obtain my pardon, you ought to be highly gratified. Leave me, insolent, this moment.

SUSAN. (*Muttering aside.*) Ha! And dare you use me in this manner? I am glad you have betrayed yourself in time, when I can take a severe revenge. (*Exit Susan.*)

LADY DINAH. I have gone too far. Now must I court my servant, to forget the resentment which her impertinence occasioned. Well, 'tis but for a short time: the marriage over and I have done with her. I must retire to my apartment to recover my composure. Perhaps he'll visit

me there—but not to talk of veneration and respect again. Oh! I'll torment him for that. Nothing gives a woman so fine an opportunity of
plaguing her lover as an affectation of jealousy. If she feels it, she's his
slave; but, whilst she affects it—his tyrant. (*Exit.*)

Enter Bella and Harriet.

HARRIET. How very unfortunate, that Mr. Drummond is absent! He
would have opposed the reasoning of Lady Dinah, and prevented
their departure. Sure, never anything was so cruel.

BELLA. Oh, there's no bearing it. Your father is quite a manageable being,
compared to this odd, provoking mortal, whose imagined flexibility
baffles art, reason, and everything.

HARRIET. Never shall I forget the look, wild yet composed, agonized
though calm, which she gave me, as her uncle led her out. Her lover
must possess strange sentiments, to resolve to marry her, in spite of
her aversion.

BELLA. Sentiments! My dear, why he's a modern fine gentleman; there is
nothing he's so much afraid of as a fond wife. If I was Miss Morley, I'd
affect a most formidable fondness, and ten to one but she'd get rid of
him.

HARRIET. I wonder where Sir Charles is. He passed me in the hall, and
said in a hasty manner, he must tear himself from me for half an hour.

BELLA. I wonder rather where your brother is—but the heart of a
woman in love, is as unnatural as the ostrich's; it is no longer alive to
any sentiment but one, and the tenderest connections are absorbed in
its passion.

HARRIET. I hope it is not in your own heart, you find this picture of love.

Enter Sir Charles.

BELLA. Oh, here's one of our truants, but where's the other? Poor
George, I suppose, is binding his brow with willows.[83]

SIR CHARLES. That's not George's style in love. He has too much spirit
to cross his arms, and talk to his shadow, when he may employ his
hours to more advantage at the feet of a fair lady.

BELLA. What do you mean?

HARRIET. Where is my brother?

---

83   Worn thus, willow became a "symbol of grief for unrequited love or the loss of a
mate" (OED).

SIR CHARLES. On the road to France.

BOTH. France!

SIR CHARLES. Unless Mr. Morley has as much valor as obstinacy, for George has pursued him, and, by this time, I dare swear, has gained possession of his niece.

BELLA. Oh! How I dote on his knight-errantry! Commend me to a lover, who, instead of patiently submitting to the circumstances that separate him from the object of his passion, boldly takes the reins of fortune in his own hands, and *governs* the accidents which he can't avoid.

HARRIET. How can you praise such a daring conduct? I tremble for the consequences!

SIR CHARLES. What consequences, madam, can he dread, who snatches the woman he loves from the arms of the man she hates?

Enter servant.

SERVANT. My master, sir, is returned. The lady fainted in the chaise, and he has carried her back to Mr. Drummond's.

SIR CHARLES. The devil! Is he at home?

SERVANT. No, sir, and Mr. Morley is come back too; he drove through the gates this minute.

BELLA. Nay, then George will lose her at last; he was a fool for not pursuing his route.

SIR CHARLES. He has no chance now, but through Mr. Drummond, and what can he hope? Mr. Drummond has only reason on his side, and the passions of three to combat.

BELLA. Aye, here he comes—and Mr. Hargrave, as loud as his huntsman.

HARRIET. Let us fly to the parlor, and then we can send intelligence of what passes to George. (*Exeunt.*)

Enter Mr. Morley and Mr. Hargrave.

MR. MORLEY. Yes, yes, 'tis fact—matter of fact, upon my honor. Your son was the person who took her out of the coach.

MR. HARGRAVE. Sir, 'tis impossible! Ha, ha, ha! My son! Why, he's under engagements that would make it madness.

MR. MORLEY. Then, sir, you may depend upon it, the fit is on him now, for he clapped Emily into a chaise, whilst an impudent puppy fastened

on me. Egad! Twenty years ago I'd have given him sauce to his
Cornish hug.[84] I could not discern his face, but t'other I'll swear to.
MR. HARGRAVE. George! Look for George there! I'll convince you, sir,
instantly. Ha, ha!

Enter Harriet.

MR. HARGRAVE. Where's George?
HARRIET. Sir, my brother is at Mr. Drummond's.
MR. HARGRAVE. There! I knew it could not be him, though you would
not be persuaded.
MR. MORLEY. What a plague! You can't persuade me out of my senses.
Your son, I aver, took her out of the coach—with her own consent, no
doubt, and on an honorable design without doubt! Sir, I give you joy
of your daughter.
MR. HARGRAVE. If it is on an honorable design, they may live on their
honor, or starve with it—not a single *sous* shall they have of me. But I
won't yet believe my George could be such a fool.
MR. MORLEY. Fool! Sir, the man who loves Emily gives no such proof
of folly neither, but she shall be punished for hers. 'Twas a concerted
affair, I see it plainly, all agreed upon, but she shall repent.
MR. HARGRAVE. Your resentment, sir, is extraordinary. I must tell you
that my son's ancestry, or the estate to which he is heir—if he has not
forfeited by his disobedience—are not objects for the contempt of any
man.
MR. MORLEY. Very likely, sir, but they are objects to which I shall never
be reconciled. What! Have I been toiling these thirty years in Spain, to
make my niece a match for any man in England, to have her fortune
settled by an adventure in a post chaise—an evening's frolic for a
young spark, who had nothing to do but push the old fellow into a
corner, and whisk off with the girl? Sir, if there was not another man
in the kingdom, your son should not have my consent to marry Emily.
MR. HARGRAVE. And if there was not another woman in England, I'd
suffer the name Hargrave to be annihilated, rather than he should

---

84   A Cornish hug was a particularly effective form of grip (the Cornish were celebrated
wrestlers). To give sauce is to subject another to the same kind of usage. Mr. Morley
means that were he twenty years younger he would have attacked George.

be husband to your niece. (*Hargrave and Morley walk about the stage disordered.*)

Enter Mr. Drummond.

MR. DRUMMOND. Gone! Her uncle arrived and the amiable girl gone. What infatuation, Mr. Hargrave, could render you so blind to the happiness that awaited your family? I'll follow this obdurate man— where's George? Look for George there; he shall hear reason.

MR. HARGRAVE. There, sir. That's the person to whom you must address your complaints.

MR. DRUMMOND. (*To Mr. Hargrave.*) Unfortunate! I have made discoveries, that must have shaken even your prejudices.—But this uncle! Surely, my dear Harriet, you might have prevailed.

HARRIET. Sir, this gentleman is Mr. Morley—Mr. Drummond, sir.

MR. DRUMMOND. Hah! I beg your pardon. Sir, I am rejoiced to see you; I understood you were gone.

MR. MORLEY. I was gone, sir, but I was robbed of my niece on the road. She was taken out of my coach, and carried off—which forced me to return.

MR. DRUMMOND. Carried off!

MR. HARGRAVE. Aye, sir, carried off by George, whom you have trained to such a knowledge of his duty.

MR. MORLEY. Stopped on the King's highway, sir, by the fiery youth, and my niece dragged from my side.

MR. DRUMMOND. Admirable!

MR. HARGRAVE. What's this right too? By heaven, it is not to be borne.

MR. DRUMMOND. Where are they?

HARRIET. At your house, sir—

MR. MORLEY. What a country am I fallen into! Can a person of your age and character approve of so rash and daring—

MR. HARGRAVE. Let George do what he will; he's sure of his approbation.

MR. DRUMMOND. Gentlemen, if you are sure Miss Morley is at my house, I am patience itself; she is too rich a prize to be gained without some warfare.

MR. MORLEY. Sir, I am resolved to—

Enter Lady Dinah. Exit Harriet frightened.

LADY DINAH. So, Mr. Hargrave! So sir! What, your son—this new insult
    deprives me of utterance. But your son—what is the reason of this
    complicated outrage?
MR. HARGRAVE. My dear lady Dinah, I am as much enraged as you can
    be. But he shall fulfill his engagements; depend on it, he shall.
MR. MORLEY. Engagements! What, the young gentleman was engaged
    too! A very fine youth, upon my word!
LADY DINAH. (*To Mr. Hargrave.*) Your honor is concerned, sir, and if I
    was sure he was drawn in by the girl's art, and that he was convinced
    of the impropriety—
MR. MORLEY. Drawn in by the girl's art! Whatever cause I may have to
    be offended with my niece's conduct, madam, no person shall speak
    of her with contempt in my presence. I presume this gentleman's son
    was engaged to your daughter, but that's not sufficient reason for—
LADY DINAH. Daughter! Impertinent! No, sir, 'twas to *me* that he was
    engaged, and, but for the arts of your niece—
MR. MORLEY. To you! A matrimonial negotiation between that young
    fellow and you! Nay then, 'fore George, I don't wonder at your ill tem-
    per. A disappointment in love at *your* time of life must be the devil.
LADY DINAH. Mr. Hargrave, do you suffer me to be thus insulted?
MR. HARGRAVE. Why, my lady, we must bear something from this gen-
    tleman; the mistake we made about his niece was a very ugly business.
MR. DRUMMOND. I entreat you, madam, to retire from a family, to
    whom, if you suffer me to explain myself—
LADY DINAH. What new insolence is this?
MR. DRUMMOND. I would spare you, my lady, but you will not spare
    yourself. Blush, then, whilst I accuse you of entering into a base
    league with your servants, to blast the reputation of an amiable young
    lady, and drive her from the protection of Mr. Hargrave's family.
MR. HARGRAVE. (*Aside.*) What! A league with her servants?
LADY DINAH. And how dare you accuse me of this? Am I to answer for
    the conduct of my servants?
MR. DRUMMOND. The *villainy* of your servants is the consequence of
    those principles with which you have poisoned their minds. Robbed
    of their religion, they were left without support—against temptations
    to which *you*, madam, have felt, philosophy opposes its shield in vain.

LADY DINAH. (*Aside.*) I feel his superiority to my inmost soul, but he
    shall not see his triumph.—Is it your virtue which prompts you to

load me with injuries, to induce Mr. Hargrave to break through every tie of honor—through the most sacred engagements!

MR. DRUMMOND. I have just heard these terms, nearly as much prostituted by your servants, who reproach you with not keeping your engagements to them.

LADY DINAH. (*Aside.*) Ha! Am I then betrayed?

Enter George, leading Emily[, followed by Bella, Harriet, and Sir Charles].

GEORGE. Miss Morley, sir, commanded me to lead her to you; I cannot ask you to pardon a rashness, of which I do not repent.

MR. HARGRAVE. Then I shall *make* you, I fancy.

MR. MORLEY. Ha! Did you really wish to return to me?

EMILY. I left Mr. Drummond's, sir, the moment I knew you were here.

MR. MORLEY. That's a good girl; I'll remember it. Come, child, the coach is at the door and we must make speed to retrieve our lost time. But have a care, young gentleman; though I have pardoned your extravagance once, a second attempt shall find me prepared for your reception.

GEORGE. If Miss Morley consents to go with you, sir, you have no second attempt to fear. But since this moment is the crisis of our fate, thus I entreat you (*kneeling*)—you, to whom I have sworn eternal love, to become my wife. Consent, my charming Emily, and every moment of my future life shall thank you.

MR. MORLEY. So, so, so

MR. HARGRAVE. What, without my leave?   } *All together*

LADY DINAH. Amazing!

EMILY. At such a moment as this, meanly to disguise my sentiments would be unworthy of the woman, to whom you offer such a sacrifice. Obtain the consent of those who have a right to dispose of us, and I'll give you my hand at the altar.

MR. MORLEY. That you will not, my frank madam, so no more ceremony but away (*seizing her arm, and going off*).

MR. DRUMMOND. And will you go, impenetrable man? I have discovered, sir, that your niece is the daughter of Major Morley, who was one of the earliest friends of my youth. He would not have borne the distress she now endures. I will be a father to his orphan Emily, and ensure the felicity of two children, on the point of being sacrificed to the ambition and avarice of those, on whose hearts Nature has graven duties, which they willfully misspell.

LADY DINAH. What, sir, are you not content with the insults you have
offered to me and Mr. Hargrave, but you must interfere with this
gentleman in the disposal of his niece!

MR. MORLEY. What right have you, sir, to dispose of our children?

MR. HARGRAVE. Aye, very true; you don't know how to value the authority of a parent.

MR. DRUMMOND. Mistaken men! Into what an abyss of misery, perhaps
of guilt, would you plunge them! They claim from you happiness,
and you withhold it; they shall receive it from me. I will settle the
jointured land of my Harriet on Miss Morley, and George shall *now*
partake that fortune to which I have already made him heir.

MR. HARGRAVE. Aye, there's no stopping him. What can these servants
have told him that makes him so warm? Egad, I'll hear their tale. (*Exit
unperceived by Lady Dinah.*)

MR. MORLEY. Why, sir, this is extraordinary friendship indeed! Settle
jointured lands! I am glad Brother Tom had prudence enough to
form such a connection; 'twas seldom he minded the main chance—
honor and a greasy knapsack, running about after ragged colors
instead—

MR. DRUMMOND. Sir, *I* have served, and I love the profession. The army
is not more the school of honor than of philosophy. A true soldier is
a citizen of the world; he considers every man of honor as his brother,
and the urbanity of his heart gains his country *subjects*, whilst his
sword only vanquishes her *foes*.

MR. MORLEY. Nay, if you have all this romance, I don't wonder at your
proposal; however, though your jointure lands might have been necessary for Major Morley's daughter, my niece, sir, if she marries with my
consent, shall be obliged to no man for a fortune.

LADY DINAH. The insolence of making me witness to all this is insupportable. Is this you, sir, who this very morning paid your vows to me?

GEORGE. Pardon, madam, the error of this morning; I imagined myself
paying my devoirs to a lady who was to become my mother.

LADY DINAH. Your mother! Sir—your mother! Mr. Hargrave—ha!
Where is Mr. Hargrave?

Enter Mr. Hargrave.

[MR. HARGRAVE.] I am here, my lady, and have just heard a tale of so
atrocious a nature from your servants, that I would not, for half my
estate, such an affair should have happened in my family.

LADY DINAH. And can you believe the malicious tale?

MR. HARGRAVE. Indeed I do.

LADY DINAH. Mr. Drummond's arts have then succeeded.

MR. HARGRAVE. *Your* arts have not succeeded, my lady, and you have *no* chance for a husband now, I believe, unless you prevail on George to run off with *you.*

LADY DINAH. Insolent wretches! Order my chaise. I will not stay another moment beneath this roof. When persons of my rank, thus condescend to mix with plebeians—like the phoenix, which sometimes appears within the ken of common birds—they are stared at, jeered and hooted, till they are forced to ascend again to their proper region to escape the flouts of ignorance and envy. (*Exit.*)

MR. MORLEY. Well said, a rare spirit; faith, I see ladies of quality have their privileges too. (*As Lady Dinah goes off, George fixes his eye on his father, and points after her.*)

MR. HARGRAVE. (*Catching George's hand.*) My dear boy, I believe we were wrong here, and I am heartily glad we have escaped. But I suppose you'll forget it, when I tell you I have no objection to your endeavoring to prevail on this gentleman—

GEORGE. Nothing, dear sir, can prevent my feeling the most unbounded gratitude for the permission. Now, may I hope, sir—

MR. MORLEY. Hope, sir! Upon my word, I don't know what to say; you have somehow contrived to carry matters to such a length—that asking my consent is become a matter of form.

MR. HARGRAVE. Upon my soul, I begin to find out, that in some cases one's children should lead. Come, sir, do keep me in countenance that I mayn't think I yielded too soon.

MR. DRUMMOND. Your consent, sir, is all we want to become a very joyous circle. Let us prevail on you to permit your beloved Emily to receive the addresses of my godson, and you will, many happy years hence, recollect his boldness on the road, as the most fortunate rencounter of your life. You shall come and live amongst us, and we'll reconcile you to your native country. Notwithstanding our ideas of the degeneracy of the times, we shall find room enough to act virtuously, and to enjoy in England, more securely than in any other country in the world, the rewards of virtue.

MR. MORLEY. Sir, I like you. Promise me your friendship and you shall dispose of my niece.

MR. DRUMMOND. I accept the condition with pleasure.

MR. MORLEY. There it is now; this is always the way—persuaded out of every resolution, a perfect proverb for flexibility.

GEORGE. Oh, sir, permit me—

MR. MORLEY. Nay, no ecstasies. Emily dislikes you now you've got me on your side. What say you? (*to Emily*). Don't you begin to feel your usual reluctance?

EMILY. The proof I have given of my sentiments, sir, admits of no disguise; or, if disguise were necessary, I could not assume it.

GEORGE. Enchanting frankness! My heart, my life must thank you for this goodness. But what shall I say to you (*to Mr. Drummond*)—to you, sir, to whom I already owe more than—

MR. DRUMMOND. To me you owe nothing. The heart, George, must have some attachments. Mine has for many years been centered in you. If I have struggled for your happiness, 'twas to gratify myself.

GEORGE. Oh, sir, why will you continually give me such feelings, and yet refuse them utterance? Seymour, behold the happiest of men!

SIR CHARLES. May your bliss, my dear George, be as permanent as 'tis great. (*To Hargrave.*) Allow me, sir, to seize this propitious moment to ask your consent to a second union. Permit me to entreat Miss Hargrave for her hand, and I'll prove George a vain boaster, when he calls himself the happiest of men.

MR. HARGRAVE. Why, Sir Charles, you have chosen a very lucky moment, but there's no moment in which I should not have heard this request with pleasure. Why, Harriet, if we may believe your eyes, you are not very angry with Sir Charles for this request.

HARRIET. A request, sir, which gives you so much pleasure ought not to give your Harriet pain.

BELLA. Lord! You look so insulting with your happiness, and seem to think I make such an awkward figure amongst you, but here (*taking a letter from her pocket*); this informs me—that a certain person—

GEORGE. Of the name of—Belville—

BELLA. Be quiet—is landed at Dover, and posting here, with all the saucy confidence our engagements inspire him with.

MR. DRUMMOND. Say you so? Then we'll have the three weddings celebrated on the same day.

BELLA. Oh mercy! I won't hear of it! *Love*, one might manage that perhaps—but *honor*, *obey*—'tis strange the ladies had never interest enough to get this ungallant form mended.

MR. DRUMMOND. The marriage vow, my dear Bella, was wisely framed for common apprehensions: love teaches a train of duties that no vow can reach, that refined minds only can perceive, but which they pay with the most delighted attention. You are now entering on this state—may you—and you (*to Bella, significantly*) and you (*to the audience*) possess the blissful envied lot of—married lovers!

FINIS

EPILOGUE.

Written by D. Garrick, Esq.
Spoken by Miss Younge. (Bella)

Post haste from Italy arrives my lover!
Shall I to you, good friends, my fears discover?
Should foreign modes his virtues mar, and mangle,
And *caro sposo*[85] prove—Sir Dingle Dangle;
No sooner *joined* than *separate* we go,
Abroad—we never shall each other know,
At home: I mope above; he'll pick his teeth below.
In sweet domestic chat we shall ne'er mingle,
And, wedded though I am, still shall live single.
However modish, I detest this plan:
For me, no mawkish creature weak and wan;
He must be *English*, and an *English*—man.
To nature, and his country, false and blind,
Should *Belville* dare to twist his form and mind,
I will discard him—and to Britain true,
A Briton choose—and maybe one of *you*!
Nay, don't be frightened; I am but in jest;
Free men in love or war, should ne'er be pressed.
If you would know my utmost expectation,
'Tis one unspoiled by travelled education;
With knowledge, taste, much kindness, and some whim,
Good sense to govern me, must keep his heart from roving;
Then I'll forgive him, if he proves too loving.
If, in these times, I should be blessed by fate
With such a *phoenix*, such a matchless mate,
I will by kindness and some small discerning,
Take care that *Hymen's* torch continues burning.
At weddings nowadays the torch thrown down,

---

85   A loving spouse (Italian).

Just makes a smoke then stinks throughout the town!
No married Puritan—I'll follow pleasure,
And even the fashion, but in moderate measure.

NOTE ON THE TEXT

The Runaway was first performed on February 15, 1776, and published anonymously in March, 1776. The British Library copy of the first edition, an octavo, is my copy text. It bears the imprint "London: Printed for the author, and sold by Mr. Dodsley, Mr. Becket, and Mr. Cadell; Mr. Langman, and Carnan and Newbery, 1776." The text is identical to that of a Huntington Library 1776 copy bearing the same imprint, now bound with other plays, and to the Yale copy that Frederick Link uses in his 1979 facsimile edition of Cowley's plays. The first edition I call O1. A 1776 second edition of the play bears the same imprint and is a reissue of the first edition with a different title page. This I call O2. A Harvard Houghton Library copy, probably 1776, also octavo, has no publisher information on the title page and seems to be a pirated copy; I call it O3. Another octavo copy (1776?), which I call O4, is presented as "A new edition" and has an engraved title page and the illustration included on p. 195; it bears the same imprint as O1. A Bodleian library octavo copy, probably 1790, is printed in London "By and for Barker and Son." This I call O5. Because the Larpent manuscript of the play, in the Huntington Library collection, contains many underlinings that parallel italics used in O1, I have reproduced the O1 italics without commenting on variations that appear in the other copies cited here. The letter to Garrick appears in all these copies. In the last years of her life, Cowley revised her plays for the publication of her *Works*, which appeared in 1813. The differences between this nineteenth-century edition and the eighteenth-century ones cited here are extensive, and I have not noted them. *The Runaway* appears after 1813 only in Frederick Link's facsimile edition (1979), a Pickering & Chatto edition (2001), and a Dodo Press edition (January, 2010). All the copies cited here note that some scenes do not appear in production; highlighted text in the play is omitted at the theater.

TEXTUAL VARIATIONS

Dedication	perceived ...
O1, O2: Unpatronized by any *name*, I presented myself to you, obscure and unknown. You	O3, O4, O5: I presented myself to you, unpatronized by any name. You perceived ...

1.1
(p. 200)
01, 02: lists
03, 04, 05: list
(p. 202)
01, 02: ardor
03, 04, 05: ardors

1.2
(p. 203)
01, 02: Enter Mr. Hargrave.
03, 04, 05: Enter Mr. Hargrave, and a servant.... (Exit servant.)
(p. 207)
01, 02: Exeunt.
03, 04, 05: Exeunt Mr. Drummond, Bella, and Harriet.
(p. 208)
01, 02: Aye, aye, a plague on all the innovations that tend to produce a race of *pretty fellows* instead of *Englishmen*—and puny girls, for the mothers of heroes. Give me
03, 04, 05: *Enter Justice* [after Mr. Hargrave's speech]. Justice: Aye, aye, you are right, 'squire. Give me
01, 02: But, what a plague, 'squire, d'ye stay here for?
03, 04, 05: But, what a plague d'ye stay here for?

1.3
(p. 209)
01, 02: fellow of a philosopher, now—would
03, 04, 05: fellow of a philosopher—would

2.1
(p. 214)
01: Your whip, sir—your bit wants lashing
02, 03, 04, 05: Your whip, sir— your wit wants lashing

2.2
(p. 215)
01, 04: impossible to have resisted
02, 03, 05: impossible, Sir, to have resisted
01, 02: my good genius—I thank her—that inspired them
03, 04, 05: my good genius—I thank her—who inspired them
(p. 217)
01, 02: lecture on vegetation
03, 04, 05: lecture on the vegetable system

2.5
(p. 229)
01, 02: I begin to think it
03, 04, 05: I began to think it

3.2
(p. 234)
01, 02: but pray leave us cards
03, 04, 05: but leave cards
(p. 235)
01, 02: Belville!
03, 04, 05: Beauchamp!
01, 02: Belville's happiness
03, 04, 05: Beauchamp's happiness
01, 02: Mr. Belville, perhaps
03, 04, 05: Mr. Beauchamp, perhaps

3.3
(p. 236)
01, 02: Ha, not here then! Sweet *resemblance*
03, 04, 05: Sweet *resemblance*
01, 02: Enter George. Catches his

hand with the picture.

O3, O4, O5: Enter George. Seizes his arm.

3.4
(p. 240)

O1, O2: Hah, my good lady, is it so? Ha, ha, ha! I must see

O3, O4, O5: Hah, my good lady, is it so? What old woman on earth could bear to see the ardors of a fine young fellow to an handsome girl—a young fellow whom she looks on as her own too— without being mad? Ha, ha, ha! I must see

O1, O2: Enter Lady Dinah, not seeing Susan.

O3, O4, O5: Enter Lady Dinah.

O1, O2: Oh, a base man! I could have trampled him

O3, O4, O5: A base man! I could have trampled him

4.3
(p. 255)

O1, O2: (*Aside.*) Ah, there it works: Susan's my own.

O3, O4, O5: [The aside does not appear in this speech but later in the scene.]
(p. 256)

O1, O2: Mr. Drummond. Why don't you follow, sir? (*Exit Justice.*)

O3, O4, O5: Mr. Drummond. Why don't you follow, sir? Justice. I will, I will.—There it works: Susan's my own (*aside*). (*Exit Justice.*)
(p. 262)

O1: and will, I believe, come under *Scan. Mag.* For 'tis a most

scandalous libel. But hold—'gad so—let me see. It can be no libel. 'Tis a false story. If it had been true, aye, then indeed—if it had been true. But I'll go home and consult Burn

O2: and will, I believe, come under *Scan. Mag.* For 'tis a most scandalous libel. But hold—let me see. It can be no libel. 'Tis a false story. If it had been true, aye, then indeed—if it had been true. Well, I'll go home and consult Burn

O3, O4, O5: and will, I believe, come under *Scan. Mag.* But I'll go home and consult Burn

5.1
(p. 273)

O1: Enter George, leading Emily.

O2, O3, O4, O5: Enter George, leading Emily, followed by Bella, Harriet, and Sir Charles.

A MISCELLANY OF CRITICISM
BY WOMEN DRAMATISTS

.

I. APHRA BEHN, EPISTLE TO THE READER,
THE DUTCH LOVER: A COMEDY (1673)

... In short, I think a play the best divertissement that wise men have: but I do also think them nothing so, who do discourse as formally about the rules of it, as if 'twere the grand affair of human life. This being my opinion of plays, I studied only to make this as entertaining as I could, which whether I have been successful in, my gentle reader, you may for your shilling judge. To tell you my thoughts of it were to little purpose, for were they very ill, you may be sure I would not have exposed it. Nor did I so till I had first consulted most of those who have a reputation for judgment of this kind, who were at least so civil (if not kind) to it as did encourage me to venture it upon the stage, and in the press. Nor did I take their single word for it, but used their reasons as a confirmation of my own.

Indeed that day 'twas acted first, there comes me into the pit a long, lither, phlegmatic, white, ill-favored wretched fop, an officer in masquerade newly transported with a scarf and feather out of France, a sorry animal that has naught else to shield it from the uttermost contempt of all mankind, but that respect which we afford to rats and toads, which though we do not well allow to live, yet when considered as a part of God's creation, we make honorable mention of them. A thing, reader—but no more of such a smelt. This thing, I tell ye, opening that which serves it for a mouth, out issued such a noise as this to those that sat about it, that they were to expect a woeful play, God damn him, for it was a woman's. Now how this came about, I am not sure but I suppose he brought it piping hot from some who had with him the reputation of a villainous wit. For creatures of his size of sense talk without all imagination, such scraps as they pick up from other folks. I would not for a world be taken arguing with such a property as this, but if I thought there were a man of any tolerable parts, who could upon mature deliberation distinguish well his right hand from his left, and justly state the difference between the number of sixteen and two, yet had this prejudice upon him, I would take a little pains to make him know how much he errs. For waiving the examination why women, having equal education with men, were not as capable of knowledge of whatever sort as well as they, I'll only say, as I have touched before, that plays have no great room for that which is men's advantage over women: that is, learning. We all know well that the immortal Shakespeare's plays (who was not guilty of much more of this than often falls to women's share) have better pleased the world than Jonson's works, though by the way 'tis said that Benjamin was no such rabbi neither, for I am informed his learning was but grammar high (sufficient indeed to rob poor Sallust[1] of his best orations), and it hath been observed, that they are apt to admire him most confoundedly, who had just such a scantling of it as he had; and I have seen a man the most severe of Jonson's sect, sit with his hat removed less than a hair's breadth from one sullen posture for almost three hours at *The Alchemist*, who at that excellent play of *Harry the Fourth*, which yet I hope is far enough from farce, hath very hardly kept his doublet whole. But affectation hath always had a greater share both in the actions and discourse of men than truth and judgment have, and for our modern ones, except our most inimitable laureate,[2] I dare to say I know of none that write at such a formidable rate, but that a woman may well hope to reach their greatest heights.

Then for their musty rules of unity, and God knows what besides; if they meant anything, they are enough intelligible and as practicable by a woman, but really methinks they that disturb their heads with any other rules of plays besides the making them pleasant, and avoiding of scurrility, might much better be employed in studying how to improve men's too imperfect knowledge of that ancient English game, which hight "Long Laurence."[3] And if comedy should be the picture of ridiculous mankind, I wonder anyone should think it such a sturdy task, whilst we are furnished with such precious originals as him I lately told you of, if at least that character do not dwindle into farce and so become too mean an entertainment for those persons who are used to think. Reader, I have a complaint or two to make to you, and I have done. Know then this play was hugely injured in the acting, for 'twas done so imperfectly as never any was before, which did more harm to this than it could have done to any other sort, the plot being busy (though I think not intricate) and so requiring a continual attention, which being interrupted by the intolerable negligence of some that acted in it, must needs much spoil the beauty on't. My Dutch Lover spoke but little of what I intended for him, but supplied it with a deal of idle stuff, which I was wholly unacquainted with till I had heard it first from him, so that Jack Pudding[4] ever used to do, which though I knew before, I gave him yet the part because I knew him so acceptable to most o' th' lighter periwigs about the town, and he indeed did vex me so I could almost be angry. Yet,

---

1   Roman historian and orator (86-34 BCE).
2   John Dryden, poet laureate 1670-88.
3   The name Lawrence was associated with idleness.
4   A buffoon character.

but reader, you remember, I suppose, a fusty piece of Latin that has passed from hand to hand this thousand years, they say (and how much longer I can't tell) in favor of the dead. I intended him a habit much more notably ridiculous, which if it can ever be important was so here, for many of the scenes in the last three acts depended upon the mistakes of the colonel for Haunce, which the ill-favored likeness of their habits is supposed to cause. Lastly, my epilogue was promised me by a person who had surely made it good, if any, but he failing of his word, deputed one, who has made it as you see, and to make out your pennyworth, you have it here. The prologue is by misfortune lost. Now, reader, I have eased my mind of all I had to say and so sans farther compliment, adieu.

2. APHRA BEHN, PROLOGUE, *THE FORCED MARRIAGE*; OR, *THE JEALOUS BRIDEGROOM* (1670)

> Gallants, our poets have of late so used ye,
> In play and prologue too, so much abused ye.
> That should we beg your aids, I justly fear,
> Y'ave so incensed you'd hardly lend it here.
> But when against a common foe we arm,
> Each will assist to guard his own concern.
> Women, those charming victors, in whose eyes,
> Lay all their arts, and their artilleries;
> Not being contented with the wounds they made,
> Would by new stratagems our light invade.
> Beauty alone goes now at too cheap rates,
> And therefore they like wise and politic states,
> Court a new power that may the old supply,
> And keep as well as gain the victory.
> They'll join the force of wit to beauty now,
> And so maintain the right they have in you;
> If the vain sex this privilege should boast
> Past cure of a declining face we're lost.
> You'll never know the bliss of change, this art
> Retrieves (when beauty fades) the wand'ring heart,
> And though the airy spirits move no more,
> Wit still invites as beauty did before.
> Today, one of their party ventures out,
> Not with design to conquer but to scout:
> Discourage but this first attempt, and then,

They'll hardly dare to sally out again.
The poetess too, they say, has spies abroad,
Which have disposed themselves in every road,
I'th'upper box, pit, galleries, every face
You find disguised, in a black velvet case.
My life on't, is her spy on purpose sent,
To hold you in a wanton compliment;
That so you may not censure what she's writ,
Which done, they'll face you down, 'twas full of wit.
Thus, while some common prize you hope to win
You let the tyrant victor enter in.
I beg today you'd lay that humor by,
Till you rencounter at the nursery,⁵
Where they, like centinels, from duty free,
May meet and wanton with the enemy.
[*Enter an actress who speaks.*]
How hast thou labored to subvert in vain,
What one poor smile of ours calls home again?
Can any see that glorious sight, and say,
    (*Woman pointing to the ladies.*)
A woman shall not victor prove today?
Who is't that to their beauty would submit
And yet refuse the fetters of their wit?
He tells you tales of stratagems and spies;
Can they need art that have such powerful eyes?
Believe me, gallants, he 'as abused you all;
There's not a vizard in our whole cabal:
Those are but pickeroons that scour for prey,
And catch up all they meet with in their way,
Who can no captives take, for all they do,
Is pillage ye, then gladly let you go.
Ours scorn the petty spoils, and do prefer,
The glory not the interest of the war:
But yet our forces shall obliging prove,
Imposing naught but constancy in love,
That's all our aim, and when we have it too,
We'll sacrifice it all to pleasure you.

---

5   A theater establishment in London for training actors.

3. APHRA BEHN, PREFACE, *THE LUCKEY CHANCE;*
OR, *AN ALDERMAN'S BARGAIN* (1686)

The little obligation I have to some of the witty sparks and poets of the town has put me on a vindication of this comedy from those centuries that malice and ill nature have thrown upon it, though in vain. The poets I heartily excuse since there is a sort of self interest in their malice, which I should rather call a witty way they have in this age of railing at everything they find with pain successful, and never to show good nature and speak well of anything, but when they are sure 'tis damned; then they afford it that worse scandal, their pity. And nothing makes them so through-stitched an enemy as a full third day.[6] That's crime enough to load it with all manner of infamy; and when they can no other way prevail with the town, they charge it with the old never- failing scandal—that 'tis not fit for the ladies. As if (if it were as they falsely give out) the ladies were obliged to hear indecencies only from their pens and plays, and some of them have ventured to treat 'em as coarsely as 'twas possible without the least reproach from them; and in some of their most celebrated plays have entertained 'em with things that if I should here strip from their wit and occasion that conducts 'em in and makes them proper, their fair cheeks would perhaps wear a natural color at the reading them; yet are never taken notice of because a man writ them, and they may hear that from them they blush at from a woman. But I make a challenge to any person of common sense and reason, that is not willfully bent on ill nature, and will in spite of sense wrest a double entendre from everything, lying upon the catch for a jest or quibble, like a rook for a cully,[7] but any unprejudiced person that knows not the author to read any of my comedies and compare 'em with the others of this age, and if they find one word that can offend the chastest ear, I will submit to all their peevish cavils. But right or wrong, they must be criminal because a woman's, condemning them without having the Christian charity to examine whether it be guilty or not, with reading, comparing, or thinking. The ladies taking up any scandal on trust from some conceited sparks, who will in spite of nature be wits and beaus, then scatter it for authentic all over the town and court, poisoning of others' judgments with their false notions, condemning it to worse than death—loss of fame. And to fortify their detraction, charge me with all the plays that have ever been offensive,

---

6   The third night's box-office takings went to the author after management's expenses were paid.

7   Like a swindler for a dupe.

though I wish, with all their faults, I had been the author of some of those they honored me with.

For the farther justification of this play, it being a comedy of intrigue, Dr. Davenant,[8] out of respect to the commands he had from court, to take great care that no indecency should be in plays, sent for it and nicely looked over it, putting out anything he but imagined the critics would play with. After that, Sir Roger L'Estrange[9] read it and licensed it, and found no such faults as 'tis charged with. Then Mr. Killigrew,[10] who more severe than any, from the strict order he had, perused it with great circumspection; and lastly, the master players, who you will I hope in some measure esteem judges of decency and their own interest, having been so many years prentice to the trade of judging.

I say, after all these supervisors the ladies may be convinced they left nothing that could offend, and the men of their unjust reflections on so many judges of wit and decencies. When it happens that I challenge any one, to point me out the least expression of what some have made their discourse, they cry that Mr. Leigh opens his nightgown, when he comes into the bed chamber. If he do, which is a jest of his own making, and which I never saw, I hope he has on his clothes underneath? And if so, where is the indecency? I have seen in that admirable play of Oedipus, the gown opened wide and the man shown in his drawers and waist coat, and never thought it an offence before. Another cries, why we know not what they mean, when the man takes a woman off the stage, and another is thereby cuckolded: is that any more than you see in the most celebrated of your plays? As the City Politiques, the Lady Mayoress, and the Old Lawyer's Wife, who goes with a man she never saw before and comes out again the joyfullest woman alive, for having made her husband a cuckold with such dexterity? And yet I see nothing unnatural or obscene: 'tis proper for the characters. So in that lucky play of the London Cuckolds, not to recite particulars. And in that good comedy of Sir Courtly Nice, the tailor to the young lady—in the famed Sir Fopling Dorimant and Bellinda, see the very words! In Valentinian, see the scene between the court bawds, and Valentinian, all loose and ruffled a moment after the rape, and all this you see without scandal and a thousand others. The Moor of Venice in many places. The Maid's Tragedy—see the

---

8   William Davenant (1606-88), English poet and playwright, one of two men granted a royal patent to produce plays in London after the Restoration.
9   English royalist and pamphleteer (1616-1704), at this time Surveyer of the Imprimery and Licenser of the Press and thus responsible for state censorship, typically of anti-monarchist pamphlets.
10   Thomas Killigrew (1612-83), the other theater patentee, a member of the court of Charles II and, from 1673, Master of the Revels.

scene of undressing the bride, and between the king and Armintor, and after between the king and Exoduc. All these I name as some of the best plays I know. If I should repeat the words expressed in these scenes I mention, I might justly be charged with coarse ill manners and very little modesty, and yet they so naturally fall into the places they are designed for, and so are proper for the business, that there is not the least fault to be found with them; though I say these things in any of mine would damn the whole piece and alarm the town. Had I a day or two's time, as I have scarce so many hours to write this (the play being all printed off and the press waiting), I would sum up all your beloved plays, and all the things in them that are passed with such silence by because written by men. Such masculine strokes in me must not be allowed. I must conclude those women (if there be any such) greater critics in that sort of conversation than myself, who find any of that sort in mine, or anything that can justly be reproached. But 'tis in vain by dint of reason or comparison to convince the obstinate critics, whose business is to find fault, if not by a loose and gross imagination to create them, for they must either find the jest or make it, and those of this sort fall to my share; they find faults of another kind for the men writers. And this one thing I will venture to say, though against my nature, because it has a vanity in it: that had the plays I have writ come forth under any man's name and never known to have been mine, I appeal to all the unbiased judges of sense, if they had not said that person had made as many good comedies, as any one man that has writ in our age. But a devil on't, the woman damns the poet.

Ladies for its further justification by you, be pleased to know that the first copy of this play was read by several ladies of very great quality, and unquestioned fame, and received their most favorable opinion, not one charging it with the crime that some have been pleased to find in the acting. Other ladies, who saw it more than once, whose quality and virtue can sufficiently justify anything they designed to favor, were pleased to say, they found an entertainment in it very far from scandalous, and for the generality of the town, I found by my receipts it was not so criminal. However, that shall not be an encouragement to me to trouble the critics with new occasion of affronting me, for endeavoring at least to divert; and at this rate, but the few poets that are left, and the players, who toil in vain, will be weary of their trade.

I cannot omit to tell you that a wit of the town, a friend of mine at Will's coffee house, the first night of the play, cried it down as much as in him lay, who before had read it and assured me he never saw a prettier comedy. So complaisant one pestilent wit will be to another, and in the full cry make his noise too. But since 'tis to the witty few I speak, I hope the better judges will take no offence to whom I am obliged for better judgments; and those

I hope will be so kind to me, knowing my conversation not at all addicted
to the indecencies alleged, that I would much less practice it in a play, that
must stand the test of the censuring world. And I must want common sense
and all the degrees of good manners renouncing my fame, all modesty and
interest for a silly saucy, fruitless jest, to make fools laugh and women blush,
and wise men ashamed, myself all the while, if I had been guilty of this
crime charged to me, remaining the only stupid insensible. Is this likely,
is this reasonable to be believed by anybody but the willfully blind? All I
ask is the privilege for my masculine part, the poet in me (if any such you
will allow me) to tread in those successful paths my predecessors have so
long thrived in, to take those measures that both the ancient and modern
writers have set me, and by which they have pleased the world so well. If I
must not, because of my sex, have this freedom, but that you will usurp all
to yourselves, I lay down my quill, and you shall hear no more of me, no not
so much as to make comparisons, because I will be kinder to my brothers of
the pen, than they have been to a defenceless woman, for I am not content
to write for a third day only. I value fame as much as if I had been born a
hero, and if you rob me of that, I can retire from the ungrateful world and
scorn its fickle favors.

4. APHRA BEHN, "TO THE READER," *SIR PATIENT FANCY* (1678)

I printed this play with all the impatient haste one ought to do, who would
be vindicated from the most unjust and silly aspersion woman could invent
to cast on woman and which only my being a woman has procured me:
that it was bawdy, the least and most excusable fault in the men writers
to whose plays they all crowd as if they come to no other end than to hear
what they condemn in this: *but from a woman it was unnatural.* But how
so cruel and unkindness came into their imaginations I can by no means
guess, unless by those whose lovers by long absence or those whom age or
ugliness have rendered a little distant from those things they would fain
imagine here. But if such as these durst profane their chaste ears without
hearing it over again or taking it into their serious consideration in their
cabinets, they would find nothing that the most innocent virgins can have
cause to blush at. But confess with me that no play ancient or modern has
less of that bug-bear bawdry in it. Others to show their breeding (as Bayes[11]
says) cried it was made out of at least four French plays, when I had but

---

11   The playwright depicted in Buckingham's *The Rehearsal*; see p. 173 above.

a very bare hint from one, the *Malade Imaginaire*,[12] which was given me translated by a gentleman infinitely to advantage. But how much of the French is in this, I leave to those who do indeed understand it and have seen it at the court. The play had no other misfortune but that of coming out for a woman's: had it been owned by a man, though the most dull unthinking rascally scribbler in town, it had been a most admirable play. Nor does its loss of fame with the ladies do it much hurt, though they ought to have had good nature and justice enough to have attributed all its faults to the author's unhappiness, who is forced to write for bread and not ashamed to own it and consequently ought to write to please (if she can) an age which had given several proofs it was by this way of writing to be obliged, though it is a way too cheap for men of wit to pursue, who write for glory, and a way which even I despise as much below me.

5. APHRA BEHN, EPILOGUE, *SIR PATIENT FANCY* (1678)

Spoken by Mrs. Gwin[13]
I here and there o'erheard a coxcomb cry (*Looking about.*)
Ah, rot it—'tis a woman's comedy,
One, who because she lately chanced to please us,
With her damned stuff will never cease to tease us.
What has poor woman done that she must be,
Debarred from sense and sacred poetry?
Why in this age has heaven allowed you more,
And women less of wit than heretofore?
We once were famed in story and could write
Equal to men, could govern, nay could fight.
We still have passive valor, and can show,
Would custom give us leave, the active too,
Since we no provocations want from you.
For who, but we, could your dull fopperies bear,
Your saucy love, and your brisk nonsense hear,
Endure your worse than womanish affectation,
Which renders you the nuisance of the nation,
Scorned even by all the misses of the town,
A jest to vizard mask, the pit buffoon;
A glass by which the admiring country fool
May learn to dress himself en ridicule—

---

12   Three-act comedy by Moliere (1673).
13   Nell Gwyn, the actress who became a mistress of Charles II.

Both striving who should most ingenious grow
In lewdness, foppery, nonsense, noise and show?
And yet to these fine things we must submit
Our reason, arms, our laurels, and our wit.
Because we do not laugh at you when lewd,
And scorn and cudgel ye when you are rude;
That we have nobler souls than you, we prove,
By how much more we're sensible of love;
Quickest in finding all the subtlest ways
To make your joys: why not to make your plays?
We best can find your foibles, know our own,
And gilts and cuckolds now best please the town;
Your way of writing's out of fashion grown.
Method and rule—you only understand,
Pursue that way of fooling and be damned.
Your learned cant of action, time, and place,
Must all give way to the unlabored farce.
To all the men of wit we will subscribe:
But for you halfwits, you unthinking tribe,
We'll let you see, what e'er besides we do,
How artfully we copy some of you:
And if you're drawn to th' life, pray tell me then
Why women should not write as well as men?

6. DELARIVIERE MANLEY, PREFACE, *THE LOST LOVER*; OR, *THE JEALOUS HUSBAND: A COMEDY* (1696)

... I am now convinced writing for the stage is no way proper for a woman, to whom all advantages but mere nature are refused. If we happen to have a genius to poetry it presently shoots to a fond desire of imitation. Though to be lamely ridiculous, mine was indulged by my flatterers who said nothing could come from me unentertaining. Like a hero not contented with applause from lesser conquests, I find myself not only disappointed of my hopes of greater, but even to have lost all the glory of the former. Had I confined my sense, as before, to some short song of Phillis, a tender billet, and the freedom of agreeable conversation, I still had preserved the character of a witty woman.

Give me leave to thank the well-natured town for damning me so suddenly. They would not suffer me to linger in suspense, nor allow me any degrees of mortification; neither my sex, dress, music, and dancing could allow it a three days' reprieve, nor the modesty of the play itself prevail with the ladies to espouse it. Here I should most justly reproach myself, for if I did not make all due acknowledgments for Sir Thomas Skipworth's civility; his native generosity and gallantry of temper, took care nothing on his part should be wanting to make it pleasing.

Once more, my offended judges, I am to appear before you, once more in possibility of giving you the like damning satisfaction; there is a tragedy of mine rehearsing, which 'tis too late to recall. I consent it meet with the same fortune: 'twill forever rid me of a vanity too natural to our sex, and make me say with a Grecian hero, "I had been lost if I had not been lost."

They object the verses wrote by me before *Agnes de Castro*, where, with poetic vanity, I seemed to think myself a champion for our sex; some of my witty critics make a jest of my proving so favorable an enemy, but let me tell them, this was not designed a consequence of that challenge being writ two years before, and cannot have a smaller share in their esteem than mine. After all, I think my treatment much severer than I deserved; I am satisfied the bare name of being a woman's play damned it beyond its own want of merit. I will conclude with Dionysius, "That Plato and philosophy have taught me to bear so great a loss (even of fame) with patience."

7. DELARIVIERE MANLEY, "TO THE AUTHOR OF *AGNES DE CASTRO*" (1696)

Orinda[14] and the fair Astrea[15] gone,
Not one was found to fill the vacant throne.
Aspiring man had quite regained the sway,
Again had taught us humbly to obey,
Till you (nature's third start, in favor of our kind)
With stronger arms, their empire have disjoined,
And snatched a laurel which they thought their prize;
Thus conqueror, with your wit, as with your eyes,
Fired by the bold example, I would try
To turn our sex's weaker destiny.
Oh! How I long, in the poetic race,
To loose the reins and give their glory chase;
For thus encouraged, and thus led by you,
Methinks we might more crowns than theirs subdue.

---

14   The poet Katherine Philips (1632-64), known as "The Matchless Orinda."
15   Aphra Behn.

8. CATHARINE TROTTER, PROLOGUE,
AGNES DE CASTRO: A TRAGEDY (1696)[16]

How strangely times are changed. I'th'latter age
Prologues were fresh complaints of critic rage:
But now, if one play hits, you straight decree
To prop a rival muse's halting poetry.
Could it but gain the crutches of your favor,
This tragedy might walk six days together.
Today, t'incite your charity the more,
A female author does your smiles implore;
Not but I fear, 'tis now a thing uncommon,
For men of wit to raise a failing woman!
Why should vain man the gift of sense engross
Since woman's wit was never at a loss?
Husbands to wives their whoring must reveal,
(For unfed passions will expect their meal)
But women's wits with ease their roving love conceal.
And faith in spite of all the hen-pecked fools can do,
They've oft the breeches worn, why not the laurel too![17]
Therefore to those of undisputed sense,
Our poetess resigns her play's defence.
Conscious of her faults, she flies to you,
To save her from the thoughtless damning crew.
She's dead, if tried by strict poetic laws,
But men of honor can't refuse a woman's cause.
Do you, the props of wit, but seem t'approve,
She cannot fear their thunder from above:
The top must stir if the foundation move.

9. SUSANNA CENTLIVRE, DEDICATION,
THE PLATONICK LADY: A COMEDY (1707)

To all the generous encouragers of female ingenuity, this play is humbly
dedicated.

Gentlemen and ladies,

---

16   The title page omits Trotter's name, and reads "Written by a Young Lady."
17   I.e., women have often been actors, so why not poets!

My muse chose to make this universal address, hoping, among the numerous crowd, to find some souls great enough to protect her against the carping malice of the vulgar world, who think it proof of their sense to dislike everything that is writ by women. I was the more induced to this general application, from the usage I have met on all sides.

A play secretly introduced to the house, whilst the author remains unknown, is approved by everybody. The actors cry it up and are in expectation of a great run, the bookseller of a second edition, and the scribbler of a sixth night. But if by chance the plot's discovered, and the brat found fatherless, immediately it flags in the opinion of those who extolled it before, and the bookseller falls in his price, with this reason only: it is a woman's. Thus they alter their judgment, by the esteem they have for the author, though the play is still the same. They ne'er reflect that we have had some male productions of this kind, void of plot and wit, and full as insipid as ever a woman's of us all.

I can't forebear inserting a story, which my bookseller that printed my *Gamester* told me, of a spark that had seen my *Gamester* three or four times, and liked it extremely. Having bought one of the books, asked who the author was, and, being told a woman, threw down the book, and put up his money, saying he had spent too much after it already, and was sure if the town had known that, it would never have run ten days. No doubt this was a wit in his own eyes. It is such as these that rob us of that which inspires the poet: praise. And it is such as these made him that printed my comedy called *Love's Contrivance; Or, Le Médecin Malgré Lui*, put two letters of a wrong name to it, which though it was the height of injustice to me, yet his imposing on the town turned to account with him; and thus passing for a man's it has been played at least a hundred times.

And why this wrath against the women's works? Perhaps, you'll answer, because they meddle with things out of their sphere. But I say, no, for since the poet is born, why not a woman as well as a man? Not that I would derogate from those great men who have a genius and learning to improve that genius: I only object against those ill-natured critics, who wanting both, think they have a sufficient claim to sense, by railing at what they don't understand. Some have armed themselves with resolution not to like the play they paid to see; and if in spite of spleen they have been pleased against their will, have maliciously reported it was none of mine, but given me by some gentleman. Nay even of my own sex, which should assert our prerogative against such detractors, are often backward to encourage a female pen.

Would these professed enemies but consider what examples we have had of women that excelled in all arts: in music, painting, poetry, also in war. Nay, to our immortal praise, what empresses and queens have filled the world? What cannot England boast from women? The mighty Romans felt the power of Boadicea's arm;[18] Eliza made Spain tremble;[19] but Anne,[20] the greatest of the three, has shook the man that aimed at universal sway.[21] After naming this miracle the glory of our sex sure none will spitefully cavil at the following scenes purely because a woman writ 'em. This I dare venture to say in their behalf, there is a plot and story in them, I hope will entertain the reader, which is the utmost ambition of,

Gentlemen and Ladies,
Your most humble servant.

10. MARY LEAPOR, "UPON HER PLAY[22] BEING RETURNED TO HER, STAINED WITH CLARET" (1751)

Welcome, dear wanderer, once more!
Thrice welcome to thy native cell!
Within this peaceful humble door
Let thou and I contented dwell!
But say, Oh whither hast thou ranged?
Why dost thou blush a crimson hue?
Thy fair complexion's greatly changed:
Why, I can scarce believe 'tis you.
Then tell, my son, Oh tell me, Where
Didst thou contract this sottish dye?
You kept ill company, I fear,
When distant from your parent's eye.
Was it for this, Oh graceless child!
Was it for this you learned to spell?
Thy face and credit both are spoiled:
Go drown thyself in yonder well.
I wonder how thy time was spent:
No news (alas!) hast thou to bring.
Hast thou not climbed the monument?

---

18   Celtic queen who led tribes of Britons against the Roman occupation in the first century AD.
19   Elizabeth I.
20   Queen Anne, who ruled 1702-14.
21   Allusion to the War of Spanish Succession, in which the French sought to unite the thrones of France and Spain under a Bourbon king.
22   *The Unhappy Father*, rejected for performance at Drury Lane. It was published in the 1751 version of *Poems on Several Occasions*.

Nor seen the lions, nor the king?
But now I'll keep you here secure:
No more you view the smoky sky;
The court was never made (I'm sure)
For idiots, like thee and I.

SELECT BIBLIOGRAPHY

Anderson, Misty G. "Women Playwrights." In *The Cambridge Companion to British Theatre, 1730-1830*. Ed. Jane Moody and Daniel Quinn. 145-58. Cambridge: Cambridge UP, 2007.

———. *Female Playwrights and Eighteenth-Century Comedy: Negotiating Marriage on the London Stage*. New York: Palgrave, 2002.

Behn, Aphra. *A Discovery of New Worlds. From the French: Made English by Mrs. A. Behn. To which is attached a Preface by way of Essay on Translated Prose; wherein the Arguments of Father Tacquet, and others, against the System of Copernicus (as to the Motions of the Earth) are likewise considered and answered: Wholly new*. London, 1688.

———. *The Rover and Other Plays*. Ed. Jane Spencer. Oxford: Oxford UP, 1995.

———. *The Rover*. Ed. Anne Russell. 2nd ed. Peterborough, ON: Broadview, 2000.

———. *The Works of Aphra Behn*. Vol. 3. Ed. Montague Summers. New York: Benjamin Blom, 1915.

Benedict, Barbara M. *Curiosity: A Cultural History of Early Modern Inquiry*. Chicago: U of Chicago P, 2001.

Bisset, Robert. *The Historical, Biographical, Literary, and Scientific Magazine: The History of Europe, for the Year 1799*. 3 vols. London, 1800[?].

Bowyer, John Wilson. *The Celebrated Mrs. Centlivre*. Durham, NC: Duke UP, 1952.

Burroughs, Catherine B., ed. *Women in British Romantic Theatre: Drama, Performance, and Society, 1790-1840*. Cambridge: Cambridge UP, 2000.

Carlson, Susan. "Aphra Behn's The Emperor of the Moon: Staging Seventeenth-Century Farce for Twentieth-Century Tastes." *Essays in Theatre/Études Théâtrales* 14.2 (1996): 116-30.

Centlivre, Susanna. *A Bold Stroke for a Wife*. Ed. Nancy Copeland. Peterborough, ON: Broadview, 1995.

———. *The Dramatic Works of the Celebrated Mrs. Centlivre, with A New Account of Her Life*. Vol. 1. New York: AMS Press, 1872.

Clive, Catherine. *The Case of Mrs. Clive, Submitted to the Publick*. London [1744].

Collier, Jeremy. *A Short View of the Immorality and Profaneness of the English Stage*. London, 1698.

Copeland, Nancy. *Staging Gender in Behn and Centlivre: Women's Comedy and the Theatre*. Burlington, VT: Ashgate, 2004.

Coppola, Al. "Retraining the Virtuoso's Gaze: Behn's *Emperor of the Moon*, the Royal Society, and the Spectacles of Science and Politics." *Eighteenth-Century Studies* 41.4 (2008): 481-506.

Corman, Brian. "What is the Canon of English Drama, 1660-1737?" *Eighteenth-Century Studies* 26.2 (1992-93): 307-21.

Cotton, Nancy. *Women Playwrights in England c. 1363-1750*. Lewisburg, PA: Bucknell UP, 1980.

Cowley, Hannah. *Eighteenth-Century Women Playwrights. Vol. 5: Hannah Cowley*. Ed. Antje Blank. London: Pickering & Chatto, 2001.

——. *The Plays of Hannah Cowley*. Ed. Frederick Link. 2 vols. New York: Garland, 1979.

——. *The Works of Mrs. Cowley: Dramas and Poems*. 3 vols. London, 1813.

de la Mahotiere, Mary. *Hannah Cowley: Tiverton's Playwright and Pioneer Feminist, 1743-1809*. Devon, UK: Devon Books, 1997.

Donkin, Ellen. *Getting into the Act: Women Playwrights in London 1776-1829*. London: Routledge, 1995.

Evans, James. "Libertine Gamblers in Late Stuart Comedy." *Restoration and Eighteenth-Century Theatre Research* 18.1 (2003): 17-30.

Finberg, Melinda C., ed. *Eighteenth-Century Women Dramatists*. Oxford: Oxford UP, 2001.

Foreman, Amanda. *Georgiana, Duchess of Devonshire*. New York: Random House, 1998.

Gagen, Jean. "The Weaker Sex: Hannah Cowley's Treatment of Men in Her Comedies of Courtship and Marriage." *Studies in English* 8 (1990): 107-16.

Garrick, David, and George Colman. *The Clandestine Marriage, Together with Two Short Plays*. Ed. Noel Chevalier. Peterborough, ON: Broadview, 1995.

Gray, Charles Harold. *Theatrical Criticism in London to 1795*. New York: Benjamin Blom, 1931.

Holland, Peter. *The Ornament of Action: Text and Performance in Restoration Comedy*. Cambridge: Cambridge UP, 1979.

Hughes, Derek. *The Theatre of Aphra Behn*. New York: Palgrave, 2001.

Hughes, Leo, and A.H. Scouten. *Ten English Farces*. Austin: U of Texas P, 1948.

Hume, Robert D. *The Development of English Drama, 1750-1800*. Cambridge: Cambridge UP, 1976.

Jenkins, Annibel. *I'll Tell You What: The Life of Elizabeth Inchbald*. Lexington: UP of Kentucky, 2003.

Jones, Stephen. *A New Biographical Dictionary: Containing a Brief Account of the Lives and Writings of the Most Eminent Persons and Remarkable Characters in Every Age and Nation*. 3rd ed. London, 1799.

Lawton, H.W. "Bishop Godwin's Man in the Moone." The *Review of English Studies* 7.25 (1931): 23-55.

Lewes, Charles Lee. *Memoirs of Charles Lee Lewes, Containing Anecdotes, Historical and Biographical, of the English and Scottish Stages, for a Period of Forty Years*. 4 vols. London, 1805.

Mellor, Anne K. *Mothers of the Nation: Women's Political Writing in England, 1780-1830*. Bloomington: Indiana UP, 2000.

Pearson, Jacqueline. *The Prostituted Muse: Images of Women and Women Dramatists,* *1642-1737.* New York: St. Martin's, 1988.

Schofield, Mary Anne, and Cecilia Macheski, eds. *Curtain Calls: British and American Women and the Theater, 1660-1820.* Athens: Ohio UP, 1991.

Todd, Janet M. *The Secret Life of Aphra Behn.* London: André Deutsch, 1996.

Warren, Victoria. "Gender and Genre in Susanna Centlivre's *The Gamester* and *The Basset Table.*" *Studies in English Literature* 43.3 (2003): 605-24.

Woolf, Virginia. *A Room of One's Own.* London: Hogarth Press, 1929.